Cadbury's Purple Reign

The Story Behind Chocolate's Best-Loved Brand

John Bradley

John Wiley & Sons, Ltd

Published in 2008 by   John Wiley & Sons Ltd,
The Atrium, Southern Gate, Chichester,
West Sussex PO19 8SQ, England
Telephone   (+44) 1243 779777

Email (for orders and customer service enquiries): cs-books@wiley.co.uk
Visit our Home Page on www.wiley.com

Other Wiley Editorial Offices

John Wiley & Sons Inc., 111 River Street, Hoboken, NJ 07030, USA

Jossey-Bass, 989 Market Street, San Francisco, CA 94103-1741, USA

Wiley-VCH Verlag GmbH, Boschstr. 12, D-69469 Weinheim, Germany

John Wiley & Sons Australia Ltd, 42 McDougall Street, Milton, Queensland 4064, Australia

John Wiley & Sons (Asia) Pte Ltd, 2 Clementi Loop #02-01, Jin Xing Distripark, Singapore 129809

John Wiley & Sons Canada Ltd, 6045 Freemont Blvd, Mississauga, Ontario, Canada L5R 4J3

Wiley also publishes its books in a variety of electronic formats. Some content that appears in print may not be available in electronic books.

British Library Cataloguing in Publication Data
A catalogue record for this book is available from the British Library
ISBN 978-0-470-72524-5 (HB)

Typeset by Thomson Press, India.
Printed and bound in Italy by Printer Trento.

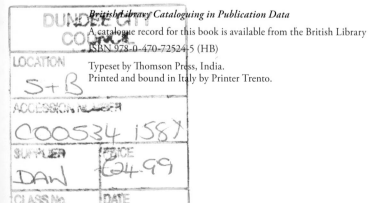

Contents

Foreword

Surprisingly, for such a well-known and venerable brand as Cadbury, there have only been two books covering the history of our company. The first was produced in 1931 to recognise the centenary of the firm, and the second, a much shorter publication, came out in 1998. A full reappraisal of the Cadbury story is therefore a welcome development.

The remarkable journey from a shop in Birmingham to becoming the world's largest confectionery company has been achieved through a unique combination of business purpose and human values. While many publications have, quite rightly, highlighted the Quaker origins of the company and the Cadburys' contribution to the addressing of social injustices, these have perhaps overshadowed the business and the brand-building story that lies at the heart of our success.

The Cadbury name has been associated with chocolate and cocoa since the early 1830's, a time when mass markets were only just emerging. Cadbury became the industry leader through harnessing the opportunities afforded by the rapid industrialisation of the United Kingdom and the emergence of a consuming class; a situation that bears many parallels with the changes occurring in India and China today.

The later stages of the Industrial Revolution, characterised by the emergence of mass produced consumer goods, was every bit as profound in its effect on industry as was the emergence of the information technology revolution towards the end of the 20th century. Cadbury rose to unparalleled heights in the way they grasped these changes and developed a business model perfectly in tune with the new consumer opportunities of the day.

We live in an era where strong brands are more important than ever. The internet is not the first new medium faced by Cadbury; popular newspapers, cinema, radio and commercial television were all as disruptive to the prevailing status quo in their day. Internationalism and global branding are challenges facing many businesses today, but are not new. There is much to be learnt from both our successes and our failures in taking the Cadbury brand beyond the British Isles.

Our history is much more to us than just a sequence of past events; it is an integral part of who we are and how we operate as a company. We have inherited a peerless set of brands and a guiding set of business principles, and it is our duty to continue to take them forward. One of the traditions of the company has been a willingness to share our past experiences for the future benefit of others. As Winston Churchill put it so succinctly, *'The farther backward you can look, the farther forward you can see.'* I hope that *Cadbury's Purple Reign* will be of interest as you face the challenges in your business today.

Sir John Sunderland

Acknowledgements

It would have been impossible to write this book without the generous help and assistance given by many people associated with the Cadbury brand. One of the most noticeable features of the Cadbury culture is a willingness to help one's colleagues, even when snowed under with work. Although I had a slight advantage of being an ex-colleague of many of the people mentioned below, I was astounded that not once did anyone tell me they were too busy to help. This really has been a team effort.

First and foremost, this book would not have been possible without the support, contributions and encouragement from three Cadbury Schweppes chairmen, past and present: Sir John Sunderland, Sir Dominic Cadbury and Sir Adrian Cadbury. All were exceptionally generous with their time in sharing their perspectives with me. Norma Boultwood deserves a special mention, both for time spent in reading various drafts and also for facilitating some key meetings during the project's genesis. I am also extremely grateful to an amazing group of PAs: Liz Atkins, Sue Li, Fern Graham, Paula Kearns, Paula Couto, Jacqueline Wheeler and Paula Grossman, who unfailingly arranged meetings to fit in with my rather inflexibly-timed research visits. In the management of the project, I benefited from an exceptional amount of support from Andrea Dawson-Shepherd, Tony Bilsborough and Chloe Haynes of the Cadbury Schweppes Corporate Communications Department, along with Mark Hodgin in the Legal Department.

In preparing the text itself, I owe an enormous debt of gratitude to Sarah Foden and Jackie Jones in the Cadbury Trebor Bassett Library and Information Services Department who very kindly tolerated my presence within their midst for weeks on end, and who also unfailingly responded to countless long-distance requests for information or photographs. In preparing the images for *Cadbury's Purple Reign*, I am also extremely thankful for the help provided by Paul Healey and Alan Hickman of the Cadbury Schweppes Design Studio and Colin Pitt of Cadbury World.

There were many Cadbury managers, past and present, who generously shared their time to search their memory banks and attics, and also to read through many drafts of various sections of the book on my behalf. Special mention must go to Chris Morgan and Neil Fozard of the Cadbury Outside Staff Pensioners Association who kindly gave me free reign through their newsletters and Christmas lunch to access the collective wisdom of the massed ranks of retired Cadbury salesmen and women. Norman Hawkins, John Tweedale, Mike Denyard, David Swain, Jim Dunkley, Jim Hay, Brian Molley, John Dwyer, Josie King and Val Davies all stepped forward to provide invaluable assistance.

In helping shape the non-Sales aspects of the U.K. part of the story, I am indebted to Robin Shaw, Stephen Ward, John Taylor, Graham Parker, Tim Cadbury, Richard Clapham, Peter Creighton, Alan Palmer and David Jones, who all spent much time in reading drafts and talking to me, helping me make sure I had got the story straight. George Dadd provided much help in making sure references to various new product recipes were correct, Bob Grundy with some terrific old brochures, and Tiphany Yokas kindly dug deep into the A.C.Nielsen data on my behalf. I am also grateful to Steve Greensted who provided a perspective from one of Cadbury's advertising agencies of the 1970s. Many of my visits to Bournville were also made much more enjoyable thanks to Sharon Boyce, Sam Bucknall, Bruce Moore, Annie Dunseith and Bob Cudd giving up their evenings to remind me of key events.

I had the pleasure of visiting Cadbury Ireland in the process of completing *Cadbury's Purple Reign*, so my thanks are due to Donal Byrne, Liam Marnane and Michael Smith for spending an inordinate amount of time, both meeting me in person and in reading drafts, and to Frank Dillon and Donna O'Herlihy for help with the illustrations. Equally hospitable and knowledgeable were the management team of Cadbury India, who also hosted a visit and read many drafts, so my thanks go to Yoginder Pal, Anand Kripalu, Ghirish Bhat, Burjor Icchaporia, Sanjay Purohit, Shawm Sengupta and the Cadbury India Marketing Department. I also received further insights from Bharat Puri and Kewel Kapoor, together with Walter Noronha, Hirol Gandhi and the team at Ogilvy & Mather in Mumbai.

My understanding of the early days of Cadbury in Australia was greatly aided by Ted Best and Frank Miller, and in more recent times by John Christophersen, Mark Smith, Peter Beales and Ian Johnston, who also gave me his perspectives on the commonalities of the Cadbury brand around the world. Robyn Newman performed miracles in getting images of the early MacRobertson brands and I am grateful to John Crawford for those from New Zealand. Bruce Creed, John Lawton and Brian Rogers were a great help in understanding the spread of the Cadbury brand globally, and I am also indebted to Vidyut Arte in China, Blair Sales in Malaysia, Andrew Baker in Africa, Jorge Stern in Argentina and Keith Sleight in Egypt, who all provided information and images from their Cadbury business units. Alan Palmer, John Christophersen, Simon Armstrong and Tim Stanford also provided much useful background on Cadbury in South East Asia, and I am grateful to Naomi Smith for patiently letting me examine her old files.

Cadbury's Eastern European ventures were described to me by Simon Baldry, Peter Knauer, Lech Rogacki and Anka Brzozowska, and I am indebted to Arlene Sheppard for digging out relevant portions of the Wedel acquisition material. Amanda Manchia gave me many useful pointers on South Africa, as did Arthur Soler on the Cadbury experience in Canada. Linda Goddard and Ted Fullona also helped me find the Canadian images. Also from Canada, Paul Lott helped me interpret the 1962 balance sheet of Cadbury Bros. and provided some useful perspectives on the operating differences between Cadbury and Mars.

Outside of Cadbury Schweppes, I am grateful to Professor Niraj Dawar of the Richard Ivey School of Business and Professor Marcel Corstjens of INSEAD who both provided much help in the early stages of the development of *Cadbury's Purple Reign*. Showing a terrific spirit of industry camaraderie, Kay Nicholls and Sue D'Arcy of Mars UK Ltd. were extremely helpful in the sourcing of images of the Mars brands; Hilary Parsons and Ann Poulter from Nestlé; Brandi Swedinovich from H.J. Heinz Company, L.P., and David Moore from the Leo Burnett Company. It has also been a pleasure to work with Claire Plimmer, Viv Wickham, Nick Mannion and Jo Golesworthy of John Wiley & Sons, and I am grateful to my agent, Robert Dudley, for his guidance through the entire process.

However, a special vote of thanks must be reserved for the team closest to me during the nearly two years from the inception of the idea for *Cadbury's Purple Reign* and its publication – Team Bradley. With unfailing help, encouragement and patience, my wife Audrey and daughter Georgina – who have heard little else but chocolate-related matters throughout that time – must take much of the credit for the appearance of *Cadbury's Purple Reign*. Also, much support from my parents John and Margaret, and my brother, Andrew. Thanks guys!

Image credits

All images supplied by Cadbury are reproduced with the permission of the Cadbury-Schweppes plc Group of Companies. The author would like to thank the picture libraries and companies below for kindly supplying and/or giving permission to use additional images for this book.

Advertising Archives for sourcing the following advertisements: Van Houten's Cocoa (p21), Rowntree's Elect Cocoa (p24), Baby Ruth (p115), Mars Bar (p118), Kit Kat Chocolate Crisp (p119), Rowntree's Fruit Gums (p120), 6d Dairy Milk (p149), Hershey Bar (p155), Milk Tray (p169), Flake (p177), Cream Egg conundrum (p239), Yorkie lorry driver (p243), Spangles (p282), and Rowntree's Fruit Pastilles (p283).

H.J. Heinz Company for the image of Heinz original clear glass horseradish bottle (p325). Reproduced by permission of H.J. Heinz, L.P.

Josephine King for the image of post-war demonstrators with Milk Tray samples (p170).

Leo Burnett Company (Canada) for the 'Creamy because of the milk' Dairy Milk advertisement (p324).

Mars UK Limited for the original Milky Way wrapper (p116), Mars Bar (p118), and Spangles (p282) advertisements. Reproduced by permission of Mars UK Limited. ®Milky Way, Mars Bar and Spangles are registered trademarks. © Mars UK Limited.

Mary Evans Picture Library for Victorian print of cocoa plant (p8), image of conching machine (p33), advertisement for Nestlé Milk Chocolate (p34), and French chocolate boxes (p40). Reproduced by permission of Mary Evans Picture Library.

Nestlé UK for Rowntree's Elect Cocoa (p24), Nestlé Milk Chocolate (p34), Kit Kat Chocolate Crisp (p119), Rowntree's Fruit Gums (p120), Yorkie lorry driver (p243), and Rowntree's Fruit Pastilles (p283). The names and images of all the Nestlé and Rowntree brands mentioned and shown are reproduced with the kind permission of Société des Produits Nestlé S.A.

Part I

THE RISE TO PROMINENCE

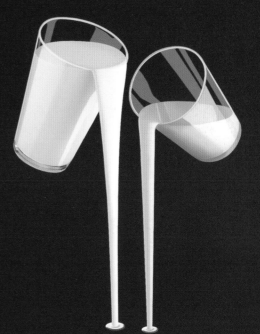

Chapter 1

GETTING ESTABLISHED: BACK FROM THE BRINK

B Fleetwood-Walke

In 1831, John Cadbury, a retailer of tea and coffee with a small sideline in cocoa, took a momentous step; one which would eventually lead to the creation of a global brand with sales counted in the billions. He switched to being a manufacturer of cocoa products.

Career Shift

This was not an obvious move for him to make. Cocoa was not in the same league as tea and coffee in terms of sales potential because it was many times more expensive. The Government had slapped on a hefty tax of 2 shillings and three pence duty per pound so, as a consequence, the UK market for cocoa remained miniscule with little more than 100 tons per annum of cocoa

beans being imported. Cocoa was not a drink for the masses, but the wealthy elite, of whom Birmingham had more than its fair share.

In the early 19th-century, Birmingham was booming and John's customer base consisted largely of successful men of industry – James Watt, son of the famous inventor, was a customer – people who thought big and acted bigger. John Cadbury cannot have failed to notice that being in the business of making rather than selling had its advantages. Being in retail meant remaining local and small whereas the potential in manufacturing seemed limitless. His confidence in making the switch was bolstered by his success in retailing his own cocoa products, painstakingly ground in a mortar and pestle, versus those bought in from the likes of Fry. Even in his first year, before he had a chance to establish much of a reputation, well over half of the cocoa takings came from the sale of his own cocoa nibs; not a bad start against the more established players.

However, the challenges of being an early manufacturer were daunting, and very different to those in retailing. As a retailer, John would have known most, if not all of his customers personally, where his rhetorical skills would have made many a sale. He was also something of a showman. To get his shop off the ground, an investment in Birmingham's first plate glass window

LIST OF
CHOCOLATES AND COCOAS,

MANUFACTURED BY

JOHN CADBURY, BIRMINGHAM.

CHOCOLATES.

Churchman's Chocolate	....		
Fine Crown	ditto	....	
Best Plain	ditto	....	
Plain	ditto	....	
British	ditto	....	
Grenada	ditto	....	
Spanish	ditto	four qrs. in each wrapper	
Ditto	ditto	in separate qrs.	
Plain London Chocolate Cakes, loose............			
Ditto	ditto	in lbs. :............	
Compressed Cocoa........................			
Soluble Chocolate Powder, in cans			
Best Chocolate, in Powder, ditto..................			
Chocolate Paste......................			
Penny Soluble Chocolate, in qrs. lbs. or 7lb. boxes			
Broma			
French Eating Chocolate			

COCOAS.

Soluble Cocoa (loose)		
Ditto, ditto (packed)		
Cocoa Paste		
Granulated Cocoa, in 14lb. boxes..................		
Improved Cocoa, (packed)		
Ditto	ditto	(ground) ....
Ditto	ditto	(flaked) ....
Rock Cocoa		
Trinidad ditto.................................		
Cocoa Nibs.................................		
Fine Cocoa Nuts (roasted)		

Show Blocks and Tins for Shop Windows.

J. C. rests his claim to the public support on his determination to maintain a character for a thoroughly good and uniform quality.

JOHN CADBURY'S PRICE LIST of 1842.

had drawn crowds from miles around – Birmingham's boom had clearly not yet encompassed much in the line of entertainment options. When John employed a Chinaman to serve behind the counter, it must have seemed like Barnum & Bailey had rolled into town. But as a manufacturer, he was in the business of selling to remote customers at the end of what could be a long and convoluted supply chain. He would need more than plate glass windows and an oriental greeter if he was to succeed.

John was to have a major stroke of luck almost immediately when, in 1832, the Government slashed import duties on cocoa. This allowed products to be priced at levels more attainable to the wage-earning classes. As a consequence, the national market was to grow more than five-fold in the next eight years, a growth that John Cadbury was much more able to tap into as a manufacturer than if he had remained a simple shopkeeper. Within another fifteen years the duty would be down to a penny a pound, further fuelling the market and John Cadbury's sales.

Perhaps the buoyant market seduced John into believing that being in the manufacturing business was a walk in the park. In truth, there was little to distinguish his goods from those of many other firms, not to mention the massive Fry company. His earlier price lists consisted mainly of generically named items such as Spanish Chocolate, Rock Cocoa, Trinidad Cocoa and the like, all of which could be expected to appear on the price lists of any reputable cocoa firm. But his product quality was ahead of the rest, which was recognised on February 4th, 1854, when he was awarded Queen Victoria's royal warrant, ahead of any other cocoa manufacturer. He wasted little time in exploiting the opportunity it offered, quickly rolling out a new line called 'Queen's Own chocolate' which complimented his existing 'British Chocolate', featuring the likenesses of Queen Victoria and Prince Albert.

But royal warrants and undifferentiated products were not enough to compete in a crowded marketplace where one company, Fry, had all the benefits of longevity, scale, retailer trust and consumer awareness. When Cadbury first opened an office in London in 1853, Fry already had men calling on the fifty largest cities and towns in the country. It was an unequal struggle. Compounded by John Cadbury having been struck two grievous blows with the death of his second wife, followed by a severe bout of rheumatic fever, the business went into decline. Without his firm hand on the tiller, product quality suffered and sales fell away. Staff levels by 1859 were half those of seven years previously, and the business had sunk into making a loss. In 1861, John handed over the reins to his sons, Richard and George, and it seemed only a matter of time before the business would be wound up.

To the Brink

Richard and George Cadbury certainly had their work cut out. Such had been the decline in the Cadbury cocoa business that three-quarters of the company turnover was coming from tea and coffee dealing, of which they had little experience. Of the thirty other cocoa manufacturers that the brothers were aware of, Cadbury Bros. was the smallest.

Richard Cadbury   *George Cadbury*

They could see others of the thirty already closing their doors, and there was a huge rate of attrition in the retail trade, with many of Cadbury's customers going bust, leaving bills unpaid. Their diminishing numbers of workers could see unsold cocoa stocks piled up in the warehouse, and were expecting to hear the worst any day.

To be thrust into such a dire situation was a severe test for two young men – Richard being twenty-five and George twenty-two. But while business was grim, the brothers had a lifeline. They had each received legacies on the passing of their mother of £5,000 each – a major fortune in those days, being together worth over £600,000 at today's prices. The brothers resolved to invest £4,000 each to see if they could weather the storm, insisting that they would not seek to borrow beyond that sum from their father or anyone else. Sales in 1860 had amounted to £27,800, so the brothers must have been reasonably confident that their combined £8,000 would provide a decent safety net for any losses.

But any possible feelings of complacency were soon swept away as a disastrous year's trading in 1861 made a severe hole in their capital, and 1862 was even worse. Every penny of expense, both business and personal, was scrutinised. George Cadbury stopped his morning paper, and then even went without coffee and tea, despite having a warehouse full of the stuff. Fourteen hour workdays were the norm. Richard declared that if the business ever made a profit of a thousand pounds a year, he would retire a happy man.

In the meantime though, things were kept going by the brothers rapidly expanding their range with a host of new products, hoping that one would find a way through the competitive minefield. The slew of innovations helped to stem the losses. The 1863 deficit had been reduced to one tenth of the previous year, and by 1865 the business was back in profit and growing, albeit not dramatically. But it had been a close run matter. Of the brothers' original investments of £4,000, Richard was down to his last £450, while George had managed to hold onto £1,500. George attributed the difference to his not having yet married, which perhaps infers that Richard's wife had not been subject to the same spending constraints that the brothers' had endured in the workplace.

Differentiate or Die

With the crisis averted at least for the time being, contingency career plans of George decamping to the Himalayas to grow tea and Richard become a draughtsman were put on hold. But, while financial implosion seemed to have been staved off, it was clear that the underlying business problem confronting them had not yet been addressed. They had no product sufficiently different to, or better than, those of the competition. The mighty Fry firm were still outselling Cadbury many times over.

Cocoa at the time was sold to be drunk: mixed with boiling water or on special occasions, milk. The basic problem was that the cocoa bean, once removed of its hard shell, consists of slightly over 50% fat. Notwithstanding the fact that fat doesn't mix well with water or milk, the absolute quantity of fat could cause gastric distress to all but the hardiest of digestive systems. Manufacturers had recognised this brake on demand, and had tried to mitigate it by mixing the cocoa with a range of substances to absorb the fat and/or mask its flavour. As a result, the only real point of difference in the products became who mixed in the least obnoxious ingredients. While Cadbury avoided the worst excesses of the adulterers – brick dust and even red lead were not uncommon additions–

CHOCOLATE.
(*Theobroma cacao.*)

Cadbury's range of cocoas left a lot to be desired. Consisting of only one part in five of cocoa, the rest being potato flour, sago and treacle, it was not something to excite the taste buds.

The breakthrough would not come from an earth-shattering innovation, but from what would become a long-term Cadbury habit of being proud and quick to borrow ideas. George Cadbury in particular was not afraid to latch onto a good idea when he saw one,

'I never looked at the small people, or people who had failed. I fixed my eye on those who had won the greatest success. It was no use studying failure. I wanted to know how men succeeded, and it was their methods I examined and, if I thought them good, applied.'

George didn't fix his eye on Fry as his role model. Although the market leader, they were also keen product adulterers and their cocoa was nothing to write home about. If the Cadbury firm was to thrive, it had to outflank Fry, not emulate them. Looking further afield, George heard about a successful cocoa brand in Europe: van Houten's.

Coenraad Johannes van Houten had opened his first cocoa factory in Amsterdam as early as 1815, and from the start had been experimenting with

ways of reducing cocoa's high fat content. Not content with the practice of boiling, skimming and adding fillers, he leveraged the burgeoning engineering knowledge of the Industrial Revolution to invent a hand-operated hydraulic press, which he patented in 1828. The vast pressures generated in the press squeezed out half of the cocoa fat, reducing the fat content from around 53% down to 27%. This dramatically improved the drinking

characteristics of the mixed final product and removed the need to add anything to make the drink more digestible.

George travelled to Holland and did a deal for a press, despite having only sign language and a dictionary with which to negotiate. This was the last throw of the dice for Cadbury Bros., even though their business was now making a small profit. The press was expensive, and would have consumed most of George's remaining capital. It also required mass production to be of benefit, so the need would be to create a level of sustained demand far above any of their existing products. No British manufacturer, including the dominant Fry firm, had gone down this route. There was no tangible evidence that there would be any market at all for such a product. If it failed, Cadbury would have gone under.

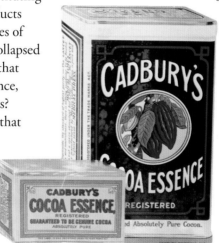

The risk of merely substituting sales of a new cocoa for existing products was high. Even worse, what if sales of Cadbury's own adulterated products collapsed and there was no market for a cocoa that would be much more expensive per ounce, as it would not include cheap fillers? There was little evidence in those days that consumers would switch to a more expensive product purely on the grounds of quality when there were far greater risks to life and limb than a cup of cocoa. But George and Richard had no doubt about it being the way forwards, and with the press installed in their Bridge Street factory in 1866, their next new product was to be the salvation of the company and the creation of an empire.

Defining the Market

Cadbury's Cocoa Essence was launched in 1866, but was not an instant success; in fact it was something of a slow seller in its first year, which tested the resolve of the brothers to breaking point. The immediate problem was one of value perception. A product range (along with everyone else's) that contained four-fifths cheap fillers had created a value for money expectation for cocoa. Because the new Cocoa Essence contained none of the additives, all of which were cheaper than raw cocoa, it was much more expensive per ounce than anything else on the market.

Cadbury's early advertising for Cocoa Essence focused on trying to head off negative value perceptions as much as it did selling the benefits of the new process,

'Cadbury Cocoa Essence (Registered) is three times the strength of the best Homeopathic cocoas ordinarily sold; consequently it is cheaper to use. Having no farinaceous substance or sugar added it does not thicken in the cup. It is guaranteed to consist solely of the extract of the cocoa nut, with the excess of fatty matter removed.'

But little headway was being made. They had yet to find a compelling benefit that would realise the sales potential of a unique and differentiated product.

Moving from Features to Benefits

The answer was to lie in making an issue of the idea of product purity. Having bombarded doctors' offices and the medical press with free samples, Cadbury were able to roll out an advertising campaign in 1867 based on the enduring technique of the medical testimonial,

'Genuine; easily prepared; economical; about three times the strength of the best cocoas ordinarily sold; free from the excess of fatty matter, and recommended by medical men as the most wholesome breakfast beverage.'

"We have carefully examined the samples brought under our notice, and find that they are genuine, and that the Essence of cocoa is just what it is declared to be by Messrs. CADBURY Brothers." – **Lancet.**

"Cocoa treated thus will, we expect, prove to be one of the most nutritious, digestible and restorative of drinks." – **British Medical Journal.**

This message, in a variety of forms, would assail the consumer at every turn, and within another year Cadbury had ceased advertising any other of its cocoas. The farm was being bet on Cocoa Essence.

Competitively, it was far from clear that George and Richard Cadbury had not just knocked the final nail into their own coffins. From the perspective of Fry, this looked like the desperate move from a company that had nothing to lose. Even after a few years, there was no compelling case to follow suit. The market for adulterated cocoas did not immediately collapse; in fact, it kept growing. Most of the growth in the market was still coming from adulterated cocoa, driven by the continuing explosion in both population and incomes. In the 1870's, the already large sales of Fry's adulterated cocoas increased by 85%, which would hardly have rung many alarm bells in their Bristol headquarters. They had been market leaders for nearly a century and would have lost no sleep had they known that Cadbury's sales, driven by Cocoa Essence, were to increase by 114% over the same period.

But Fry would soon be jolted from their reverie when Cadbury forced a sea-change in the government's attitude to the adulteration of cocoa.

Although *The Lancet* had announced the creation of a health commission for the analysis of foods way back in 1850, the subject had not really gripped the nation, even after the passing of the British Food and Drug Act in 1860. This act was designed to prevent manufacturers using harmful additives, so did nothing to change opinions or practice on the uses of sago and flour, which could hardly be considered life-threatening. However, the poor administration of that Act led to much more comprehensive measures in 1872 and then 1875 with the Adulteration of Food Acts.

George Cadbury had long been lobbying for more government action on the issue, leading the case for the 'extractors' while being opposed by most of the rest of the industry who could be categorised as the 'mixers'. George's argument was that the addition of flour and starch, while not necessarily harmful, tended to make the prepared cocoa more indigestible. The plausible-sounding counter-argument of the 'mixers' was that the extraction of the cocoa fat – known as cocoa butter – robbed the cocoa of its nourishment. The Government found George Cadbury's argument to be the more compelling, with 'mixed' cocoas falling under the remit of the new Act.

It was not an obvious move for George to have lobbied so hard on the issue. Cadbury had a unique and meaningfully differentiated product, so it would seem that the longer everyone else continued to make inferior products, the better it would be for Cadbury. But the new Acts would demand the stating on the label of any and all adulterants used, harmful or not. This would give the maximum awareness to Cadbury's selling point, and is a powerful mechanism even today. Be it calories, Recommended Daily Allowances, Genetically Modified ingredients, or allergens, changes in labelling requirements have been shown time and time again to be enormously powerful drivers of changes in consumer behaviours.

Defining the Category

The Act, and George Cadbury's role in its development, generated acres of free publicity for Cadbury's Cocoa Essence, and also prompted a flood of advertisements from Cadbury's competitors, protesting that they only mixed cocoa with the most wholesome of ingredients. But they were now on the back foot; a situation that would

get much worse for them when hit by Cadbury's next move, which was the progressive cancelling of their range of adulterated cocoas, even though most were still selling well. In 1878 Cadbury's Homeopathic, Pearl and Breakfast Cocoas were cancelled, soon to be followed by the rest of the range. Such was the initial hit to the Cadbury sales line that the company was prompted to make special payments to their travellers in recompense for the substantial commissions that would be lost.

But the lost sales and extra commissions would soon be repaid many times over. This move by Cadbury to purge their product range of any adulterated lines was to become hugely significant. They did not have to do it; it was not against the law

AN EPOCH-MAKING DECISION

"ABSOLUTELY PURE: THEREFORE BEST"

to add wholesome foodstuffs to raw cocoa, as long as they were declared on the label. Nor was there an immediate business case for doing so; they were giving up profitable volume, in fact were handing it straight over to their competitors. Cadbury could easily have kept advertising Cocoa Essence as *'Absolutely Pure, therefore Best'* while still promoting the cheaper cocoas to the lower end of the market. But to have done so would have missed out on the huge benefit that was to come from the move: the building of the Cadbury brand reputation and that it would define how consumers should view the cocoa category.

The outcome of Cadbury's move to cancel their adulterated cocoas was to give a meaning to the Cadbury name. They were saying that the ideals of product purity were so important, they would not sell anything that was anything less than pure. While the Cocoa Essence product brand stood for purity, the Cadbury name would stand for quality, integrity and trust. At the time, very few, if any, manufacturer names stood for anything at all beyond a basic level of quality. In the cocoa category, the name of the market leader, Fry, didn't even stand for that. Driven by an advertising campaign, the scale of which dwarfed those of the competition, Cadbury turned the screw.

With a punch-line that summed everything up succinctly: *'Absolutely Pure, therefore Best'*, it was to be a thirty year advertising campaign that would drum into consumers that the cocoa market was all about purity. We have seen in more recent times the benefits that can come by raising the importance in consumers' minds of one's own brand feature into a category-defining benefit. Volkswagen a generation ago almost single-handedly redefined the American car market with their *'Think Small'* campaign. More recently, Volvo triumphed by raising the importance of safety in car-buying decision-making.

Now Cadbury had shifted the debate to the issue of purity, both Fry and Rowntree were forced to launch their own versions, although both waited far too long before doing so. It was not until 1880 that Rowntree brought out Elect Cocoa, but it soon struggled as it could not match the Cadbury product. While Joseph Rowntree searched the continent for a suitable supplier of pressing machinery, in 1883 Fry brought out Fry's Pure Concentrated Cocoa, the recipe for which had been supervised by Albert Fry himself.

Fry finally realised they had a competitor on their hands and replicated every one of the sales tools that Cadbury had used so effectively over the last half-century. Cadbury's royal warrant from Queen Victoria had been matched by an identical one for Fry, and then decisively trumped as Fry signed up every Head of State they could lay their hands on. In addition to their star signing, the Prince of Wales, Fry could boast royalty from Emperor Napoleon III to the King of Siam and most points in between.

Cadbury's by now ancient *Lancet* quote was matched by one from Fry's own tame medic, a Dr. Andrew Wilson,

*'I have had **Fry's Pure Concentrated Cocoa** again analysed, and as a result I find **no flaw or weakness in my constant claim for it**, that it represents an ABSOLUTELY PURE AND PERFECT FOOD.'*

In other ads they were soon adding the claim that,

'The MEDICAL PRESS, including the "LANCET," "BRITISH MEDICAL JOURNAL," and "MEDICAL ANNUAL," testifies to its ABSOLUTE PURITY.'

Fry were also playing at every turn their many quality awards gained from various exhibitions and fairs across Europe and America; a practice that Cadbury had ignored. As time went by, the number of medals being trumpeted was to eventually exceed 300.

Over in York, Rowntree had eventually launched their own brand of pressed cocoa in 1886, calling it once again 'Elect.' But by the end of the century, having been constrained from being able to compete effectively with Cadbury's Cocoa due to Joseph Rowntree's antipathy to the concept of advertising, they were having to fight by other means. This involved buying business for the Elect brand by offering discounts to customers well outside the limits fixed between the main manufacturers in their collusive agreements. In eschewing the single biggest driver of mass markets – advertising – Rowntree had been forced to adopt a 'push' model.

But neither Fry nor Rowntree made much headway against Cocoa Essence with which Cadbury had had eighteen years head start. Both the Fry's Pure Concentrated Cocoa and the improved Rowntree Elect Cocoa were at best parity products, so there was no danger that they would damage sales of the much better known Cadbury's Cocoa Essence. Sales of Cadbury's Cocoa Essence had trebled during the 1880's and were to double again in the 1890's.

Cadbury's investment in van Houten's hydraulic press had been a bold move, but one driven by the company's failure to make headway by offering products little different to the multitude already available. Although affordability was still an effective path to growth for the industry as a whole, there was little point in Cadbury being just another also-ran trailing in the wake of Fry. Cadbury, through their cancellation of their adulterated cheaper cocoas, had given their name a brand platform which provided them with insurance against some unforeseen market shift sidelining the Cocoa Essence brand. This distinction was to pay huge dividends when a potentially fatal threat to the Cadbury's Cocoa Essence brand did in fact arise. And it was to be another output of Coenraad's van Houten's inventive mind that was to precipitate the crisis: alkalised cocoa.

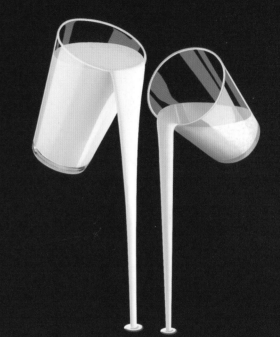

Chapter 2

MARKET CHANGES: MOVING ON FROM COCOA ESSENCE

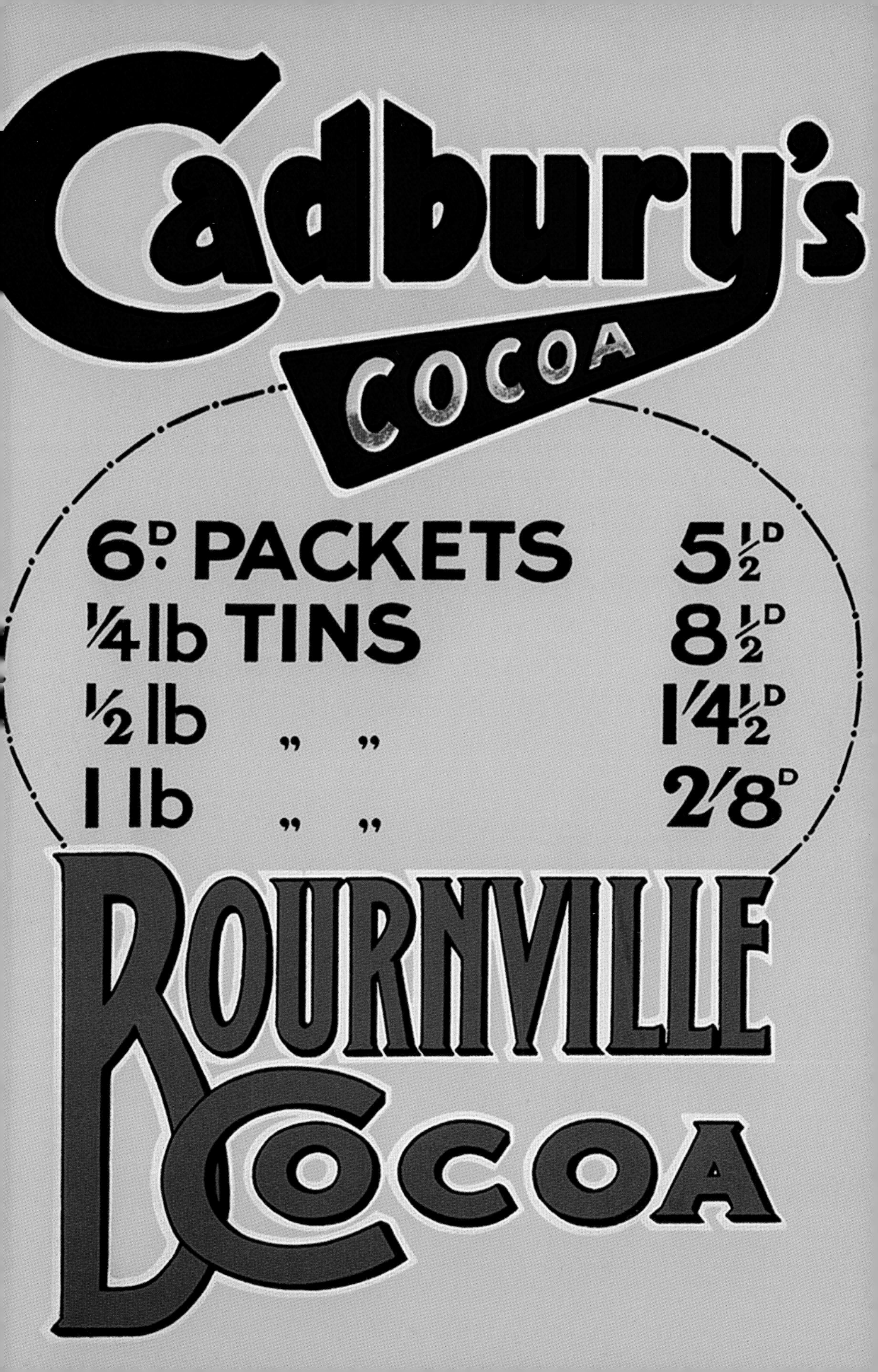
Cadbury's
COCOA
6D PACKETS 5½D
¼lb TINS 8½D
½lb ,, ,, 1/4½D
1 lb ,, ,, 2/8D
BOURNVILLE
COCOA

Built on the success of Cocoa Essence, the Cadbury business came on leaps and bounds in the late 19th-century. By 1895, the dozen employees inherited by George and Richard had turned into a small army of over 1,800. Cocoa Essence had been the company's driving force for thirty years and was still increasing at a rate of 15% a year. Weekly outputs were now up to around half the level of Fry's and it became an obsession to overtake them. But it was beginning to look like Cocoa Essence would not be up to that task.

While the absolutely pure cocoa powder emerging from the Van Houten press was a lot easier on the stomach than had been the previous full-fat versions, it was by no means fully optimised. Firstly, the drink was coarse and grainy, as the granules did not fully dissolve, but were held in suspension in the hot water or milk. Secondly, the fermentation process undergone by all cocoa beans raised their acidity level, such that the resulting product had quite a strong bitter taste. While Cocoa Essence suffered from these two drawbacks, they had in fact already been solved in one stroke.

Van Houten had discovered that the acid taste of the cocoa nibs (the de-shelled cocoa bean) could be neutralised by adding an alkali – carbonate of potash – prior to the roasting process. To his surprise, not only did the bitter taste disappear, but the powder became more miscible, in that it dispersed in the milk or water to create a more homogenous solution. Not only that, but the colour was darkened, the mixed drink frothed up better, and also tasted milder – what we would describe today as more 'chocolatey.'

By keeping the process to himself, Coenraad Van Houten could put out onto the market a product that was a superior drinking experience along just about every dimension that mattered. He managed to keep the secret until the end of the 19th-century, when the seemingly inexorable success of Van Houten Cocoa in the British marketplace alerted local manufacturers that something had to be done. In addition to discovering how to improve cocoa, Van Houten had also discovered the vast consumer market that was the British Isles. The Industrial Revolution had created the largest concentrated consumer market the world had ever known, which had become a magnet for every European manufacturer. For the next twenty years, all the new competitive threats to Cadbury's growing business would come from the innovative and aggressive European firms.

George Cadbury had long been aware that Van Houten was using chemicals to alter the product, and he had made unsuccessful efforts to have alkalisation declared a harmful adulterant. As early

as 1888, Cadbury were already feeling the pressure, altering their famous slogan to say 'Absolutely Pure and Soluble' in an attempt to pre-emptively own solubility, despite the fact that their product clearly failed to deliver. The next tactic was to launch an all-out assault on alkalis, warning the public to increase their vigilance,

Cadburys caution the Public against adulterated Cocoas sold as pure Cocoa, to which about 4 per cent of Alkali and other agents are added, to give apparent strength to the liquor, by making it a dark colour. This addition may be detected by the scent when a tin is freshly opened. No Cocoa can be stronger than Cadbury's which is guaranteed absolutely pure.

Cadbury were also not shy in pointing out to the public who the culprits were,

Improvements effected in recent years in the manufacture of Cocoa have been brought about "without any admixture of alkalies, starch, sugar or sago, but simply as the result of more scientific treatment." The cocoa that perfectly answers this description is Cadbury's Cocoa, which is guaranteed absolutely pure; among the Cocoas that do not answer this description are those of foreign make, notably the Dutch, in which alkalies and other injurious colouring matters are introduced.

Cadbury in their advertisements also focused in on the apparent dangers of potash,

Mr. T. Eustace Hill, M.B., Analyst, Birmingham, certifies that in the foreign cocoas there is a large excess of potash salts over that contained in the nibs of Cadbury's Cocoa Essence. The excess of alkali, he adds, must be undesirable from a dietetic point of view.

Fearing that a local food analyst might not carry enough gravitas, the reliable tactic of signing up doctors made a re-appearance,

Dr. A.J.H. Crespi says: "Perfectly pure brands, like Cadbury's Cocoa Essence, never thicken on the application of heat, nor do they, like foreign Cocoas, contain dangerous and objectionable alkaline salts."

But these efforts failed to have much impact. By 1892, Cadbury ads had, in a typeface bigger than the 'Absolutely Pure....' slogan, the crystal-clear message, 'NO CHEMICALS USED.'

There are two interesting points about this turn of events. Firstly, Cadbury in its advertising had by now dropped most references to the name Cocoa Essence, and was promoting it simply as Cadbury's Cocoa, even though the Cocoa Essence brand name on the packaging remained unchanged. As the non-pure cocoas had been cancelled, Cocoa Essence was the only Cadbury line of cocoa, so could be boldly promoted as such. However, as a result, the battle with alkalisation was not just an issue of one product versus another, such as VHS versus Betamax, it was the Cadbury name and reputation that was going in to bat. The Cadbury brand itself was making this stand.

Secondly, Cadbury had failed to realise that the benefit of purity was now past its sell-by date. While it had been a terrific selling point in the days of rampant adulteration,

the Food Adulteration Act of 1872 had forced all manufacturers to clean up their acts, so consumers no longer saw purity as the major benefit it had been when sawdust and sago could make up 4/5ths of the product. Van Houten was convincing the cocoa-buying public that the next big benefits in the category were taste and solubility. While companies can become too attached to brands, recipes, factories and the like, Cadbury had become too attached to a market positioning. They were making a stand on an issue that in reality had been overtaken by events, for which there was an accumulating body of evidence

The strong sales growth of Cocoa Essence in the 1890's, while seemingly providing evidence that the brand was in rude health had, in fact, been driven more by market expansion than by continuing competitive advantage. Although measurement of these things was not possible in those days, the anecdotal evidence coming back from the sharp end indicated that Cadbury was losing market share.

But companies don't take market share to the bank. What really focused the minds at Cadbury Bros. was the fact that the first few years of the 20th-century saw sales for Cocoa Essence grinding to a standstill, and then going backwards. A 5% decline in 1903 got worse in 1904 when sales fell by a further 8%. Cadbury sales declined

in every one of their most important 21 towns and cities. Cocoa Essence and its peerless advertising campaign, 'Absolutely Pure, therefore Best' had been the dominant force in the company for a generation, and had not only saved the business, but created a very successful and large enterprise.

So what were Cadbury to do? That Cocoa Essence might have run its course was a thought that had to be taken on board. More difficult to accept was that purity itself might no longer be as potent a selling point. Cadbury stood unequivocally for purity, and thirty years of increasingly massive advertising budgets had been sunk into this one thought. A *volte-face* on this issue was unthinkable, but it could not be argued that the communication strategy that had put purity at the top of the decision tree was being found wanting in trying to convince the public that Van Houten's superior-tasting product was in fact inferior.

Reasons behind the sales declines were sought from the travellers at a national conference, and they weren't slow in coming: Van Houten being fingered as the main culprit, with Rowntree, Fry, Suchard and even Dutch cocoa being imported in bulk and packed under grocers own labels not helping matters. While there was a fair degree of consensus as to the problem, agreement as to what to do about it was harder to come by.

The initial response from the floor betrayed a large element of the company believing its own publicity. The question was asked as to why the Food and Drugs Act could not be forcefully applied to drive Van Houten's cocoa from the market. Cadbury's chemical analyst sheepishly responded that to do so, it would have to be proved that the addition of alkali would be harmful to the consumer, and that, contrary to what the last ten years of advertising had been saying, the quantity added by Van Houten (3.5 to 4%) would have no impact whatsoever on the food value of the cocoa nor on the health of its drinker. In short, a great deal that had been inferred against alkali by Cadbury could not be supported.

Another school of thought was that direct competitor-bashing was both wasteful and a diversion from the real opportunity. Figures were presented showing that, even after a six-fold increase in Cocoa Essence sales in the last two decades of the 19th-century, only one family in 32 were drinking Cocoa Essence. Surely being first to reach the other 31 families would be more productive than slugging it out with Van Houten? 'Not so,' was the response of many. Sales were in decline directly as a result of the impact of Van Houten's cocoa, so an effective response was deemed a top priority.

The Cadbury Board were hugely influenced by this feedback from their Travellers and announced there was no objection in principle to the company selling a slightly Alkalised product, but that the stumbling blocks were entirely practical. The main one being that there now existed only one Cadbury's cocoa, that being Cocoa Essence, which by now was widely advertised as 'Cadbury's Cocoa.' If Cadbury were to launch an alkalised cocoa, 'We could not sell two different kinds under the name 'Cadbury's Cocoa.'

But the audience was in no mood to be fobbed off with esoteric branding issues. A traveller from Scotland, Mr. Port, took the floor with a no-holds-barred description of the scale of problem facing the company,

'There is little doubt that Van Houten take 50% of (the) trade, so they are by far our most formidable opponents. After Van Houten come Cadbury, Fry and Rowntree, (with volume) somewhere about equal between the three.'

If the sales position versus Van Houten wasn't bad enough, what was no doubt shocking to Head Office was the news that the Dutch company's sales came virtually without effort or expense,

'This position has been obtained, or rather I should say maintained, not only without the goodwill of the retail trade, but without travellers and with very little advertising. The grocer tells you he would not have a tin of it in his shop if he could help it, that he gets practically no profit from it. If a grocer wants to introduce any other cocoa, he invariably says it is as good as Van Houten's. The public demand is the vital point of the question.'

Here was the nub of the issue. The public's perception of what defined 'best' when it came to cocoa had initially been shaped by Cadbury to mean 'purest.' But times had changed, and given that virtually all cocoas were pure by the government's definition, the public's perception of 'best' had shifted to 'best tasting.'

The insightful Mr. Port brought the issue to a head,

'This leaves two courses open. The first is to convince them that absolutely pure cocoa is best, the second course is to make an Alkalised cocoa. (As to the first course) the firm have already spent large sums of money in this endeavour. Business is conducted for the purpose of making a profit and therefore it is only commercial prudence that the expenditure should not exceed an amount which will leave a margin.'

His insight and clarity on the way forwards, even though on the day he assumed that launching an alkalised cocoa was out of the question, swayed the Board.

It was at this stage that the next generation of the Cadbury family move to the fore in the management of the company. When Richard Cadbury died unexpectedly from diphtheria in 1899, George had turned the business into a private limited liability company.

Back row: George Cadbury Jnr., Dorothy Cadbury, William Cadbury, Walter Barrow, Paul Cadbury, Laurence Cadbury
Front row: Edward Cadbury, George Cadbury, Barrow Cadbury

George took the role of chairman, together with whom four sons of Richard and George comprised the board. Richard's eldest son, Barrow, had joined as early as 1879, and was responsible for finance, accounts and advertising. Richard's second son, William, after an apprenticeship in engineering partly served at the German chocolate company, Stollwerk, joined in 1887. George, having married later than Richard, was not to have his offspring join until the turn of the 20th-century, and it was to be his sons, Edward and George Jnr., who were to play significant roles in dealing with the Van Houten problem.

Edward Cadbury was soon writing to his fellow directors, *I think there are signs of a growing demand for Alkalised cocoa, and that in the near future "absolutely pure cocoa" will not hold first place.'* If indeed it still did. But having accepted the commercial reality, the nettle was finally grasped, *I do not, of course, suggest altering our Cocoa Essence, but should the public taste for Alkalised cocoa continue to increase I think something should be done to meet it.'* This was good open thinking from Edward, especially as, for his entire lifetime to that point, he will have been steeped in the folklore of the business and the central role played by Cocoa Essence and the concept of purity.

Even so, it cannot have been far from Edward's mind, or those of his fellow directors, that such a move would almost certainly accelerate the decline of their iconic Cadbury's Cocoa Essence brand, and this cannot have been an easy decision to take. But having been prepared once before to grasp the opportunities of the new at the expense of the old, when Cocoa Essence itself had sent Cadbury's original range of cocoas into an early grave, they did not shy away. George Cadbury Jnr., a qualified chemist was deputised to head up the project of developing an alkalised cocoa at least as good as Van Houten's (who had not yet shared his secret process.)

George came up with the goods in 1905, but company records state that the launch of what was to be called Bournville Cocoa was put off until 1906, as the company was busy launching another new product at the time (one we shall examine in the next chapter.) But this explanation is somewhat less than credible. No new product opportunity could have been seen to be as important to the company as what was happening to the sales of cocoa. It was the most important issue the company had faced since the loss-making years of the early 1860s. George Jnr. had been given only a year to come up with a product as good as one that was sweeping all before it. Surely it is more likely that t's were crossed and i's dotted in ensuring that all the key elements were in place to ensure victory against Van Houten.

Everyone knew that Bournville Cocoa would hole Cocoa Essence beneath the waterline, so it would have been only good business sense to pause the finger on the firing button, as there would only be one opportunity to get it right. The risks were enormous. What if George Junior's recipe didn't match up? Even with today's highly sophisticated market research techniques, over 90% of all new products fail within three years. What if Van Houten had an even better one up their sleeves? What if the public refused to accept an impure product from Cadbury? It would have been easy for the company to be paralysed or to be half-hearted, but they were neither.

The delay was also helpful in that it gave time to consider the one remaining problem with launching an alkalised cocoa – how to promote it in the context of Cocoa Essence. The first issue to address was how to communicate both in the price list. For the previous thirty years, Cadbury's price list had informed the retailer that, *'We guarantee our Cocoa Essence to be absolutely pure and that no chemicals are used in its manufacture.'* The 1906 Christmas Season price list – the first in which Bournville Cocoa appeared – had dropped the reference to chemicals. The only reference to Bournville Cocoa's product difference was the word 'flavoured.' Never again would an adverse reference to chemicals appear in any Cadbury sales or advertising materials.

But the real difficulty came in deciding how to advertise the two brands to the consumer. Dropping the references to chemicals was the easy part; where it got tricky was in how to sell the benefits of the one without denigrating the other. The more they trumpeted Cocoa Essence as being pure, the more they begged the question as to what exactly went into Bournville Cocoa. Equally, by raising the profile of Bournville Cocoa's superior taste, the more they highlighted the bitterness of Cocoa Essence. This issue would still be exercising the collective minds of the travellers as late as 1911, when a proposed advertisement showing the two together was given the thumbs down as it seemed only to suggest that Cocoa Essence had no flavour and Bournville Cocoa no purity.

However, such details had to be worked out on the hoof as the opportunity highlighted by Van Houten was enormous. With a substantial focus on sampling the new Bournville Cocoa, its sales soon took off despite the lack of clarity on how to advertise. By 1911, only six years after launch, sales of Bournville Cocoa were exceeding those of the original Cocoa Essence formula, whose sales had halved compared to 1904. By 1920 Bournville Cocoa was twice the volume that Cocoa Essence had ever been. Van Houten saw their sales in Britain decimated by the First World War and were unable to put a significant dent into Cadbury's position once normal trade resumed. Cadbury's dominance of the cocoa market was assured for another generation.

Cadbury Bros. had faced its biggest challenge since being saved by the Van Houten press, and had come through with flying colours. Now that the constraint of purity had been dropped, which had restricted the company to only having one definitive brand of cocoa, the company soon felt emboldened enough to launch another brand into the cheaper part of the market in 1910; Welfare Cocoa. This, combined with Bournville Cocoa, squeezed Rowntree's Elect and Fry's Pure Concentrated in a pincer attack, and both competitors' brands were to go into terminal decline from that point onwards; Elect not being alkalised until 1920, by when it was too late.

The launch of Bournville Cocoa was a turning point for Cadbury Bros. Although it had been prompted by competitive pressure from abroad, the willingness to forget past glories and move on was decisive. But its importance would soon be masked by the other new product that allegedly bumped Bournville Cocoa from being launched in 1905. What could have been an interesting, but niche opportunity would turn out to be the brand that would take over the mantle of defining the Cadbury name from Cocoa Essence, but in a way that was much more transferable to the rest of the product portfolio: Cadbury's Dairy Milk.

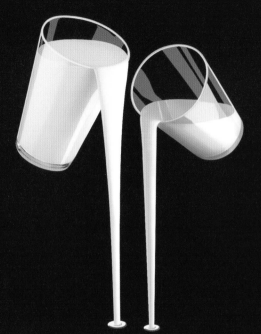

Chapter 3

NEW CATEGORIES: EXTENDING THE CADBURY BRAND BEYOND COCOA

Just as Cadbury had not invented pressed cocoa or alkalised cocoa, they did not invent milk chocolate. Confectioners had long pondered combating the acidity of fermented cocoa by adding nature's natural alkali, milk. The first person known to have combined milk with cocoa was an Englishman, Nicholas Sanders. In 1727, working under the direction of the eminent botanist and physician, Sir Hans Sloane, he developed a recipe for cocoa that made it suitable for adding to hot milk. This was sold in the usual patent medicine style as coming *'Greatly recommended by several eminent physicians, especially those of Sir Hans Sloane's acquaintance (!) for its lightness on the stomach and great use in all consumptive cases.'*

Although the drink was widely appreciated far beyond the chronically consumptive, Sir Hans Sloane's fame – he being the Sloane of London's Sloane Square and Street – was such that over a century later it still carried enough weight for John Cadbury to indulge in a co-branding exercise, selling a product called *'Sir Hans Sloane's Milk chocolate, prepared after the original recipe by Cadbury Brothers.'* This product pre-dated the Cocoa Essence revolution, having been launched in 1849 and lasted a surprisingly long time until 1885.

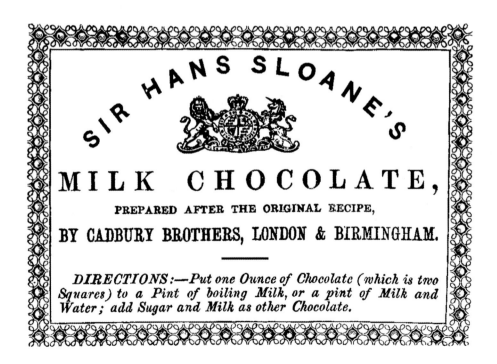

Raising the Bar

But a drink only scratched the surface of the potential that could result from combining milk with cocoa. It had long been realised that by having a delicious chocolate product in bar form, the consumer would be freed from the constraints of necessitating a kettle, heat supply, cups etc. to partake in the category. As a bar, the product would be both portable and ready to eat; this would open up a volume opportunity far greater than the market for cocoa beverages. The addition of milk to such a creation would result in a creamy flavour that could be appreciated by everyone, increasing the potential even further.

But the initial problem was in creating a bar of any chocolate that wasn't as dry and crumbly as cocoa powder. The solution was to come from the cocoa butter that Van Houten's hydraulic press had been invented to remove. While unpressed cocoa nibs – cocoa liquor – contained too much fat to make a palatable drink, they contained too little fat to make a palatable chocolate bar. Somewhat counter-intuitively, given the zeal that had been applied to removing cocoa butter, it dawned on confectioners that adding more cocoa butter to the liquor could solve the problem. Cocoa butter is the secret ingredient that gives chocolate bars their magic. Solid at room temperature, by adding more cocoa butter to the liquor, the crumbliness would be overcome by the firmness of the extra butter. But cocoa butter has the additional property that it melts very quickly at body temperature, and it is the extra quantities of cocoa butter that create the melt in the mouth sensation loved by chocolate eaters the world over.

The development of the first solid bar of eating chocolate, a dark chocolate containing no milk, had been mastered as early as 1847 by Cadbury's Bristol-based rivals, Fry & Sons. Although it was pretty poor by today's standards, being somewhat coarse and bitter, other manufacturers could see the potential if the problems encountered by Fry could be ironed out. In 1879, Cadbury had begun moulding plain chocolate lines, but sales were disappointing at around five tons per week. That same year, Rudolphe Lindt invented a process called '*conching*' which worked to increase the smoothness of chocolate, drive off unwanted volatile flavours and make the chocolate much easier to mould. Chocolate liquor which had been through Lindt's *conche* achieved the smoothness of texture and flavour we would recognise today.

Milking the Idea

But dark chocolate was, and still is, too bitter for many palates. Another Swiss invention at around the same time opened the way for the successful addition of milk, resulting in the first bars of milk chocolate. The trick was in being able to successfully combine water-based milk with fat-based cocoa liquor. The solution was many years in the making and came when chocolate-maker, Daniel Peter, joined forces with his neighbour, who happened to be the inventor of condensed milk, Henri Nestlé. A milk chocolate bar under the Nestlé name was launched, although it was to be another twenty years before Nestlé and Peter had mastered the technology sufficiently to be able to build sales in a serious way.

CHOC-FULL OF GOODNESS !

Cadbury had been experimenting since around 1889 in making milk chocolate at Bournville, but struggled to master the process, not launching a milk chocolate bar until 1897. The resulting product, while comparable with many other early offerings, didn't catch on and sales remained small. After installing an improved milk condensing plant at Bournville in 1902, the company launched a new milk chocolate bar that still didn't manage to put a dent into the Peter recipe being sold by Nestlé, even though it was advertised on the label as being 'Made with pure English milk and cream only.' Sales amounted to under a ton per week, which at the time was less than 1% of Cadbury's business, while the Cadbury board estimated that the Swiss, led by Nestlé/Peter, were sending thirty times that amount into Britain every week.

Cadbury's interest in the idea would be rekindled in 1904 when they spotted a new milk chocolate from the Swiss firm of Cailler that contained a much larger percentage of milk. They immediately saw in the Cailler product the key insight behind the appeal of milk chocolate that would endure up to the present day. The breakthrough in thinking was that the best milk chocolate would be defined by having the best milk credentials, as opposed to the best chocolate credentials.

The board turned to their resident qualified chemist, George Cadbury Jnr., to add the development of a milk chocolate superior to that of the latest Swiss offering to his to-do list, along with beating the Dutch on alkalised cocoa. The direction in which to steer the product research was clear: parity products were clearly no use, so the next Cadbury milk chocolate had to have a far higher milk content than any previously available. By the use of large quantities of fresh full cream milk from British pastures, they would not only have a flavour to beat the Swiss, but the potential to leverage the quality, quantity and the British-ness of the milk in their advertising. By late 1904 the product recipe had been settled and attention switched to the engineering challenges of building an infrastructure for milk collection, delivery, evaporation, conching and moulding. George Cadbury Jnr. went to the board and reported that the product was ready; the process defined, and was given the go-ahead to launch in 1905.

The next question was what capacity should the company gear up for? The technology was large, complex and expensive, making it a very difficult decision. Too little capacity and the opportunity might be lost to others; both Rowntree and Fry already had milk chocolate products in the market, and although neither was close to matching the Swiss products, they too must have been aware of the trends in the market. On the other hand, too much capacity would be money down the drain, as it would have had little other use if the new milk chocolate didn't take off. It was also a category in which the company had had very little experience, so detailed projections were thin on the ground.

The board must have thought they were being bullish in suggesting the installation of a capacity of five tons per week – a 500% increase on their current business and the most they had ever achieved with a chocolate bar. George Jnr. however was passionate that the much milkier recipe would trounce the Swiss and argued vociferously for quadruple that amount – twenty tons a week, i.e. twenty times their current sales and two thirds of the sales of all the Swiss companies combined. With nothing other to go on than their feeling for the market, it is remarkable that, at a time when the Cocoa Essence headache had not yet been solved, the company would commit the resources for such a figure, which represented an incremental 20% total manufacturing capacity of the entire company. But George got his twenty tons.

The one remaining problem was the name – an important factor in communicating the key product benefit of milk – which was to be solved by the daughter of one of their

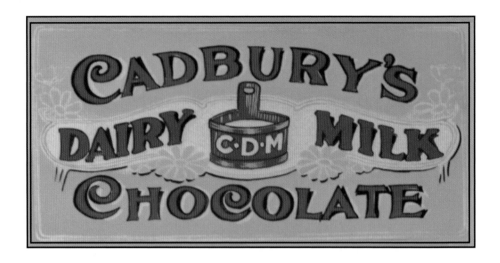

customers in Plymouth, a Mrs. Creacy. Suggested names such as Jersey, Highland Milk and Dairy Maid were jettisoned in favour of Mrs. Creacy's suggestion to her local Cadbury traveller of 'Dairy Milk'. A wise decision; the milk to be used in the new bar would be coming from within a fifty-mile radius around Birmingham rather than from the Scottish Highlands or Channel Islands.

Cadbury's Dairy Milk Chocolate would be a stealth success for the company. It made its appearance in June 1905, the Travellers circular announcing that although *the milk chocolate that we have been making during the last year or so is almost precisely similar in its character to Peters, but the new kind will sell even where Peters have the monopoly. It is evident that the demand for Milk Chocolate is larger than ever.'*

The company believed that the future of milk chocolate lay in giving the public the best possible value for money. They designed the plainest possible box which contained one gross of unwrapped blocks, each of which could be broken into six 1 penny bars. A similar parsimony also applied to the allocation of advertising and trade promotional budgets, which were heavily directed in favour of Bournville Cocoa as it fought its epic battle with Van Houten. Although the Travellers had declared almost to a man that the cheap box with little advertising wouldn't sell, it became one of the most successful lines in the company's history.

But success was to come somewhat slower than would be demanded of such an initiative today. In the first three years after launch sales had doubled to two tons a week, which must have had George Jnr. somewhat nervous given his bullishness, and not only were the Swiss not vanquished, their sales had continued to grow as well. But the policy of putting quality and value ahead of presentation and advertising created a groundswell of momentum as more and more consumers discovered the product. Along with the success of Bournville Cocoa, by 1910, Cadbury Bros. had overtaken Fry to become Britain's largest manufacturer of cocoa and chocolate. By the outbreak of World War One, Cadbury's Dairy Milk had become the firm's largest selling line, accounting for over half of total output by weight; such a vindication of George's optimism that further capacity had had to be installed. In 1917, Cadbury's original, much darker milk chocolate product was quietly dropped, enabling the company to focus on one milk chocolate recipe.

It is remarkable, given the iconic role the Dairy Milk brand would play in the subsequent development of the Cadbury business, just how little of the early success of the brand could be attributed to advertising. Initially, there was a lack of clarity in what to say about the new product. The box labels for Dairy Milk featured rosy-

cheeked dairymaids ferrying gallons of creamy milk into the kitchen, but with the punch-line, '*Rich Nutty Flavour.*' However, this was a temporary lapse from the key insight that it was all about the milk, so advertising for Cadbury's Dairy Milk from that point on was focused solely on reinforcing the brand's grip on milk credentials. A year after launch, the label and advertisements were featuring a pixie skimming the cream off containers of milk in a dairy with the punch-line amended to say, '*Rich in Cream*'.

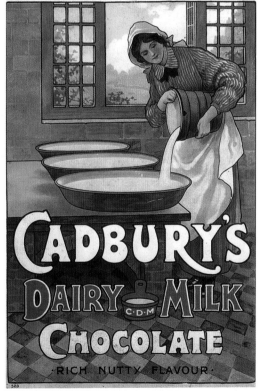

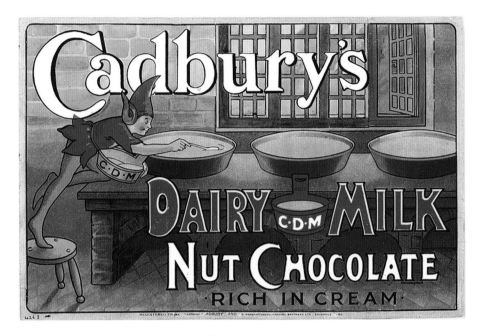

Advertising support remained small as the company stuck to its value policy. Even in the years after 1913 when it had become the company's best seller, significantly more funds were being spent advertising and promoting cocoa than milk chocolate. It would not be until 1928 that substantial funds would be invested, by which time the brand was already far and away the biggest selling chocolate product in Britain. Edward Cadbury, reflecting many years later, stated that *'Advertising up until 1928 had been generally in small spaces, unexciting in presentation and layout.'* Edward was clear that the success of Dairy Milk was built on the recipe and quality of the line itself (which remains virtually unchanged to this day), together with its cheapness.

So what did the competition make of Dairy Milk? Fry had launched their milk powder-based bar in 1902 under the brand name 'Five Boys.' While the famous visual depicting the little tyke's journey from Desperation (induced in the picture by the photographer's use of an ammonia-soaked rag) to Pacification, Expectation, Acclamation, and ultimately the Realisation.... its Fry, resonated with the public, the product never matched that of Dairy Milk.

Up in York, Rowntree's powder-based Swiss Milk Chocolate and Mountain Milk Chocolate had neither the product credentials nor the advertising support to survive the Cadbury onslaught. Cadbury had compounded

FRY'S MILK CHOCOLATE

DESPERATION. PACIFICATION. EXPECTATION. ACCLAMATION. REALIZATION.
"IT'S FRY'S"

J.S. FRY & SONS L.TD. BRISTOL & LONDON.

Rowntree's misery by reducing prices on their original, darker milk chocolate, again squeezing the competition from both ends as they were doing with their Bournville and Welfare cocoas. The Nestlé business was decimated by the insuperable supply problems caused by the First World War. Swiss imports dried up to a trickle, during which time Cadbury's Dairy Milk had completely sewn up the market, such that in the aftermath the Swiss were restricted to small, niche roles. By the early 1920's, Cadbury's Dairy Milk was the country's pre-eminent milk chocolate with sales 20 times larger than those of Rowntree's, and Nestlé having virtually disappeared. Only Fry's Five Boys, by now made with condensed milk, could be considered a competitor.

For the third time in fifty years, Cadbury had launched a product that would transform their business, and for the third time it would not be in a category they had invented or played any role in developing. Cadbury's success was not that they were chocolate innovators, but rather the way in which they entered, exploited and grew markets developed by others. This required the mindset of being willing to move on, as we saw with Bournville Cocoa, but the real secrets were their obsession with beating existing product formulations – driven by sufficient investment in the technical ability to do so – along with a 'think big' mentality, which led them to place large bets when other manufacturers vacillated.

All Because the Lady Loves…

Although Dairy Milk and Bournville Cocoa were driving the success of the firm, the Cadbury product portfolio had broadened out beyond cocoa beverages and chocolate bars into areas where they did have a couple of notable innovations to their name.

The third section of the chocolate market – boxes of chocolates – that would fall before the Cadbury onslaught, had initially been dominated by yet more foreigners, this time the French. But it was not to be a simple task of identifying the leading product, and then briefing George Jnr.'s specialists to beat it. This was because the category itself consisted of a multitude of different products, manufactured by a diverse bunch of companies from the large, industrialised set-up to the small *chocolatier*. There was not so much a definitive product as an overall class of products whose appeal resided in their diversity of individual chocolates, and a romantic, almost exotic imagery that more often than not was more important than the product.

George and Richard knew their work so far on building the Cadbury name would be insufficient to have an impact in this category where high quality in effect meant 'French-ness.' The first initiative to move the Cadbury name upscale was the opening of a depot in Paris. The goal was not so much to sell large

THE COMING OF THE FANCY BOX.

The idea that chocolate boxes should bear pictures instead of printed labels was conceived by Richard Cadbury in 1868. His artistic talent was always invaluable to the business, and it was he who designed the first fancy boxes introduced, as well as numerous box-labels and advertisements. The picture box readily caught the public fancy, and did much to popularise the firm's lines generally. The designs shown are reproduced as a record of his talent as they appear on a page in the "Cadbury Family Book."

itself up by the bootstraps with the launch of Cocoa Essence, Richard Cadbury had hit on a unique notion for increasing the appeal of chocolate boxes. Boxes from the continent by this time came with a modest printed label stuck on the lid, featuring designs that children could cut out and stick in scrapbooks. Printers sold such designs by the sheet to whoever wanted to buy, which of course meant that a manufacturer could well find the same design appearing on a competitor's box. Richard realised that recent developments in lithography had opened up the possibility of a manufacturer commissioning their own designs of picture labels.

Not content with just coming up with the idea, Richard brought his hobby as an amateur artist into play by painting many of the pictures himself. An advertisement placed in the *Birmingham Gazette* on 8th January, 1869 proudly announced,

volumes into the French market, but more the fact of being able to put Birmingham, London *and Paris* on the Cadbury labels. Next was the task of launching products with French-sounding names into the market. *'Chocolat du Mexique'* had been one of their early cocoa lines, and the same strategy was to be employed by assortment products such as *'Chocolat des Delices aux Fruits'* which appeared in 1867 under a separate section in the price list, headed 'Fancy Boxes.'

The presentation of boxed chocolates – known as Assortments in the industry – was an area of the market where Cadbury would be more the innovator rather than the follower/exploiter. As early as 1868, only two years after the company had dragged

'Messrs Cadbury's four-ounce box of chocolate crèmes is among the pictorial novelties offered to the trade. Chaste yet simple, it consists of a blue-eyed maiden some six summers old….designed and drawn by Mr Richard Cadbury.'

Richard turned out many more designs such as vases of flowers, alpine scenes from his holidays in Europe, and the rest of his children – the blue-eyed maiden having been his own daughter, Jessie. Accessible pricing of the small boxes at threepence and sixpence meant they appealed more to the everyday consumer rather than the art connoisseur and were an instant hit. Defining a genre that lives on to this day, Richard had created the beginnings of a mass market for special, but affordable chocolate gifts, and in the process, adding special-ness to Cadbury's growing reputation for quality and value.

The explosion in the range of fancy box Assortments Cadbury put out into the market was astounding. By 1887, the range had expanded to over a hundred lines. Only ten years later, the range had more than doubled in size up to 264 lines while, by 1904, the range had doubled again up to over 450 lines.

But volumes of boxed chocolates, while significant to Cadbury, were not of the scale to which we are accustomed today. The packaging and labour intensive manufacturing process costs combined to keep all but the cheapest assortments an infrequent purchase, which was further reinforced by many of the lines only being available in shops in the run up to Christmas. Plus Cadbury were hardly benefiting from economies of scale with such a vast range of relatively small volume lines. What was needed was a chocolate box for the masses.

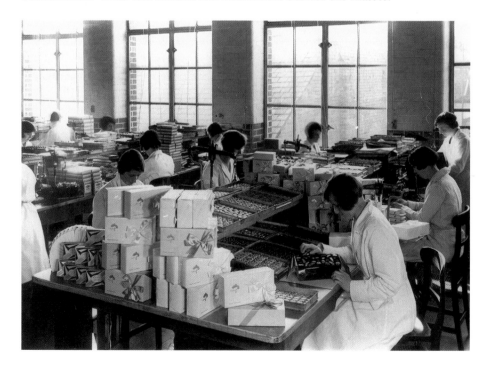

The company's range of loose assortments was made available covered in both milk and plain chocolate and sold to the retailer in 5½lb boxes. These were then laid out in front of the consumer in display trays and sold for 3½d a lb. To keep things simple, the two lines were called Milk Tray and Plain Tray. In 1916, Cadbury decided to package the products into ½lb, rather plainly decorated cardboard boxes and soon had a runaway success on their hands from the much more popular-tasting Milk Tray. Being boxed rather than loose, the effect was special enough to be considered a gift for a wide range of occasions such as birthdays, anniversaries and the like. But the relatively low cost of the packaging compared to fancy boxes made the price low enough to appeal to a broad section of the population, and by being available all year, the volume potential was increased even further.

This concept proved to be an instant hit. The ½lb was followed eight years later by a 1lb box; two formats of the Milk Tray brand that live on to this day, even after metrication, albeit now renamed 227gms and 454gms. The company were quick to discontinue selling the loose chocolates, because the appeal of unwrapped chocolates had moved downmarket, making it very difficult to uphold the image

2111-12
Milk Tray Chocolate Assortment
1 lb. ¼ dozen

2109-12
Tray Chocolate Assortment
1 lb. ¼ dozen

of quality that had been a driving force for Cadbury entering the chocolate assortments category in the first place. Similarly, the highly successful unwrapped 1 pence Dairy Milk bars were also replaced by wrapped product.

Taking the Biscuit

The last sector of the market in which Cadbury's would have a significant presence would be the one in which they were most definitely the innovator. In 1891 the company successfully submitted a patent for the idea of a chocolate biscuit,

The object of our invention is to produce what we term a "chocolate biscuit." The chocolate biscuits constructed in accordance with our present invention consist of one, two or more biscuits surrounded by chocolate, which, whilst possessing all the nourishing and food sustaining properties of ordinary biscuits are very palatable and will serve as a very nourishing and tempting article of diet for travellers, invalids and others.

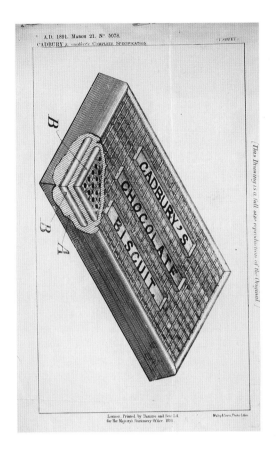

Somewhat perversely, Cadbury completely missed the significance of their invention and put next to no effort into developing the category. Their first chocolate biscuit lines to appear after the awarding of the patent on 25th April, 1891 were the somewhat unimaginatively named, '1d Biscuits' and '2d Biscuits.' These were buried in a section headed 'Best Quality Fancy Goods' and were the 983rd and 985th lines in a by then bulging order catalogue. This new category was not getting the major push that it needed to become quickly established, so, perhaps unsurprisingly,

by 1902 it was only accounting for 2% of their production.

In Dairy Milk, Bournville Cocoa and Milk Tray, Cadbury now had in place the leading brands in the three main categories of the market, and a foothold with a new category of their own invention. But for Cadbury to continue its impressive growth of the late 19th- and early 20th-centuries, it had to create much larger markets for its strong brands. But to do that, Cadbury had to have an infrastructure capable of doing so.

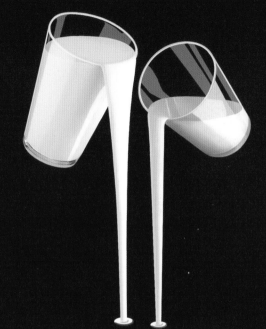

Chapter 4

CREATING BUSINESS ADVANTAGE: ALIGNING INFRASTRUCTURE WITH STRATEGY

It is hard to imagine today the El Dorado that was late 19th-century Britain. In his seminal book, *Scale and Scope*, Alfred Chandler describes the opportunity that presented itself to the Victorian businessman,

'In Britain, the rapid internal migration from country to city and from agriculture to industry, resulted in the largest concentrated consumer market yet created. By 1850, more than 10 million persons living within the geographical small quadrangle bounded by London, Cardiff, Glasgow and Edinburgh depended on money wages to obtain their entire supplies of food, drink, clothing, and housing. That golden quadrangle remained the world's richest consumer market for more than a century.'[1]

Where the Cadbury brothers were to triumph was in their grasp of this opportunity by aligning their business infrastructure, key processes and people with their over-arching consumer strategy of quality and value.

Bournville – The Ideal Base

As 19th-century markets continued to grow, a main preoccupation for most successful business owners was investing in their production, distribution and selling capabilities. But in those boom times, no-one could predict just how big a business could become. No sooner would a factory be built than it was too small. Previously ideal locations would soon become cramped as nearby businesses also rapidly expanded. Many businesses would ultimately fail because, while they planned for growth, they were unable to cope with exponential growth.

Added to the uncertainty of what size of business to plan for, the issue of being located in a city centre went far beyond dealing with the smog belching from the neighbouring foundries and factories. Having inherited their father's zeal for tackling head-on the social ills of the Industrial Revolution, both George and Richard never accepted what, at the time, appeared to be the inevitable consequences of rapid industrialisation. Seeing the rural location of their

---

[1]   Alfred D. Chandler Jnr., *Scale and Scope: The Dynamics of Industrial Capitalism*, (Harvard University Press, Cambridge Mass. 1990) p251

upbringing disappear under a tidal wave of factories and slum houses, they were appalled at the impact on both the physical and moral well-being of the people who flocked to live and work there.

As with most of their initiatives on the product side of the business, George and Richard would not have claimed to have been the originators of the ideas they were to employ. Many businessmen had had second thoughts about the typical employment practices of the time. Richard Arkwright, the inventor of the factory system, had employed children as young as eight; but his son was to abandon the practice. Robert Owen, with his New Lanarkshire Mills, had pioneered a more reformist approach to motivating workers, as opposed to working them like slaves, and the Cadbury Brothers were certainly aware of his work. But it was to be the bringing together of the separate strands of business efficiency and moral duty that would make the Cadbury business uniquely successful.

Where their philanthropic and business agendas merged was in their belief that the existing factory practices they saw elsewhere in Birmingham were not only shameful, but were appallingly wasteful. Their thoughts about a replacement for the increasingly cramped Bridge Street factory would be decisively influenced by almost messianic convictions that industry need not be inextricably associated with slum houses; that factories need not be dark and airless; that workers need not be treated worse than cattle; that progress need not lower living standards. From a pure business perspective, Richard and George Cadbury also believed that these commonplace features of late 19th-century industrialisation made workers less willing and able to add anything to their work beyond the bare minimum, and as a consequence, reduced profits.

The decision of what to do with their Bridge Street factory was to assume enormous significance for the brothers. Many issues had to be considered before a final decision could be made. They needed vast amounts of space for possible future growth; a location away from slum-ridden Birmingham to be able to provide ideal working conditions, and most crucially, excellent transportation links. After extensive prospecting, much of it done by Richard spending his weekends walking alongside the tracks of the various railway lines that radiated from Birmingham, a 14-acre plot of rural farmland 4 miles southwest of Birmingham was purchased on June 18th, 1878.

Bordered on one side by the Birmingham West Suburban Railway, alongside which lay the Worcester and Birmingham canal, the site was ideally placed for getting raw materials in and finished products out. The Bourn stream, which ran through the property, would provide more than ample fresh, clear water for the generation of steam, and the location was a delight to the eye. The Bourn stream also lent its name to the factory, albeit in the Gallic version of Bournville as another strand to Cadbury's quest for upmarket imagery

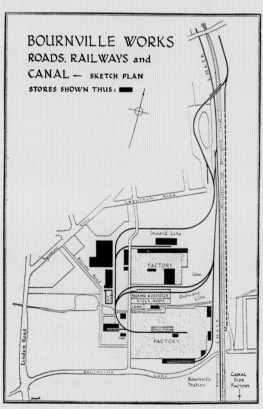

The sidings are represented by a single line. In actuality there are at many points two, three, or four sets of tracks.

George helped design a factory many times bigger than the Bridge Street premises (over two million bricks would be used in its construction) and the move in September 1879 had financially stretched the company's resources almost to breaking point. The factory was many times bigger than it needed to be for the existing level of sales, and matters were not helped by a surge in the prices for raw cocoa that year. Consequently, the brothers had to work harder and longer than ever before. So tight were finances that the brothers' lunches for weeks on end consisted of one leg of mutton that by Fridays would yield only the toughest of meagre scraps.

But the crisis passed as sales of Cocoa Essence continued to grow, so much so that within five years the brothers were investing more into their new location. Aided by the upgrading of the local rail line to double-track, and its connection to the main routes that serviced Britain's rapidly expanding cities, Cadbury constructed their own siding so that trains could pull right alongside the warehouse decks. Built at standard gauge to eliminate unnecessary unloading and reloading, this internal railway was to grow into a six-mile network operated by the company's own locomotives. Eventually, three trains a day of sixty cars each would be leaving Bournville packed with product; quite a change from the one horse-drawn van used on the opening of Bournville to transport goods from the factory to the railway station. Meanwhile on the raw materials side, cocoa beans and sugar made their stately way to the factory via the nearby canal from the ports of Liverpool and Bristol.

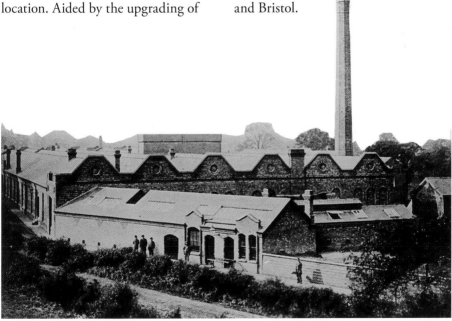

This logistically efficient set-up was to give Cadbury decisive cost advantages over their city-bound competitor, Fry. Although Fry were still the much larger of the two, they stayed on in their central Bristol location where they had none of the advantages of Bournville. Cadbury had discovered for themselves the concept of economies of scale. They could easily accommodate their growing sales in their large and efficient factory at virtually no extra cost other than ingredients and some labour. On the other hand, Fry grew piecemeal by building a succession of extra factories that were cramped and inefficient when compared to Bournville. Consequently, the extra sales that came to both companies from the growing affluence in the 'Golden Quadrangle' were much more profitable to Cadbury than they were to Fry. This was the beginnings of a virtuous circle for Cadbury, where they would be able to offer better products, at lower prices, and with much more advertising than their competitors.

The scale and speed of Cadbury's subsequent success was staggering. By 1889, ten years after moving to Bournville (a factory deemed far too large at the time,) floor space had needed to be doubled, and the number of workers had gone up five-fold. Another ten years later, the workforce had more than doubled again and, having had to buy further land to increase the factory, the floor space was seven times bigger than originally built.

The company's launch of Dairy Milk in 1905 simultaneously solved old and created new logistical problems. Prior to Dairy Milk, the hundreds of tons of cocoa butter that flowed from the presses in the manufacture of cocoa were a waste product and had been sold off at commodity prices on the London markets. But the production of milk chocolate bars required the use of extra cocoa butter, so seemingly here was a perfect match. Cadbury redoubled their efforts to sell more cocoa and keep the production of cocoa and Dairy Milk in tandem, where cocoa butter was neither bought nor sold off. This aim of keeping a balance between the two was to influence the company's thinking for decades. George Cadbury was to constantly remark that selling chocolate bars was easy whereas selling enough cocoa was the big challenge.

Another logistical impact from the success of Dairy Milk came from the use of fresh milk, which had involved the creation of a whole new infrastructure for its collection, transportation, receipt, storage, condensation and processing. By 1910 they were using over a million gallons of milk a year. Again led by George Jnr., who was something of a transportation expert in addition to being a chemist, the company decided that there had to be a better way than transporting such massive volumes of milk into an increasingly complex factory. Since the milk was to be evaporated anyway, it seemed to make little sense to ship a substance that was seven-eighths of unwanted water over such distances. Also, on warm summer days, up to half of a day's milk could spoil before it reached Bournville, and the unwanted effluent was polluting the Bourn stream, making it useless for other manufacturing purposes.

So in 1911, Cadbury took the momentous step of taking the cocoa to the milk and processing it there, rather than bringing the milk (and water) to the cocoa. Their first milk processing factory was opened in 1911 near the Staffordshire town of Knighton, an area surrounded by dairy farms. Now that Cadbury were operating much closer to the source of the milk, they were able to exercise much greater control over its quality, with regular inspections of both dairies and cows. The company then were able to further enhance the selling story for Dairy Milk with the claim that Cadbury's Dairy Milk was made from fresh, full-cream British milk, and made at once without delay. This was a fine example of a logistics strategy being in perfect harmony with a brand strategy, which was a concept that the company would carry through into its sourcing of its principle raw material – cocoa.

African Gold – Ensuring Quality in the Supply Chain

As their business had expanded prior to the First World War, Cadbury could not necessarily assume that their rapidly increasing sales volumes would be automatically matched by similar increases in supplies of the higher quality cocoa used for their products. The company needed ever increasing quantities of Grade A cocoa at predictable prices if the Bournville machine was to run efficiently and the Cadbury brand reputation be protected.

Apart from owning a small cocoa-growing plantation in the West Indies, Cadbury sourced all their cocoa from the main dealing markets in London and Liverpool. But the revelation that the cocoa sold at these markets partly originated from sources strongly reputed to use slavery in its cultivation prompted the company to look for alternatives. They sent one of their men from Trinidad over to the Gold Coast in 1907 for some initial prospecting, but the news was not encouraging: African beans were of such poor quality they did not even qualify for the lowest grade of usable cocoa.

Returning to Bournville in 1908, the Cadbury expert recommended an approach that was to transform the company's cocoa sourcing strategy. The key elements to the proposal were:

- Gold Coast conditions were perfect for the growing of cocoa.
- There was no inherent defect in the Gold Coast beans; it was the farming and transportation methods that were causing the problem.
- The company should invest in two or three strategically located drying houses, as the main quality problems were the result of poor practices in drying the harvested beans.

- The evangelising of quality improvement would have local government support and had every prospect of yielding results in the foreseeable future.

- The company should buy a small estate to set up a model plantation, and buying stations should be set up at suitable locations.
- The market was dominated by a cabal of buyers who paid in 'chits' which could only be redeemed in local stores for shoddy merchandise. Therefore, if the company were to pay in cash and at a level above the going rate, they would have first choice of the crop.

The proposal was agreed in its entirety and a beefed-up team was sent back to the Gold Coast to begin its implementation, which was not without teething troubles. The quality of bean being brought to the buying stations varied dramatically, even within the same sack, making the buying process much more laborious than anticipated, Unsurprisingly, the local buyers deeply resented Cadbury paying over the odds and in hard cash, and, as they controlled transport to the coast, were able to restrict Cadbury to buying and shipping a mere eight tons of the 1908 crop to Bournville. The only good news in the enterprise was that Bournville discovered the quality to be significantly above the cocoa still being bought in the London and Liverpool cocoa markets.

Developing from this modest start was not made any easier by the difficult conditions being experienced by the Cadbury men. The visiting of cocoa-growing villages involved being carried in a sling chair through miles of steaming jungle, while an small army of porters followed up with the luggage. Malaria, guinea-worm, tsetse flies and Blackwater Fever all took their toll and made the Gold Coast not the cushiest job on the company payroll. But the hard work seemed to pay dividends quickly. Supported by the colonial government and the travelling inspectors of the Department of Agriculture, Cadbury's evangelising of the benefits of growing high quality cocoa resulted in the country's annual crop rising to over 26,000 tons in 1911, from which Cadbury selected the highest quality 1,767 tons to ship over to Bournville.

In a report on the 1912 buying season, the senior Cadbury Gold Coast man provided further encouragement,

'We are still the principle influence in the production and maintenance of a higher grade of cocoa, and it is from this aspect that the enterprise in the Gold Coast is worth going on with.'

Which of course was the nub of the issue: the Gold Coast presented Cadbury with the opportunity to create competitive advantage in the sourcing of their principal raw ingredient. By advocating and tangibly assisting in the raising of quality standards in one of the most ideal cocoa-growing locations in the world, and by short-circuiting the buying markets, Cadbury were developing a highly advantaged sourcing strategy.

There were many temptations for Cadbury not to stay the course. Cadbury were accused of being far to picky in their standards, sending many growers into the arms of other traders who bought, with no questions asked, supplies that Cadbury had refused outright to consider. Local traders also began shipping cocoa to Liverpool on their own behalf which, while not meeting Cadbury standards, opened up to Cadbury's competitors some of the advantages of the Gold Coast adventure. Last, but not least, Cadbury were losing money on the venture, as their purchases were well below the level demanded by the level of their investments to date.

But the following season provided encouragement that the strategy was correct. Purchases more than doubled, and the quality was exceptional: 92% of their Gold Coast purchases were rated within the top two quality grades, compared with only 24% for the Gold Coast cocoa that made its own way to the Liverpool markets – a figure typical for the purchases of their competitors. Fry, among others, had not been slow to see the benefits that Cadbury were beginning to accrue. Some of the European chocolate firms set up their own buying organisations in the Gold Coast, and Fry had begun buying direct from local traders. While they didn't have the pick of the crop, Cadbury's evangelising was raising standards all round, making the Gold Coast a popular cocoa source.

Clearly, Cadbury could not keep Fry out, but they soon realised that the key to long term benefit from their investments was going to be their relationship of trust and respect with the local growers. Consequently, rather than compete head on with Fry for purchases, it was decided to invite Fry to let Cadbury buy for them. It was a win-win. Fry would be spared the expense of setting up their own infrastructure, while Cadbury would have greater throughput to help pay off their investment; Fry would gain access to better quality cocoa, but Cadbury would keep the all-important direct relationship with the buyers. A subsequent contract to supply Rowntree with cocoa further solidified Cadbury's Gold Coast strategy.

By 1936, the Gold Coast had become the world's largest producer of cocoa beans with a crop of over 300,000 tons. Two years later, 98% of Cadbury's bean requirements were sourced from there, with 64% of the Cadbury-Fry-Rowntree organisation's purchases being Grade I beans, compared to an industry average of only 21%. Cadbury's Gold Coast involvement had given the company an unrivalled access to ever-increasing quantities of the highest grade of cocoa over a prolonged period of time. But while Bournville and the Gold Coast provided

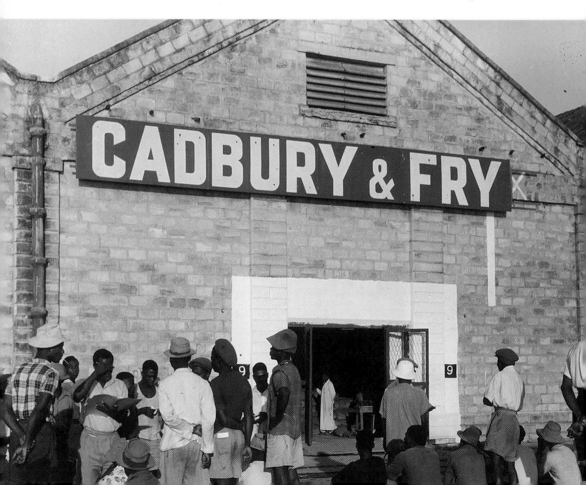

a fantastic logistics base, their effectiveness would be massively enhanced by Cadbury's philosophy towards their people, and how that translated into workplace practices. They were to overcome the biggest limitation of industrialisation – the dehumanisation and disengagement of employees.

Employee Engagement: Getting People to Give Their Best

The popular perception today of Cadbury in the early 20th-century is that of a quaintly paternalistic enterprise. While it is true that George Cadbury certainly had some strong views about how the adult males of Birmingham could and should improve their lifestyles, Bournville in the first thirty years of the 20th-century was anything but a sleepy, bucolic haven for the work-shy. The Concise Oxford Dictionary defines paternalism as, 'limiting the freedom of the subject by well-meant regulations.' In contrast, working at Bournville involved the unleashing of the potential of each and every employee by far-sighted and leading edge employment practices, and in the process driving further business success.

The 'Bournville Experiment' as it was always called by its originators, came in two distinct phases. Up until the death of Richard Cadbury in 1899, the approach taken to the firm's employees could be fairly described as enlightened paternalism, and differed little from those of Lever Bros., Rowntree's and others. It was to be the reorganisation of the management of Cadbury Bros. that followed Richard's death that was the catalyst for the second, much more revolutionary phase.

Responsibility for running the business was now devolved down to Edward, George Jnr., William and Barrow.

They were keenly aware that the size of the business and the industrialisation of its production processes had made their fathers' personal approach untenable. But they were equally aware that the success of the business was also rapidly changing the relationship between company and employee, in their view to the detriment of both. Mechanisation, if left to its own devices, would inevitably reduce the ability and motivation of the employee to contribute anything to the job apart from the bare minimum. The destructive notion that workers do just enough to avoid being sacked and employers pay just enough to prevent employees leaving would not be allowed to take root at Bournville.

This second phase was not implemented as a fully worked out plan but grew over time as new ideas were encountered and then assimilated into the emerging Cadbury way. The four sons of Richard and George were prodigious travellers, both at home and abroad, and were always on the lookout for new ideas. The deciding factor as to what would be incorporated back at Bournville always came back to the goal of improving the Cadbury brand attributes of quality and value. By 1912, Edward Cadbury, subsequently honoured as being one of management's key fifty figures,[2] was able to write a book[3] defining in great detail all the components of their model. The purpose of the whole exercise, wrote Edward, was that of efficiency,

The efficiency of the employees shows itself in many ways, one of the most striking being the elimination of waste and the reduction of cost in the various departments. Where discipline is good and elicits the goodwill and efficiency of the employees, the staff and foremen can give practically all their attention to organizing their departments…The increased intelligence of employees, obtained by method of selection and the (Cadbury) educational system, facilitates the scientific organization of their work.[4]

---

[2] Morgen Witzel, *Fifty Key Figures in Management*, (Routledge Key Guides, New York, 2003) pp43–48

[3] Edward Cadbury, *Experiments in Industrial Organization*, (Longman's, Green & Co., New York 1912)

[4] Cadbury, pxviii

> From Education Department   To Fred Brown,
>   Bournville.   Post Boy.
>
> 'Many skilled trades are carried on at Bournville, and the Firm encourages youths to apprentice themselves to these. Vacancies will shortly occur and an examination will be held. All apprentices must attend a Day Continuation School or a Technical School until they are 21, and all time spent at school will be paid for by the firm.'
>
>   (Signed) C.A.H.
>   Director of Education.

The first and most obvious component – that of choosing the cream of the crop of people seeking employment with the firm – largely looked after itself, due to their success and reputation as a good employer. But leaving school at the age of fourteen was, in Cadbury's view, a wholly insufficient preparation for an empowered and contributing worker. They believed that continued education would develop initiative, adaptation, self-control and a general knowledge of mechanical and scientific principles; valuable attributes in the ever-changing, fully industrialised business that Cadbury had rapidly become.

Consequently, the parents or guardians of all successful applicants under the age of 18 years received a letter informing them that evening classes would be a compulsory feature of their offspring's employment. The unskilled workman, who would have the most limited opportunity to demonstrate initiative and adaptation, was allowed a wide choice of subjects designed to compensate for his depressingly monotonous working day. Even the least capable employee would have his outlook on life broadened and deepened by courses in such subjects as music, art, science, literature, political economy and social philosophy. Classes focused on specific workplace tasks were also run, such as a three year course in cardboard box making. With such in-depth education, there was really no excuse not to be stunningly efficient at making boxes, and having plenty to think about while doing so.

Most tasks in the factory for women, who constituted over half the workforce, involved precise manual dexterity. Consequently, their compulsory PT focused on gymnastics and ball games to improve eye-hand coordination. In all such activities, which constituted two half hour sessions a week, taken in work time with no loss of pay, the aim was *'to develop alertness and decision, with that perfect control of the body which develops a consciousness of power, inspiring courage, confidence and resolution'*, all of which would reap benefits when tending their machines. Henry Ford's strategy of increasing the speed of the production line and firing anyone who couldn't keep up seems somewhat primitive in comparison.

The visible and long-term commitment of the firm to their welfare agenda was massive. As one example, in 1902 a staggering 30% of the company's annual capital expenditure was on welfare facilities. The Girl's Swimming Baths

(which still stand today) cost seven times more than was spent on extending the management offices. The baths were the best equipped in Birmingham, if not the country: crystal-clear water kept at a rather bracing 74 degrees Fahrenheit in summer (76 in winter), with slipper baths and spray baths, together with permanent instructors, to complete the impressive facility.

The *quid pro quo* was employee commitment and loyalty, so that skills in even the most mundane jobs would be honed to the finest of degrees and retained by the company. Virtually the only turnover at Bournville came from retirements and prospective brides – Cadbury following the usual practice at the time of not employing married women. In contrast, over in Detroit in 1913, the Ford Motor Company had an annual turnover of over 380%. Ford management had been stunned to learn that only 640 out of their 15,000 workforce qualified for a newly-instituted three year loyalty bonus;[5] a situation Ford only managed to address by doubling wages overnight.

---

[5] Robert Lacey, *Ford – The men and the machines*, (Little, Brown & Co., Boston 1986), pp117–130

But Cadbury were much smarter than Ford in how they structured monetary rewards. They paid a better than average basic wage, though not dramatically so. This was then augmented by an element of piece rates for the exceeding of personal output targets. On top of that, the company came up in 1923 with an innovative profit sharing scheme. As dividend payments were made to family shareholders, the same dividend rate was paid on a hypothetical block of shares into the company's Welfare Fund. First call on these funds went to employees who were put on short time working. After short time claims had been met, the balance was distributed as an annual bonus among employees in proportion based on age and length of service, and to a lesser extent, sex.

This reward programme was finely tuned to work at three levels. Firstly, the higher basic wage encouraged the best applicants to join; secondly, piece rates encouraged personal achievement; and lastly, the profit sharing encouraged loyalty. That short time working existed at Bournville demonstrates Cadbury Bros. was primarily focused on being firstly a profitable business, and not a provider of out-relief for the disadvantaged. As the business entered the economically turbulent 1920's, permanent lay-offs were also not unknown. The company softened the blow by providing its own non-contributory unemployment scheme to augment what it considered to be the government's woefully inadequate Unemployment Insurance Act. The Pension Fund and a Savings Fund rounded out what was without doubt one of the most comprehensive and well-thought through package of benefits in the country.

But having high calibre, well rounded, loyal employees, highly-trained in their field, and cleverly incentivised to work harder and smarter was not the end of the Cadbury system. The true prize was the active mental engagement of all employees in the goals and strategy of the company. The key component required for that was exceptionally well-structured channels of communication between management and employees. The Bournville Works Magazine was begun by the company in November 1902 with the stated aim, *'To promote what for lack of a better word we may describe as the Bournville "Spirit" – to foster comradeship and good fellowship, and to add one more to the links binding together the community at Bournville in mutual service.'*

Having become aware of Lever Bros' 'Progress' magazine, which had been launched in 1899, Cadbury as they had done so often before, were not slow to know a good idea when they saw one and adopt it into their approach. People needed to know that the company was about quality and value. The task of the Works Magazine was to encourage everyone to think around that very simple proposition, which it did in subtle and imaginative ways. But without doubt its greatest triumph was as cheerleader and focal point for what would become Cadbury's secret weapon, their suggestion scheme.

It is difficult to imagine the impact the scheme was to have. Up to that point, British workers would never have dreamt that they might be asked for ideas on how things could be improved, let alone see them implemented and be paid a monetary prize for doing so. In 1901, George Cadbury Jnr., who had been on a trip to America, had seen the emergence in a few enlightened firms of the practice where employees could make known to management their ideas and suggestions about improving products or processes. He passionately advocated the idea to his fellow Directors, who were equally enthused, and the Cadbury scheme was launched in May 1902.

The company went to extreme lengths to ensure the process was transparent and fair. Two committees were formed to review the suggestions, one each for the men and the women. The Chairman of each committee was appointed by the firm, two representatives of the foremen elected by ballot, and three employees also elected, one each from manufacturing, offices and trades. A suggestion box was placed in each department along with a duplicate book of suggestion forms. Employees filled in their name, clock number, department and date, along with the suggestion, and posted a copy in the box, keeping the duplicate for themselves. No ideas would get 'lost in the post.' An acknowledgement was then sent to the employee that it had been received. After being entered into the master suggestions book and allocated a number, the idea itself would be transcribed onto a report form, omitting all the details of its originator, and then sent to the committee member allocated to evaluate suggestions for the department or class of work concerned. This anonymity was crucial as it ensured every suggestion was taken seriously – it could have come from George Cadbury himself.

The committee member, and also the head of the department concerned, would pass opinion with both opinions being forwarded to the committee, who met once a week and would vote on the idea. Suggestors were then quickly informed as to the outcome, with reasons given for all ideas that were declined. Girls suggestors were deemed to require slightly more incentive to come forwards than the men, so any of theirs that were accepted resulted in the payment of a shilling the end of the following week. Both men's and girl's successful suggestions were then entered into a six-monthly prize evaluation.

A month after an accepted suggestion had been approved for implementation, the committee followed up with the department concerned, firstly to ascertain that the work had been done, and secondly to ask for an evaluation of the financial benefits. Each suggestion was then awarded a prize proportional to the resulting benefit. To avoid any misunderstandings in this area, the suggestor was also sent a form asking whether the idea had been carried out to their satisfaction, and what he or she considers has been its success. Even employees who had since left the firm got their prize in full. There was also an appeals process through the secretary of the scheme.

The success of the scheme was staggering. By 1929, the company had received 141,000 suggestions – nearly five for every single employee who had ever worked at Bournville. It is difficult to believe there could have been anything left to improve. One that has lived down to this day was a suggestion that the Cadbury's Dairy Milk bars be divided into bite-sized chunks.

The outcome of the 'Bournville Experiment' was that Cadbury were more successful in harnessing the potential of their thousands of manual workers than any company before them and most since. Herbert Casson, one of the 20th-century's great management thinkers[6], wrote in 1929,

The improvement in design shown by the lower cake of chocolate over that appearing above is an interesting example of a worker's suggestion affecting a factory product.

[6] Witzel, pp48–55

'I have seen many factories in six countries over the last thirty years. I have made reports or carried out reorganizations in more than 150 of them, and the one factory which comes nearest to the scientific ideal is not in my opinion in America. It is the factory of Cadbury Brothers at Bournville, England….There is a larger nucleus of creative thinkers in Cadbury's than there is in any other firm in the world. The whole firm thinks. There is an efficient many, not an efficient few…. Now that Cadbury's has become established, the Professors of Economics can put up their shutters. Cadbury's is Economics. It is not empty theory, but fact. The Cadbury Brothers did what all the Professors and idealists have been talking about for centuries…Cadbury's put people before machinery. They put health before profit. They put character before profit. Then, to their own surprise, no doubt, they got all six – people, machinery, health, profit, character and output.'[7]

It would take the rise of the Japanese car industry before a similar phenomenon would be seen again.

Cadbury Bros. would be able to accelerate far ahead of their rivals during the first four decades of the 20th-century because of their ability to develop and harness the capabilities of their workforce. Cadbury employees were better selected, educated, trained, motivated, informed and engaged than in any other company at the time. Edward Cadbury, when reviewing the last fifty years of the firm in 1931 stated that *the well-being and success of this business has turned mainly on the personnel.*

The Bournville infrastructure, the cocoa sourcing and the entire workforce were all aligned with Cadbury's brand benefits of quality and value. Thus, it can be argued, although the terminology did not exist then, that Cadbury made themselves into the first true branded company. This mix was to reap massive dividends as Cadbury embarked on their next big step forwards: the creation of a mass market for chocolate.

---

[7] Herbert N. Casson, *Creative Thinkers*, (Cosimo Business Classics, New York, 2005) pp194–197

Part 1 – Summary

It had been a remarkable turnaround for Cadbury. From being on the verge of ruin, they had emerged triumphant as the industry leader when seemingly all the odds had been stacked against them. Cadbury had not been the first cocoa manufacturers in Britain; Fry had had nearly a century in which to build up a head start. Nor did Cadbury come into the market with some secret new wonder-product; for the first eighty years of their existence, Cadbury contributed little to the innovations that would drive the industry. By the beginning of the First World War, they would dominate all four of the categories in which they competed: cocoa, chocolate bars, boxed chocolates and chocolate biscuits, without having played any role in the invention of three of them.

Cadbury triumphed through better management of their product range and infrastructure, specifically through the convergence of several key attributes:

- Their strong external radar.
- A willingness to change direction, even at the expense of existing products.
- Speed of decision-making.
- A commitment to produce better products, backed up by appropriate resource.

- Strong promotional and advertising skills, particularly in building up the Cadbury name.
- The huge advantages that flowed from the move to a green-field production site.

With these attributes, Cadbury didn't need to be the most inventive; demonstrating that product innovation was not, and is not, a necessary component for success. Microsoft invented very little of their product range, yet became the dominant force in their industry. The product that made the company, the operating system MS-DOS, was acquired for the princely sum of $50,000 under its original guise of QDOS (Quick and Dirty Operating System) from its original author, Tim Paterson, who understood that invention and exploitation are two distinct skill-sets, *"It was a good deal as far as I'm concerned. DOS became big only because of Microsoft's muscle."*[8] Today, at a time when many business plans rely on unspecified 'breakthrough' innovations to achieve their growth targets, it can be questioned if that is the right focus. Having the right management attributes in place is far more important.

Cadbury's success also demonstrates the value that can flow from turning one's own particular brand benefit into the unit of currency of the entire category. By being the U.K.'s first adopter of the Van Houten press,

---

[8]   Tim Paterson, "The Dross of DOS", http://www.forbes.com/asap/1997/1201/070.html; Accessed December 18th, 2005

quality would become an enduring key plank of the Cadbury brand. Market forces rewarded Cadbury for putting quality at their core, mostly because of enormous amounts of time and money employed by Cadbury in their campaign against adulterants. Cadbury were the first UK cocoa firm to stake such a claim, and they were aided by Fry and Rowntree not effectively countering with anything like as effective. The Cadbury campaign resonated with the public and political moods of the time, and the result was that any thinking person had purity at the top of their list of decision factors.

All other brands were judged against the criterion which Cadbury owned, and most were found wanting. Even though both Fry and Rowntree were eventually to launch pressed cocoas, it did not give them a stake in owning the benefit of purity. While the expansion of the market meant both companies were still growing in volume, they were in fact becoming progressively weaker as brands in relation to Cadbury. The more Cadbury stood for something and made it important in people's minds, the more Fry and Rowntree seemed insipid and irrelevant. With a single-minded focus, brands can raise the profile of their particular USP into being of significance across the industry.

But nothing lasts forever, and Cadbury were somewhat fortunate that it took forty years for a new category-leading benefit to emerge, that of superior taste and texture. It is to Cadbury's credit and benefit that they responded so quickly to this new turn of events. While sales of Cadbury's Cocoa were beginning to suffer, the fall had hardly been calamitous, but they did see it as a turning point. It was a situation where fortune favoured the brave. Van Houten's success in sales terms was not being matched by their grasping ownership of the taste benefit. They hardly advertised at all and retailers resented having to stock them. So the opportunity was still there to follow Van Houten in product terms but to lead them in claiming ownership of the taste benefit, which Cadbury duly did.

What had changed in the market was the definition of quality, from purity to taste. This kind of shift is not uncommon. Quality for mobile phones used to lie in optimising the trade-off between battery size and battery life, whereas now we take both for granted, and judge the quality of mobile phones by their additional communication and MP3 features. Tomorrow, we may judge them by something completely different.

Cadbury were also on top of an even bigger shift in the market: that from cocoa beverages to milk chocolate bars. Here Cadbury's were helped by the fact that they were already in the chocolate business through their range of assortments, and had developed skills in chocolate-making. But Cadbury could easily have remained the leading brand in cocoa and assortments and ignored the emerging milk chocolate bar category. Participation necessitated a diversion of technical resource at a critical stage in the company's history, and also involved the development of a substantial infrastructure and skill-set in collecting, transporting and processing oceans of fresh milk. But the potential of the new category was seen, and Cadbury entered the category with the best product and a seemingly ambitious production capacity.

Cadbury also had the huge advantage of having been the first to address key industry limitations in ways that maximised their future flexibility. In the late 19th-century, logistics and high rates of growth were far bigger headaches than brands or products. Cadbury's solution of the move to Bournville was highly risky, defied accepted business norms, but solved both problems while giving significant business advantage without tying the company into a solution for that era only. Bournville is still Cadbury's main UK production site today.

Another limitation to the Victorian and Edwardian businessman was that, because of their own employment practices, their thousands of workers contributed absolutely nothing to the improvement of the business. Cadbury's approach to employee selection, training, motivation,

reward and empowerment gave them a continuous improvement culture decades ahead of their peers. It also equipped the business to be able to cope well with future changing conditions.

Their approach to the sourcing of their principal raw ingredient, cocoa, gave significant quality advantages while not tying them irrevocably to one source. Cadbury were able to take their West African experience and help develop cocoa-growing industries elsewhere. They were not tied to large, company-owned estates in one region and hostage to some unforeseen localised problem such as crop disease, political instability or suchlike.

By the First World War, the Cadbury business as set up by George and Richard Cadbury had largely reached its potential. But it was to scale new heights from a major strategic shift: moving from one based on the selling of better products to one of selling products better. Chocolate in 1920 was still a relatively expensive and infrequent purchase compared to what we are familiar with today. Between 1920 and the Second World War, Cadbury were to change all that and, in the process, quadruple the size of the business, make their brand unassailable to direct competition, and then take the battle to overseas markets.

Part II

MAKING CHOCOLATE A MASS MARKET

Chapter 5

CREATING A MASS MARKET: THE FORD OF CHOCOLATE

The First World War had a major impact on the Cadbury business. Competitively, it greatly eased the pressure from the troublesome continental competitors as the hostilities prevented their exporting into the U.K. In addition, the government placed massive orders for Bournville Cocoa and Dairy Milk to supply the millions in uniform. This surge in demand had necessitated the company to reconfigure their product range and manufacturing methods such that efficiency in production became the priority. A range of 706 lines at the beginning of 1914 had been reduced by almost three-quarters to 195 lines only two years later.

Cadbury found that their key products of cocoa and milk chocolate were well suited to mass production processes. When it came time to resume normal business after the cessation of hostilities, the benefits of true mass production were to fundamentally alter the mindset of the Directors, placing cost control and manufacturing efficiency at the heart of their operational agenda. However, it would not be easy to implement their new thinking. In 1920, while Cadbury's sales were eight-fold the level of twenty years prior, there were still some major challenges.

Passing on the Costs

After the War, the price of raw cocoa was double the level of 1914, while sugar had increased six-fold. Such increases could not be offset by the increased throughput or more efficient planning, so Cadbury, along with Rowntree and Fry, had to increase their prices: a 1lb tin of Bournville Cocoa rising from its pre-war level of 2/6d to 3/-, and the ½lb. bar of Dairy Milk up from1/- to 2/2d. Sales did not appear to have suffered as a result, with both selling substantially higher volumes than had been the case pre-war, so it would have been reasonable for Cadbury to consider the market to be quite price inelastic and perhaps consider dropping value from their strategy.

But they fully understood that the increased volumes had been caused, both directly and indirectly, by the war. The drying up of international trade resulted in the virtual disappearance from the UK market of continental firms such as Nestlé and the leading French firm, Menier. But Cadbury could not count on such big players not making a comeback, and if that happened, they did not want to be caught out by potentially cheaper alternatives. So when raw material prices went into virtual freefall between 1920 and 1924, with cocoa bottoming out at half of its pre-war level, these reductions were passed on in the form of lower prices such that by 1924, both Bournville Cocoa and Dairy Milk were back to their pre-war price levels.

While sales volumes had increased as a result of these reductions, it was by no means a direct, linear relationship; volumes of Dairy Milk had doubled but those of Bournville cocoa remained almost static. Although Cadbury was not to know at the time, the market for cocoa beverages in the UK had peaked and would remain largely unchanged for the next fifty years. Dairy Milk was now unequivocally the product on which Cadbury would depend for its fortunes.

The next five years saw another rise and fall in raw material prices, and during these five years Cadbury's manufacturing costs were to reduce but, having got the ½ pound block down to the apparently attractive price point of 1/- in 1925, this price was maintained and the savings that resulted from a bout of mechanisation in the factory were spent on extra advertising and more Travellers. Unfortunately, this investment achieved nothing as sales of Dairy Milk became as sluggish as indeed Bournville Cocoa had become. With their largest two brands stalled, the overall business suffered. Between 1925 and 1928, top line sales decreased by 9% and trading profit halved despite advertising spend rising by over 50%. For the first time since the 1860's, the business was in some trouble.

But the company believed the per capita consumption in Britain, although stalled after doubling in the previous twenty years, still had much potential as it was less than that pertaining in America and in Germany. But they had lost faith in the power of selling and advertising to make up the difference, as the anonymous author of Cadbury's 1930's publication, *'Industrial Record'* was to summarise, *'In the case of standardised articles of known quality and unit price, the certainty of getting value for money is by far the most important consideration in the eyes of the consumer.'*

Mass Production

Seeing that they could not rely on wildly fluctuating raw material input prices to set the value given to the consumer, Cadbury set about an enormous investment in the Bournville site to apply fully the efficiency lessons of the First World War, and to make it a true mass production environment where huge efficiency savings could be passed onto the consumer. Electrification of manufacturing processes was now possible and offered cost and efficiency benefits that had been almost undreamt of. But it would all cost money.

A STRIKING CONTRAST BETWEEN NEW AND OLD.

Recognising that the basic chocolate and cocoa manufacturing technologies had not changed since the days of Lindt and Peter, nor were likely to in the foreseeable future, the company saw the opportunity to invest heavily in a much more efficient manufacturing infrastructure, relatively safe in the knowledge that it would not be made redundant by some earth-shattering innovation. With efficient sales and planning processes in place, such an investment could be sweated heavily to produce prodigious savings that could be passed onto the consumer to reignite both Cadbury and market growth. A massive rebuilding of Bournville was initiated where dozens of cramped two-storey buildings were bulldozed to make way for state-of-the-art five- and six-storey edifices, designed to optimise the efficiency of the key production processes.

A new chocolate-making building entailed the overhauling of the entire chocolate-making process, with new automatic moulding machines, for which Cadbury had negotiated a five-year exclusive right to use, together with automatic wrapping machines doubling the output of each employee. The other key process of cocoa-making was to undergo a similarly impressive makeover. The new Cocoa Block was the largest and most efficient of its kind in the world. Designed to be a continuous flow operation that eliminated as much handling and transport as possible, it was to be a model of manufacturing efficiency. Utilising over a mile of electric conveyor belts, bags of cocoa beans were deposited direct from

trains into one end of the building and tins of Bournville Cocoa loaded onto
trains at the other, while rivers of cocoa butter were transferred over to the
Chocolate Block.

Further major redevelopments were to follow in the mid-1930s such that by the
Second World War, only one quarter of the Bournville that George Cadbury
would have recognised prior to his death in 1922 still stood. The original 14 acre
site had expanded to 81 acres, with another 110 acres devoted to recreation. The
factory floor space had doubled in just 16 years. The entire network of works
railway had been re-laid, 1,600 electric motors were in place, and 30,000 tons
of coal, together with 19 million cubic feet of gas, was used annually to power
this colossal enterprise. In 1931 a British weekly paper listed its Seven Wonders
of Britain, and sixth behind the Bank of England, Lloyd's, the British Museum,
Southampton's Floating Docks and the new Piccadilly Tube Station was
Cadbury's Chocolate Works.

The needs of the workers were not overlooked in this rebuilding period. A
new Dining Block was erected which also contained such facilities as dressing
rooms for 5,000 girls, various library, club and rest rooms together with a

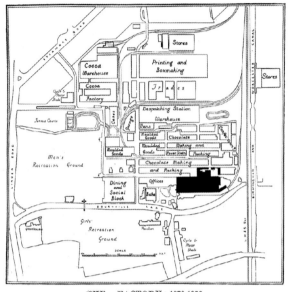

THE FACTORY—1879-1930.
The black portion shows the area covered by the original factory.

1,000-seater concert hall with fully equipped stage and pipe organ. Such further visible commitment to worker facilities was timely as much of the cost-savings from the new Chocolate and Cocoa blocks, together with other such rebuilding, was to come from reductions in headcount.

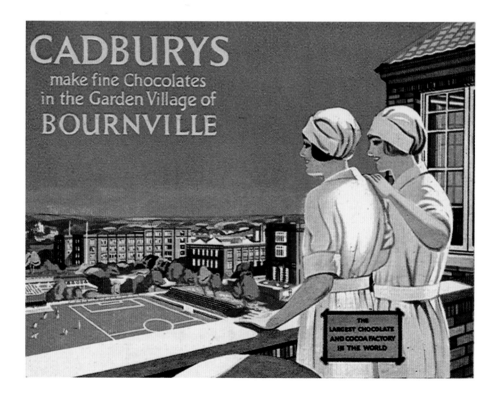

Efficiency rules

The company firmly believed that cost reductions were the way forwards, even if that meant a radical downsizing of the workforce. The Bournville workforce, apart from during the First World War, had grown every year between 1880 and 1925 when it had peaked at 11,000. Only four years later, due to the investments in mechanisation, that had shrunk by over 25% to just over 8,000, and by 1931 the number had reduced further to 7,327. Also within those numbers were large amounts of short-time working and the reallocation of employees onto tasks such as excavating railway cuttings, preparing sites for future buildings and even some road building for the Bournville Village. The cost benefits of the investment into Bournville were substantial. Between 1924 and 1938, Cadbury's labour costs and overheads fell in real terms by 56%;[1] output per worker of Milk Tray doubled, while that of chocolate bars increased more than four-fold.

Over approximately the same time period Cadbury's also nearly halved their distribution costs. At the end of World War One, a new Transport Department under the guidance of the indefatigable George Jnr. revolutionised the company's ability to service its customers at a much lower cost than could be achieved by competitors. Transportation of finished product had always been controlled centrally at Bournville, along with all the ancillary operations of order receipt, collation, handling of queries, invoicing and so on. With the ballooning size of the business, this had become both expensive and unwieldy to manage. The solution was to be a powerful mixture of leveraging the Bournville location in harmony with the need to stop these customer-related activities from clogging the

---

[1] Robert Fitzgerald, *Products, Firms and Consumption: Cadbury and the Development of Marketing, 1900–1939, Business History,* Volume 47, Number 4 / October 2005, 511–531

place up. The answer lay in a network of railhead distribution depots around the country which could be serviced by full trainloads from Bournville.

Having set up the first railhead in London in 1921, by the end of the decade Cadbury were serving Britain and Ireland with a network of fourteen such depots from which orders were delivered by a combined fleet of over sixty Cadbury vans. The benefits were immediate and substantial. Many activities were removed from Bournville creating more space so that stock could be built in the run up to the busier Easter and Christmas selling periods. Bulk rates were negotiated with the rail companies for full trainloads. Packaging costs were slashed as the reduction in handling meant that, with reusable large railcar packing cases to protect the product for most of the journey to the customer, much cheaper packaging could be applied at the depots for the final truck journey.

Cadbury had been very clear from the start that cost savings from the mechanisation of Bournville and the new distribution system had to be quickly translated into lower prices. Edward Cadbury, in an address to the employees in 1924, laid out the company's philosophy,

As regards price, there are three parties to be considered – ourselves, our customers and the public. As regards ourselves, we believe in a moderate profit, not based on the

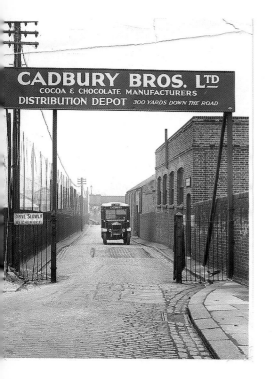

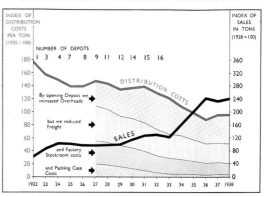

ECONOMIES ACHIEVED BY RAILHEAD DEPOT DISTRIBUTION COMPARED WITH SALES

utmost we can get out of the public, but based on giving the best possible value. We must not despise the public and think that anything will sell provided we have a big enough staff of Travellers, and the article is well advertised.

Edward went on to outline the strategy for the years ahead,

First, the best possible quality – nothing is too good for the public.

Second, a fair profit to ourselves, giving the public the economies we make in buying or manufacture.

Third, a fair profit to the trade, not an excessive profit for which the public pays.

Fourth, an adequate but carefully selected advertising programme.

With this clear direction, Cadbury implemented a series of price cuts that would totally change the UK chocolate market and Cadbury's position within it.

Having already reduced the price of a half-pound block of Dairy Milk from 2/2d to 1/- between 1920 and 1926, which was then held for a further three years, Cadbury used their cost savings to progressively drop the price at a penny a time down to 8d in 1934, the last 2d being funded by reductions in selling and advertising costs. Much of the still substantial advertising budget was devoted to publicising each new price cut, many coming fully illustrated with graphs showing the rapidly rising volumes. And impressive graphs they were too. The overall reduction in the price of Dairy Milk between 1920 and 1934 was a staggering 70%. Although the country was in a period of price deflation, Cadbury's price reductions were more than double the average for consumer prices over that 14-year period.

The result was a five-fold increase in the sales of Dairy Milk. Cadbury's themselves were surprised at the

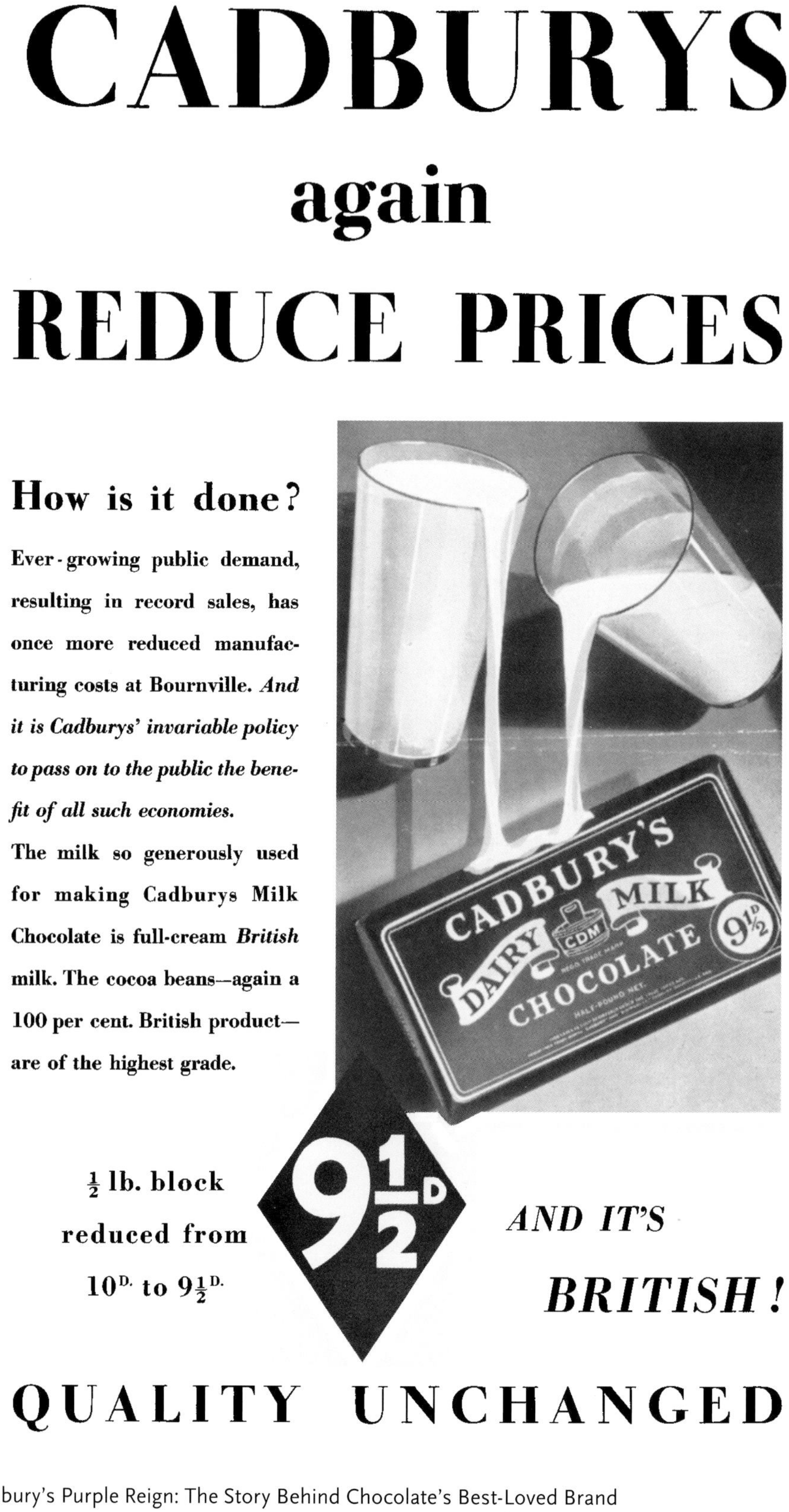
CADBURYS
again
REDUCE PRICES
How is it done?
Ever-growing public demand, resulting in record sales, has once more reduced manufacturing costs at Bournville. *And it is Cadburys' invariable policy to pass on to the public the benefit of all such economies.*
The milk so generously used for making Cadburys Milk Chocolate is full-cream *British* milk. The cocoa beans—again a 100 per cent. British product—are of the highest grade.
CADBURY'S
DAIRY
CDM
MILK
CHOCOLATE
9½D
HALF-POUND NET.
½ lb. block reduced from 10D. to 9½D.
9½D
AND IT'S BRITISH!
QUALITY UNCHANGED

scale of the increase. Their research in the mid-1930's led them to believe that chocolate was now consumed by 90% of the British population – a far cry from the one household in 30 that had been the case at the turn of the century. Weekly consumption of confectionery had increased from 4ozs per head in 1920 to 7ozs in 1938, almost entirely due to Cadbury's strategy. What had been a luxury product for the well-to-do had been transformed into food for the masses, as explained in the March 1934 Works Magazine,

At Bournville we cater for the man in the street, his wife and family – the poor man at the gate rather than the rich man in his castle. For though we are pleased to sell the landlord a box of 'Carnival', our prosperity depends far more on selling the farmer who rents the land a box of 'Milk Tray', the ploughman who tills it a '2d bar', and his wife a tin of cocoa.

Quite simply, they had created a mass market for chocolate by making the best products of their day affordable to all. A modern-day equivalent of what Cadbury had achieved would be if iMacs were available at Dell prices. Cadbury's saw no dissonance between quality and value as consumer propositions, and they felt their ads could communicate both simultaneously. Edward Cadbury described the company's view in July 1930 as, '*The Prestige (placement of) advertising*

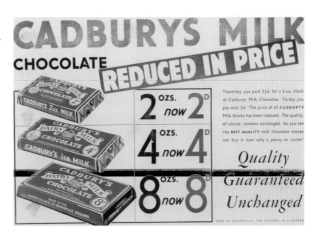

had emphasised the *quality* of the goods, while the reduction in prices of the blocks (i.e. the message) exemplified the *value* the Firm was able to give as a result of better marketing and scientific production.'

And he seemed to be right. Pouring from the new Bournville production lines were over a million bars

Pre-war marketing was against a background of falling prices

of Dairy Milk a day, two million individual chocolate assortments a day and a million tins of Bournville Cocoa a week. The head of Cadbury's London-based advertising agency was hauled up to Bournville in 1934 to explain to the managers the dramatic shift that had taken place in just a few short years, *'Chocolate has been taken above the battle for luxury goods and become a candidate for basic expenditure.'* The consequence of this was that Cadbury's competition was as much the cinema, theatre and petrol pump as it was the likes of Rowntree. The 2oz bar priced at 2d became the company's flagship product. Annual volume of that format increased by 10,000 tons in the two years after achievement of the 2d price point, and by 1936 was accounting for nearly 40% of sales of finished products. It was by far the best-selling chocolate bar in Britain.

The effect on Cadbury's bottom line was equally impressive. As early as 1930, Cadbury had become Britain's 24th largest manufacturing firm and the sixth-largest of packaged goods.[2] Volume increases more than compensated for the lower cash margins brought about by price reductions. Between 1934 and 1936, tonnage increased by 33% and top line sales by a still healthy 20%. Overall profits increased during the period of price cuts from £709,061 in 1930 to £979,995 in 1935.

Cadbury's performance compared to their competitors was equally impressive. Throughout the period 1929–1938 Cadbury Bros. delivered a return on total assets of 17% – more than double that of Rowntree and Mackintosh – and a return on shareholder capital of 40%, which was triple that of Mackintosh and five times that of Rowntree.[3]

---

[2] Fitzgerald, *Business History*
[3] Fitzgerald, *Business History*

When Cadbury had increased their advertising spend in the 1920's, Arnold Rowntree was to complain that its scale was such as to constitute a barrier to entry into the market. His staff suggested that Cadbury might be approached so that some kind of agreement restricting ballooning advertising budgets could be worked out. Arnold vetoed the plan as he did not want Cadbury to realise that their strategy had driven his business almost to the brink.[4]

As Cadbury were outselling Rowntree in milk chocolate by over ten to one, Rowntree gamely tried to fight on by developing an even milkier chocolate that would trump Dairy Milk and its 'Glass and a Half' claim.[5] By May 1931, Rowntree had a recipe which their research showed had a slight taste preference over Dairy Milk, but was not yet at the 65% preference level they felt they needed. Christened Extra Creamy Milk, the idea was well received by Rowntree's travellers and also the retail trade, who were far from convinced that Dairy Milk's stranglehold and constant price-cutting was in their best interests.

Much work was put in by Rowntree to further optimise their product, but the whole plan was scuppered by Cadbury's price cuts in 1932/3, which drove the price below the point where Rowntree could make any profit at all. Rowntree were faced with either launching a loss leader, which could well prompt further Cadbury price cuts, or cheapening the product such that it would be a very poor offering in comparison. Cadbury had taken their advantages of huge scale and efficiency, and simply made it impossible for their main rival even to compete in the milk chocolate market.

Cadbury's embracing of the concepts of scale and efficiency through mechanisation might sound like a production-led strategy, especially as described by the company's head of advertising to the 1934 Conference of the firm's Representatives. It was stressed that the Representatives job was not so much to ascertain their customers' needs, but to direct their customers towards the lines that Bournville could make most efficiently, which were the ones the firm advertised,

'Otherwise the factory would be at the mercy of the individual preferences of our Representatives, our trade customers, and members of the public, and we would have to sell four

---

[4] Robert Fitzgerald, *Rowntree and the Marketing Revolution, 1862–1969*, (Cambridge University Press, New York, 1995) pp173–175
[5] Fitzgerald, *Marketing Revolution*, p310

thousand articles instead of four hundred. Advertising focused public demand where value could best be given. It helped the Representative to carry out the firm's policy by inducing the public to ask the shopkeeper for the lines on which the manufacturer wished to concentrate. The Representative should not merely make sales for lines but should "sell" to his customers the ideals for which the Firm stood, and the policies which underlay the Firm's advertising.'

Ruling out catering to every customer's and consumer's whims was the route to the most potent consumer benefit of the time – affordability. During this period, when Cadbury were making milk chocolate affordable to the masses for the first time in their lives, there was no problem with channelling demand into products and formats where the company was best able to execute its strategy to bring down prices even further. If consumers had been given the option of Dairy Milk at 2d versus a wider range of choices at, say, 5d, there is no doubt which way most will have voted at a time when money was tight.

Cadbury's alertness to the changes being wrought by the electrification and mechanisation of factories transformed the fortunes of the company and the entire confectionery market. But they were not the sole weapons in the Cadbury armoury. Simultaneously, Cadbury had developed a huge advantage over their rivals in their selling and advertising capabilities which would build the Cadbury brand name to being the best-loved in the country.

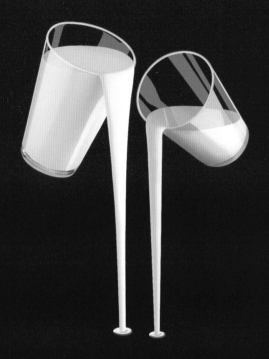

Chapter 6

BUILDING THE CADBURY BRAND

Eat more milk
in
Cadbury's

1½

GLASSES OF ENGLISH

FULL CREAM MILK

IN EVERY SIX

2ᴰ BARS

ALSO IN ½ lb BLOCKS 1/-

The Cadbury success in the U.K. between the wars had been fundamentally driven by having the best products at the lowest prices. By these means they were able to build a mass market for what had previously been a luxury item. But their efficiency model alone would not have built such a strong bond with the consumer. If anything, such a scenario tends to weaken brands as it makes price

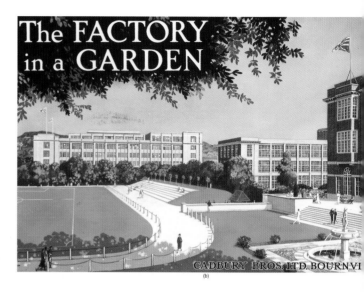

the key decision factor. But Cadbury came through their period of price-cutting with a much stronger bond with the consumer. Cadbury cemented their long-term position in the consumers' affections by employing an impressive array of advertising and marketing techniques that would endear the Cadbury name to the British consumer in a way that would be matched only by Marks & Spencer.

People Come to Cadbury

A cornerstone of Cadbury's marketing efforts had long been the location and nature of the Bournville site itself. But consumers' experience of the 'Factory in a Garden' and the surrounding Bournville Village would not be restricted to reading reports in the press or viewing the countless illustrations in the company's advertisements. Cadbury were also very keen on the idea of attracting people

as visitors to immerse themselves in the Bournville factory and environment. A Visitors Department had been set up in 1902 and at first ran separate tours around the factory and the village, which

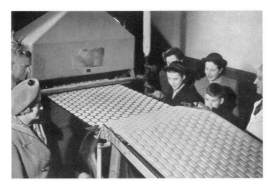

seemed to be equally popular. In 1911, there had been 7,102 factory visitors and 6,037 for the village.

After the First World War, Cadbury cranked up the visitors programme. A charabanc tour of the village was combined with the visit to the factory in 1920, and in 1928 the numbers of visitors rocketed upwards with the introduction of highly popular, scheduled railway excursions. By 1938, 150,000 people a year were taking the tour. Photographs of the time show such massive crowds milling through the production rooms it is surprising that anyone could get any work done. But the company believed that such an up close and personal experience was essential, as reported in the May 1939 Works Magazine,

The personal touch enters into every visit, and links which are both intimate and lasting are thus forged between the Firm and consumers of Bournville goods.

The tour was not for the faint-hearted, being a two and a half hour walk, but energy levels were topped up with a constant supply of free samples. Each visit ended with lunch or tea, and it was not unusual, prior to George Cadbury's death, for him to wander around handing out single roses to the massed ranks of Women's Institutes and Mothers' Unions members from across the country. If that didn't get them buying Cadbury's, nothing would. The Cadbury brand values of trust, integrity and quality were deeply ingrained by a visit to Bournville.

Cadbury Comes to the People

Each visit to Bournville had begun with a showing in the 1,100 seat factory Concert Hall of a film showing cocoa

cultivation in the Gold Coast. This was one of many films that the company had been commissioning since prior to the First World War, and took out on the road to as wide an audience as possible. Four fully-equipped cinema-units continuously toured the country conducting three showings a day in cinemas and town halls of what were state-of-the-art productions. Well-known actors and technicians from Hollywood were employed in their production, ensuring that standards were of the highest. In the 1930's the company had commissioned the first full-length sound film to be made for advertising. The public loved it; in 1935 alone, half a million people saw a Cadbury film.

The company had also used a parallel strategy of employing only the best when it had commissioned ten famous artists of the day to design unique chocolate boxes, including Arthur Rackham, the country's definitive illustrator of fairy stories and such classic books as Peter Pan and Aesop's Fables. But this proved to be a step too far for the British consumer with sales being extremely disappointing and the exercise not being repeated. Cadbury found that the artistic *genre* of the Beano was more in tune than their venture into the world of modern art. The inclusion of a range of small toys – the Cadbury Cococubs – in tins of Bournville Cocoa was supported by a comic strip written and drawn by one of the country's leading comic book illustrators. The strip appeared daily in the national press and was an immediate hit. A Cococub Club was formed in 1935 and a year later thousands of Cococub newsletters were being issued to excited members from the club's mythical secretary, 'Jonathan'.

Cadbury's inter-war marketing strategy of enveloping the consumer with a series of high-quality, close-up-and-personal branded experiences reached out to almost everywhere the public gathered. Racecourses, markets, pet shows, Grand Prix races and village

fetes could usually
expect to see a Cadbury
van pull up from which
company demonstrators
would sell mugs of hot
cocoa and Bournvita to
chilled holidaymakers at
the bargain price of 6d.
Young men in company
blazers at Britain's seaside
resorts would announce the
presence of the 'Chocolate
Mystery Man' who would,
on the production of a bar
of Dairy Milk, hand over a prize.

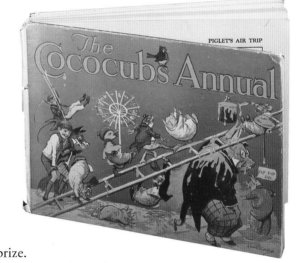

This would prompt armies of bored holidaymakers,
each clutching a bar of Dairy Milk, to spend the day approaching
any likely-looking suspects. When the sun finally peeked through, teams of

company sand artists would supervise sand-drawing contests of the famous Glass-and-a-half logo.

It is easy to see why Cadbury not only dominated sales during the period between the wars, but came to dominate consumers' affections. Experiential marketing was the mainstay of the company's efforts to build the Cadbury brand between the Wars, with no other manufacturer going to such lengths to directly engage so many consumers with such a large array of personal and enduring touch-points. This breadth and depth of engagement was in perfect harmony with how Cadbury developed their product range.

The Product Portfolio

Cadbury's product portfolio did not evolve as a range of distinct brands, each with its own niche in the market, but was driven by their efficiency focus around the optimal use of the existing manufacturing infrastructure. Bournville had been built to make cocoa powders, Moulded bars and chocolate assortments, and any new products would come from these technologies. In 1920 had come the first new product that added inclusions into the chocolate bars, with the launch of Bournville Fruit & Nut. This was minimally disruptive to the main bar moulding process, and the company was already sourcing and preparing nuts for some of its Milk Tray centres. Brazil Nut Chocolate was launched in 1924; milk chocolate Fruit & Nut in 1926 and Wholenut in 1930. Although these were later to be marketed as distinct brands, at the time such products were positioned as essentially being Dairy Milk with bits in, and thus just extensions of the Dairy Milk brand itself.

Cadbury's approach to promoting this range of Moulded lines leveraged the strength of the Cadbury name and the reputation of Dairy Milk as the best milk chocolate, the two being visually combined onto the packaging of the large range of somewhat similar products. Dairy Milk, Fruit & Nut, Whole Nut and Brazil Nut wrappers all used the same high quality, purple paper and, to keep the costs down, one additional colour – gold. The commonality of the look across the Moulded range reflected the commonality of Dairy Milk chocolate as the primary ingredient and the reassurance of quality inherent in the Cadbury name.

Once all the obvious Moulded line extensions had been launched, Cadbury had to look more imaginatively at its limited Bournville toolkit if the asset-based innovations were to continue. The next successful concept was to come from the combination of two of their core technologies – bar moulding and assortment centres – to create a range of bars filled with the kind of centres popular in Milk Tray. The process had started in 1932 with a range of Filled Blocks with centres such as Orange Crème, Peppermint Crème, Vanilla Crème, Caramello, Lemon Delight, Ginger Delight, Marzipan and Truffle. All these sold entirely off the back of the strength of the Cadbury name. The logical extension of the idea was the launch of Milk Tray Block in 1947 which combined a range of such centres into different segments of one moulded bar.

Apart from the Moulded and Filled Block line up, two new products launched in the 1920s that become strong, brands in although neither positioned as the 1960s. managed to

there had been would eventually stand-alone their own right, would be such until Both achieve real

uniqueness while also leveraging the existing infrastructure. In 1920 Cadbury launched Flake which was made on part of the chocolate-making equipment that processed the chocolate crumb. Packaged in a clear wrapper to highlight the product's unique texture, the product was called Dairy Milk Flake to benefit from the power of the Dairy Milk brand. A few years later, a product closely resembling the future Cadbury's Creme Eggs brand appeared in the Easter range, this being manufactured by adapting the Milk Tray technology of depositing a creme centre in a chocolate shell.

The incessant desire to increase sales of cocoa-based products, so that the surplus cocoa butter from the product process could match the needs of the ever-increasing sales of Dairy Milk and its derivatives, led to a spurt of innovation by Cadbury in the early 1930's. First to be developed was a

product called Cup Chocolate, which, rather than being powder-based, consisted of crumbled Flake that could be mixed with hot milk for an instantaneous chocolate beverage.

The second new beverage mix brand was Bournvita, which was launched in 1932 partly to combat Ovaltine head-on. Another triumph of asset utilisation,  Bournvita used Bournville cocoa powder and was further processed in the ovens used to dry chocolate crumb. Cup Chocolate proved to be a fleeting success, but Bournvita would prove to be a valuable new addition to the Cadbury range. Even despite such new launches, in 1936, Dairy Milk and its nut derivatives were still accounting for two-thirds of Cadbury's U.K. sales.

Recognising the Range

In a world where the average grocery store has 25,000 products and where we are assaulted by hundreds, if not thousands of advertising messages a day, standing out is a challenge that defeats most ordinary brands. But the Cadbury signature, purple wrappers and Glass and a Half logo are instantly-recognisable icons, and have been for decades. It was not until the early 20th-century, prior to which there was no consistency at all, that Cadbury gave much thought to such matters. But the solutions they developed have certainly stood the test of time.

In 1905, William Cadbury, on a visit to Paris, commissioned the first properly designed Cadbury logo from the noted French designer, Georges Auriol, an acquaintance of Toulouse Lautrec and famous in typographical circles for his eponymous typeface used for the Paris Metro signs. His effort for William Cadbury, while pleasing to the eye, was perhaps less distinctive: a bold Cadbury name is somewhat brought to life with the 'y' inter-twined around a stylised cocoa tree. But consumers of the early 20th-century, or even today, would struggle to identify a cocoa tree, or perhaps even know that cocoa grows on trees, so the allusion was wasted.

The logo first appeared on tins of the newly-launched Bournville Cocoa in 1906 and, while appearing on the company's van fleet, stationery and the like, was restricted on the product range largely, but not entirely, to the Bournville brand. While there was a degree of consistency on the typeface of the Cadbury name on packaging, the company was simultaneously using many different typefaces for the Cadbury name on the products themselves.

The famous Cadbury script logo that would replace the tree design and all the other Cadbury typefaces originated in 1921. Like most of Cadbury's successful initiatives, the idea of using a signature as the brand logo was borrowed from a competitor, and then executed far more proficiently. Macpherson Robertson had originally branded his products in Australia using, on his proud mother's advice, his entire name. In the interests of being able to fit something else on his wrappers, he soon shortened this to MacRobertson, but felt it was still lacking something. Then he hit on the idea in the early 1880's of using his signature, which became the branding device encountered by Cadbury when their travellers entered the market.

The use of a signature brings some very important benefits versus a simple typeface. Firstly, it is almost certainly unique. It also has a degree of approachability and familiarity lacking in bold typefaces. There is also an element of a personal guarantee if each bar is signed by the business owner. However, the use of a real signature also has some limitations, not least visibility. Replete with multiple whorls and flourishes, the MacRobertson signature

is certainly unique but at any distance it becomes a mass of squiggles – not necessarily a benefit in an impulse category.

Cadbury maintained that their script logo was based on the signature of William Cadbury. But even a cursory glance at the 1921 design, when set alongside William's actual signature, shows that it was largely the creation of a designer, in this case being a member of Cadbury's design department, Ashley Cooper. Certainly, key elements of William's signature informed the design, but it is clear that it was developed to retain all the strengths of MacRobertson's while being much more legible and thus effective as a branding device.

A year before the development of the script logo, the packaging colour of Dairy Milk had been changed from lilac to purple. Ever since the days of Rome when only the emperor was allowed to wear a purple toga, purple has been associated with royalty. It was felt that Dairy Milk was equally deserving of such recognition, and turned out to have been an inspired choice: the richness of the colour perfectly compliments the eating experience itself. Within the same decade, the last of Cadbury's icons, the 'Glass and a Half' symbol, had made its appearance in a series of advertisements for Dairy Milk.

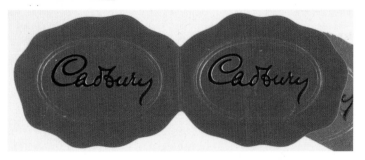

Advertising the Range

Because Cadbury's range had mostly evolved as a consequence of their factory model, as opposed to identified consumer needs, it was largely dependent on the Cadbury name and/or Cadbury's Dairy Milk for its appeal. With a plethora of experiential marketing activities to promote the Cadbury name, there was regular advertising on only three lines between the Wars: Dairy Milk, Bournville Cocoa and Milk Tray. Both Cup Chocolate and Bournvita were added to the advertising roster following their launches, and Bournvita became a permanent addition, making four lines in total that had their own advertising.

But even within the four, there was a large reliance on Dairy Milk as a key part of the message, as was later described in the September, 1955 edition of the Bournville Works Magazine,

…the whole of our milk chocolate advertising for thirty years had been built on the theme of a pure food product, made under ideal conditions, and value for money.…We know that the main reason for the popularity of Milk Tray is the thick coating of milk chocolate. This is why we use, "See how Cadbury's Milk Tray are thickly covered with Cadbury's Dairy Milk Chocolate."…

You can't take a dairy cow motoring

**but . . .
you can take the glass-and-a-half
of milk in a ½ lb block of
Cadbury's milk chocolate**

Our biscuit advertising is based on the same principle as that for Assortments.

As a consequence, the advertising of Dairy Milk was of paramount importance to Cadbury, and was the single most visible manifestation of Cadbury to the public. The ever-decreasing prices meant that Dairy Milk would be most people's first exposure to milk chocolate and thus was able to mould a nation's taste preference. The Dairy Milk brand was to fulfil the same role as had Cocoa Essence fifty years before, that of a proxy for the Cadbury brand itself. This was a roll far better suited to Dairy Milk than had been the case for Cocoa Essence. Apart from a small selection of plain chocolate lines, Dairy Milk's unique and distinguishable taste could be found on or in every product that carried the Cadbury name.

Dairy Milk's 'Glass and a Half' logo and slogan were initially accompanied by a series of other advertising tacks for the brand. In1928, the Minister of Health –

the future Prime Minister, Neville Chamberlain – was being quoted in Cadbury ads exhorting the nation to, *"Eat more milk – it is the perfect food."* In 1929 the company was advertising the contents of a report to the Scottish Board of Health on the benefits of giving milk to children, with Dairy Milk being not only a delicious, convenient and concentrated form of milk, but one having twice the amount of 'sunshine vitamin D' than fresh milk. Other ads showed highly-contented Cadbury cows getting one of their twice-daily hand brushings in what looks like the cattle barn equivalent of the Ritz.

MINISTER OF HEALTH

SAYS:

"EAT MORE MILK"

"Eat more milk—it is a perfect food," said The Rt. Hon. Neville C. Chamberlain, Minister of Health, in a recent speech.

(a)

In the mid-1930s, Cadbury employed throwbacks to the kinds of advertising used for Cocoa Essence.

Under a heading of 'Why doctors like chocolate', an eminent specialist wrote, "*Chocolate is a good food, and not merely an extra. It is suitable for children as well as adults.*" Further ads showed the mid-morning energy kick from chocolate and the surprising news that a 2d bar equalled three horse-power of energy. It seemed like Cadbury alone were providing for the nation's health and well-being. Eating milk chocolate, and by default that meant Dairy Milk, had become almost a sacred duty of every household in the country.

But by the late-1930s, the company's advertising strategy had evolved to having three main aims. The quality message was put across with such themes as 'Cadbury Means Quality', 'The Factory in a Garden', and 'See the Cadbury Name on Every Piece of Chocolate'. The second aim was to establish Dairy Milk as the nation's leading brand via the 'Glass and a Half' campaign. The third was to emphasise value by advertising the successive price reductions. All three worked synergistically as a general umbrella for the hundred's of other Cadbury lines.

Making the Sale

The pre-war success of Cadbury in the U.K. had been built not only on the impressive Bournville factory, the peerless Dairy Milk chocolate and a hugely effective advertising approach, but had been equally reliant on the Cadbury selling and distribution system. The enormous volumes, together with the

efficiencies of their railhead distribution system, meant that Cadbury could cost-effectively send a representative to one in every two shops in the country that sold chocolate. Cadbury had over 500 Representatives calling once a month on over 120,000 individual shops and reached another 150,000 through wholesalers – a number that dwarfed the retail coverage of their competitors. To announce the presence of Cadbury products, legions of

Cadbury display men were plastering every High Street with Cadbury lettering on shop fronts and Cadbury displays in shop windows.

By being so large, the Cadbury sales force was also more cost efficient. With much smaller individual territories to cover, they could make more calls per day by having much less travelling time. In contrast, Jim Hay, who joined the Fry sales force in 1949, found himself working a territory that included one third of Glasgow, all of Argyllshire and the Western Islands from Arran to Tobermoray, and all without a car! Rowntree Representatives were no better off.

The outcome of this system was that Cadbury products were far more available to the consumer than were those of their competitors. With much smaller sales forces, Cadbury's competitors had to rely on retailers topping up their range by buying other major  brands from Wholesalers, a process that could be very hit or miss. It was a huge competitive advantage for Cadbury. By the late 1930s, Cadbury completely dominated the British chocolate market, and had done so by developing a business model that could deliver an unmatchable combination of both quality and value, and by developing a brand that had an unparalleled breadth and depth of engagement with the British population. The impact on their competitors was devastating.

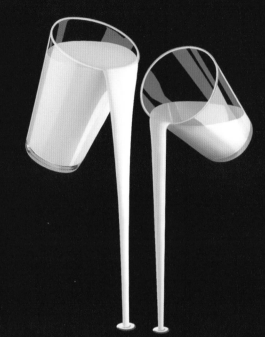

Chapter 7

A CHANGING U.K. MARKET: CADBURY'S COMPETITORS EVOLVE

taste the cream!

Although the First World War had removed the continental firms from the U.K. market, Cadbury worried long and hard about their return post-hostilities, especially the innovative Swiss firms who had grabbed half of the world market for chocolate prior to the War.[1] Adding to Cadbury's concerns was the fact that, just prior to the war, the Swiss confectionery industry had undergone a series of consolidations. The inventor of milk chocolate, Daniel Peter had merged with Kohler in 1904, with Nestlé investing capital into the merged concern a year later. In 1911, Peter-Kohler merged again with Cailler to create a Swiss confectionery powerhouse.

Sleeping With the Enemy

Even after the successes of Bournville Cocoa and Dairy Milk, Cadbury were daunted by the prospect of resuming battle with this colossus. Who knew what new innovations they would come up with? And further over the horizon lay the emerging giant of the U.S. market, Hershey, who could well be tempted to take a run at what was still the most concentrated consumer market in the world. The last thing Cadbury wanted to do was to be spending massive sums of money competing head on with their British rivals while the real threat lay in the return of the Swiss to the fray.

We should remember that attitudes to competition were very different in those days when it was commonplace to see it as wasteful and ultimately to the detriment of the consumer. J.P. Morgan in America was messianic in his advocacy of mergers and trusts. In the consumer goods industry, both Lever Bros. and Procter & Gamble had bought up most of their competitors to free themselves from the spectre of endless price competition. As the Cadbury board were not interested in hostile takeovers of businesses run by fellow Quakers, it was almost inevitable that their minds would gradually turn to amalgamation.

Cadbury, Fry and Rowntree had worked closely over a number of years on matters of cocoa sourcing, bonuses

Cadbury and Fry Boards in the 1920s. Back: Miss Dorothy Cadbury, Charles Gillet, Laurence Cadbury, Major Egbert Cadbury, Paul Cadbury, Walter Barrow. Centre: William Cadbury, M. Tatham, R. Algernon Fry, A. E. Carter, R. J. Fry, Barrow Cadbury, Conrad P. Fry. Front: Edward Cadbury, George Cadbury, Cecil R. Fry, Claude Fry, G. H. Bowden

---

[1] www.Swissworld.org; accessed April 12th, 2007

paid to retailers and so on, but it was Cadbury who took the initiative to explore much closer cooperation. In January 1917, the Cadbury Board Minutes reported that a meeting had been held with Fry and it was decided to approach Rowntree as well. A month later a letter jointly signed by Cadbury and Fry was sent to Rowntree and in the first paragraph went straight to the point,

We the undersigned have been discussing the possibility of a nearer working arrangement, chiefly with the purpose of abolishing all needless competition and making our organisation more complete to face foreign competition at home and abroad after the war.

Rowntree were not so enthusiastic in their response, favouring a continuation of current arrangements. On April 18th the Cadbury Board had agreed that they would go it alone with Fry if Rowntree could not see their way to participating. In June, having reached no agreement with Rowntree, Cadbury and Fry signed their joint agreement.

But during the negotiations, it had become apparent to the Cadbury directors that their Fry counterparts, who were now several generations on from the original founder, were lukewarm about remaining independent. Fearing that Fry could be tempted to sell out to the Peter-Kohler-Cailler-Nestlé combine, Cadbury proposed a full merger.

Both firms consulted their London-based accountants to evaluate the possibility, but full amalgamation proved impossible and the solution lay in the formation of a joint holding company that would take over the assets of both businesses. The formation of the British Cocoa and Chocolate Company was announced to the press on October 19th, 1918 and the next month's edition of the Bournville Works Magazine outlined how things would work,

The two companies, Cadbury Brothers, Limited, and J.S. Fry and Sons, Limited, will continue to carry on business in their own names and under their own management, and the identity and goodwill of each company, as they now exist, will therefore be maintained.

In the final split of BC&C equity between the two families, the Frys benefited greatly from the generosity of the then Cadbury chairman, Barrow Cadbury. In the days before in-depth due diligences, Cadbury had not realised that the Fry business was not all it seemed and a far cry from the confectionery powerhouse it had been in the 19th–century. Fry's glory days as the industry innovator and leader were far behind them. By chance, a son of George Cadbury – Egbert – on return from war service had been taken on at Fry, and was able to describe the state of Cadbury's new partner,

They never had much regard for quality, but during the war they abandoned any pretence at maintaining it…they came out with the terrible reputation as the manufacturers of gritty and almost unpleasant chocolate.[2]

If that wasn't bad enough, on closer inspection Fry was a ramshackle organisation with a somewhat laissez-faire approach to the business of delighting customers,

Fry's had far more orders for their goods than they could possibly supply and this especially applied before Christmas. It was not an uncommon practice if, at the end of the day, there were more orders than could be coped with, for the clerks in the office to gather them up in armfuls and put them on the open coal fires which used to warm the rooms. Obviously, this state of affairs could only have one end.

---

[2] John F. Crosfield, *A History of The Cadbury Family,* University Press, Cambridge, 1985; pp719–733

THE BRISTOL FACTORIES (GROUPED)

Egbert Cadbury, who had been decorated in the War for having shot down two zeppelins, must have yearned for the simpler world of aerial combat when he saw what confronted him in Bristol.

If Cadbury had known all this beforehand, it is questionable whether they still would have seen Fry as their salvation against the Swiss. Interestingly, George Cadbury himself had been utterly unconvinced that the merger was a good idea, irrespective of the state of Fry's. At a joint meeting of the Bournville and Bristol directors, he outlined his concern,

You may wonder how it is, seeing that we have worked for so many years so harmoniously, that I should not enter heartily into the amalgamation….We had much opposition years ago from the English manufacturers,

and you did not show us any mercy. We had also severe opposition from Van Houtens and the French manufacturers. You younger men are now afraid of Nestlés and the Swiss manufacturers who were not known then. If we could fight Van Houten and the other foreign houses and more than hold our own against them, I have no fear of foreign competition now. I cannot believe that with a combination, there will be the

BIRD'S-EYE VIEW OF THE FRY FACTORIES AT BRISTOL.

same energy thrown by either firm into their business, as if it was the only one in which they had an interest.

Fry's use of unfilled orders to heat the building turned out to be the least of Egbert's problems. Accustomed to seeing on the Fry wrappers an idyllic-looking factory in vast open spaces, seemingly next door to Bristol's docks, the reality was 24 cramped factory buildings squashed into the middle of Bristol. Not one building had a single right angle, all built on curves and odd shapes following the pattern of Bristol's streets. Partially manufactured goods had to be moved by horse and cart through narrow, congested streets from one building to the next. The place was hopelessly inefficient and as far from the slickly organised Bournville as was possible to imagine.

Just 18 months after amalgamation, the combined board of BC&C agreed to start again in a new factory outside of Bristol. Using the tried and tested method of walking along the railway lines, a suitable site was found in the village of Keynsham, and over £160,000 was invested in building a new factory named Somerdale. George Cadbury in a letter to Egbert highlighted another aspect of the huge favour Cadbury had done for Fry with the generous merger,

It always seemed to me very doubtful if the Bristol business could afford the enormous expense of giving up the costly buildings in the centre of the city and moving into the country.[3]

But far from solving Fry's problems the new factory became something of an albatross because of a calamitous fall in Fry's sales. Fry's business went into freefall as they were the one most hit by Cadbury's success. Fry responded by launching vast numbers of new products, 165 between 1930 and 1936,[4] nearly four-times as many as were launched by Cadbury, but to no avail. By 1935 the once mighty Fry firm was losing money, let alone paying back the investment in Somerdale. This disastrous state of affairs forced Cadbury to initiate a full takeover of the Fry business in 1935.

The long catalogue of problems post the amalgamation must have been even more galling for the Cadbury management as the reason for getting together in the first place – post-war competition from the Swiss or Americans – never materialised. The Swiss businesses took much longer to recover from the conflict than had been imagined, and Hershey remained resolutely insular. The amalgamation

---

[3] Crosfield; pp719–733
[4] Crosfield; pp719–733

with Fry had thus turned completely sour. Far from strengthening Cadbury to face new threats, it had weakened and distracted the business.

George Cadbury had been concerned that taking defensive measures against threats that had not yet emerged was not the action of a committed market leader. But the move was understandable. A business that had greatly benefited from the enforced absence of proven tough competitors should have worried about the possibility of their return post-hostilities. However, running the businesses independently after the full Cadbury takeover was a strategic error. Several good suggestions had been made at that time on how to streamline the two operations and further enhance productivity at Bournville:

- Transferring all Somerdale Moulded and cocoa production to Bournville.
- Moving the labour intensive production of biscuits to Somerdale.
- Using Fry to produce a cheaper range of goods specifically for the wholesaler – a channel that Cadbury's railhead depot system almost completely neglected.
- Using Somerdale to produce all of Bournville's export lines.

But none of these were implemented. Fry continued to be run separately, largely charting its own course. Fry would still be competing rather than cooperating with Cadbury until the mid-1960s to the detriment of both. However, the Cadbury board had learned that merging with weak competitors was an exercise not to be repeated. Rowntree, who had passed on the invitation to join BC&C in 1917, had spent the next decade increasingly rueing the decision as their business was almost crushed by the Bournville machine. In 1930, they came back asking if the original invitation still stood, but were given a firm 'no'. Cadbury had no desire to take on the problems of another seemingly lame duck. Rowntree would have to find another solution to their problems.

A New Market Sector

Within the bloated Fry range of sub-standard products were a handful of products that had no direct equivalent in the Cadbury range. Fry's Chocolate Cream had an extremely long heritage, having been developed by Fry's in the 1850's at the same time as their initial experiments in making a Moulded bar. Fry's Turkish Delight had come along much later, being launched in 1914. Fry's Crunchie had a typical Cadbury parentage; the basic idea having been spotted by Cadbury-Fry-Pascall in Australia, where another local manufacturer, Hoadley's, had invented and launched a honeycombed bar in 1913 called Violet Crumble.

By the time Cadbury in the U.K. had perfected the technology to make their own version, it had been deemed only fair to give the product idea to Fry as recompense for their business having been decimated by Cadbury.

Such products, known by the manufacturers as Countlines, had emerged in the United States during the First World War. The American army were ordering vast quantities of candy bars, made of nougat, wafer and other such confections, which were delivered in large blocks. Army personnel would then cut these into smaller chunks for individual consumption, but soon tired of that burdensome task, asking their American suppliers to cut and wrap them before shipping. It was soon realised that covering the bars with a thin layer of chocolate on all sides improved the taste and

the keeping qualities, and a new category of product was born: Countlines, so called because they were sold by count rather than by weights, as the weights of the different kinds of Countline could vary tremendously. Many such brands began to emerge in the U.S. market as millions of soldiers were decommissioned after the war.

Paul Cadbury had noticed an already vibrant group of Countline brands on a visit to Canada in 1928,

'The sale of 5c and 10c pieces in Canada is something that has not got its parallel in either England or Australia. On the counter of every Candy and Drug store, restaurant or grocer's shop there is a great array of these lines. Size and variety seem to be all important factors and all are, of course, wrapped. The most popular lines have a mixture of maple fudge caramel and marshmallow on the inside and are wrapped round with peanuts bedded in soft toffee. The names by which these bars are known are some indication of the appeal they make, e.g. "O'Henry", "Fat Molly", "Sweet Marie".

Here was a concise description of all the attributes that would make Countlines a success: key price points, variety, widespread distribution, prominent display, familiar and widely accepted ingredients, and a name that strove for individuality around which a brand personality could be built. Even the dimmest of advertising agencies could make hay with a brand called Fat Molly. But the potential for Countlines in the U.K. market was not immediately realised.

Novelty chocolate-covered bars, as Countlines were known at that time, had been around for a while, but had not taken the market by storm. Many other manufacturers had produced novelty bars, but most lasted only a few months before the public returned to their staple diet of Dairy Milk.

The Man From Mars

All this was to change in 1933 with the launch in the U.K. of Mars Bar. Forrest Mars, an American, had originally worked for his father's confectionery business in the U.S. where he had come up with the idea for a new product. The concept was the solidification of a popular malt drink of the time into a bar of nougat, and then covering it with a layer of caramel and a coating of chocolate. Christened

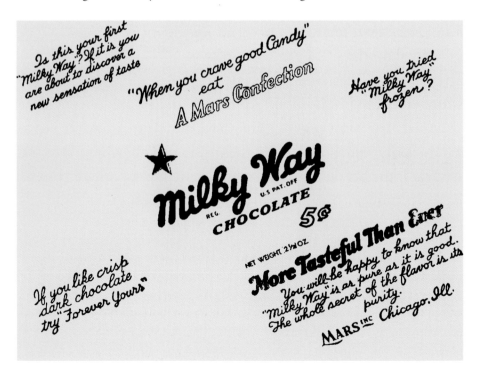

'Milky Way' and launched in America in 1924, it was an instant hit that transformed the fortunes of his father's company, racking up sales of $800,000 in its first year.[5] Followed by Snickers in 1928 and Three Musketeers in 1930, the Mars family were clearly onto a good thing and were rapidly becoming a significant force on the U.S. confectionery scene.

They had also grasped the importance of configuring products to run as efficiently as possible on modern machinery. All three products were made on essentially the same equipment and the large volumes of standardised product generated substantial cost efficiencies. In addition, nougat and caramel were also much cheaper ingredients than chocolate, so Mars had plenty of profit margin to play with, which they would need to accomplish the two factors which lay at the heart of the success of their products. Firstly, they were able to offer the consumer a substantially bigger product for the same price than the market leading Hershey Bar – a moulded milk chocolate line. Secondly, total advertising costs were much higher as each Mars product had to be communicated separately. There was no spin off effect from one to the other as they were very distinct brands in their own right, with no 'House Name' to do the heavy lifting of generating consumer trust and appeal.

In 1933, after a row with his father, Forrest Mars headed to Slough, England, where he re-christened the Milky Way as Mars Bar and began making it in his kitchen. Cadbury were soon aware of his presence, not least because he negotiated a contract with their industrial coatings people to supply him with chocolate. Together with some adaptations to the original Milky Way recipe to suit the British sweet tooth, he soon had a product that was bringing in substantial orders.

Rowntree Strike Back

Up in York Rowntree viewed the early success of Mars Bar with more interest than did Cadbury. Following their being rebuffed from joining BC&C, Rowntree had already decided that competing head on with Cadbury any further on Moulded, assortments and Cocoa would lead to ruin, and that the best way to compete with Cadbury was to avoid them. Countlines appeared to offer such a route, especially as Rowntree's advertising agency were also telling them that, despite the seeming unstoppability of Dairy Milk and its variants, the public would soon be

---

[5] Joël Glenn Brenner, *The Emperors of Chocolate*, (Broadway Book, New York, 2000) p55

craving more variety in their confectionery consumption. But switching to a Countline strategy was not an easy decision for Rowntree to take, as it would involve a complete reorientation of their business with what seemed like some substantial risks.

Rowntree's new approach was to systematically research the consumer to find out what other confections they might like to eat, either as an alternative, or in addition to, Dairy Milk.[6] Such an approach was unheard of in the British confectionery market. For decades the market had revolved around Moulded bars, assortments, cocoa drinks and chocolate-covered biscuits. Competition was conducted at the company level, each striving to convince shopkeepers and consumers that their versions of these product formats were the more desirable – a contest that Cadbury were winning hands down. That there may be an untapped mass market for other types of chocolate confectionery had not crossed anyone's minds.

For the new strategy to work, Rowntree would have to come up with several new, large volume Countlines in a short space of time, of which there could be no guarantees that they would succeed. They would also have to increase their advertising costs many times over, as every new Countline would require its own large scale advertising campaign. They would then have to clear out from their product range many of the me-too products that were struggling against Cadbury's market leaders. Lastly, there would be a conscious scaling back of the prominence of the Rowntree name on the remaining lines.

---

[6] Robert Fitzgerald, *Rowntree and the Marketing Revolution, 1862–1969,* (Cambridge University Press, New York, 1995) p521

With a Countline, the brand name is everything and the house name virtually redundant, which was the converse of the Moulded market where names such as Cadbury's Brazil Nut relied very heavily on the house name. Consumers neither knew nor cared who made Countlines, a situation that still largely applies today. This worked to the advantage of Forrest Mars, as it neatly avoided having to spend fifty years building up a house name to match that of Cadbury. But it was a major issue for Rowntree who had invested time and effort, if not much advertising money, in patiently building up the Rowntree name. Deprioritising the one real link they had with the consumer was a tough decision that created major misgivings on the part of some Rowntree family members, but it went through as there were no other ideas with which to stave off seemingly inevitable bankruptcy.

Picture Post, December 9, 1939

2 hours' steady nourishment for 2d

FOUR big wafer biscuits, oven-crisp and crunchy; a lacing of the finest butter and creamy milk chocolate in between, *and* a thick coating of milk chocolate all round! Isn't that the most amazing 2d. worth you ever heard of? And, you know, this particular type of chocolate block produces a *slower* rise of blood-sugar, which gives you longer endurance and staying power. That's why we call Chocolate Crisp the biggest little meal in Britain. It gives you energy to make a *good* job of whatever you're doing.

THE BIGGEST LITTLE MEAL IN BRITAIN 2d

The opportunity for Rowntree lay in the fact that, such had been the success of Dairy Milk, it was being used for many different eating occasions. Rowntree saw that with a well segmented range of Countlines they could begin to pick off some of Dairy Milk's usage occasions if, firstly, each product was different enough from Dairy Milk, and secondly, had been designed to meet specific needs, as identified by their consumer research programmes. In other words, Rowntree felt they were better able to compete with Cadbury through their research and advertising capabilities than through cost structure and efficiencies.

Soon to flow from Rowntree's new product pipeline were two winning countlines, both launched in 1935. 'Wafer Crisp', a product whose name would soon morph into 'Chocolate Crisp', then 'Kit Kat Chocolate Crisp', and eventually to 'Kit Kat', delivered a lighter eat than Dairy Milk that made it more suitable for between meal snacks. The second blockbuster was Aero, for which the name itself had been politely handed over by Cadbury who could see no use for it for themselves.

Taste the fruit!

While 'Wafer Crisp' did not initially cause many sleepless nights at Bournville, Aero certainly did. Cadbury were soon objecting to the validity of Rowntree's aeration patent, and were outraged that Rowntree's advertisements claimed aerated chocolate to be more digestible than solid chocolate. Cadbury's vociferous complaints forced Rowntree to consider other advertising messages that would avoid all references to competitors' Moulded bars. This ended up doing Rowntree a huge favour as it pushed them further down the road of building unique brand messages and personalities.

Rowntree were soon looking around for advertising propositions which would make no reference, direct or indirect, to the ubiquitous Dairy Milk, but would acclaim the unique benefits of their new lines. Thus, in 1939 Chocolate Crisp Kit Kat advertisements were encouraging consumers to 'Give Yourself a Break at Tea-time', seeking to define and own a usage occasion. Aero also had soon zeroed in on its benefit of lightness, as supported by the unique product feature of bubbles. Both approaches live on to this day and have never been seriously challenged. Within a year, the success of Rowntree's approach had encouraged them to increase their advertising budget, and also look around for any other products they

could make into branded Countlines, while at the same time expanding their range of branded assortments which had already benefited from the launch of Black Magic.

1936 saw two more new brands in their range: Dairy Box and Blue Riband, and in 1937, an existing product called 'Chocolate Beans' was rebranded as 'Smarties Chocolate Beans', soon shortened to Smarties. This was originally a technology invented by an Austrian firm who had offered it initially to Cadbury. Since Cadbury at the time had no interest in cluttering up Bournville with any new processes for unproven lines, they had passed on it. To round out a very successful five years of innovation, Rowntree's venerable gums and pastilles were put into branded packs and renamed 'Fruit Gums' and 'Fruit Pastilles', with Polo coming along in 1939. Elsewhere, two second tier manufacturers, Mackintoshes and Caley's, had merged their companies and also their core capabilities – Mackintoshes being caramel and Caley's chocolate – to get in on the act with a new Countline, Rolo.

Although the trend towards Countlines was now clear, it had worked to Cadbury's short-term advantage. Far from having to compete head on with Fry, Rowntree and the Swiss firms on Moulded and cocoa, Cadbury had a completely free run in

those two categories. So strong was the Bournville machine that it had seen off all its direct competitors. So aside from the Fry nightmare, the inter-war period had turned out much better for Cadbury than could have been expected. By the outbreak of war, U.K. volumes and profits were at an all-time high with no direct competitors on their key lines. The Bournville machine was humming.

While Rowntree, Mars and Mackintosh/Caley were launching all their Countlines, Cadbury were still increasing sales of Dairy Milk with no additional advertising costs, so Cadbury's growth was far more profitable at that stage than was Rowntree's. From Cadbury's perspective, the Rowntree strategy would have looked like a very large bet on an unproven idea that was making little money. As to Mars, they had entered the market but apparently posed little threat to Cadbury; they would be slugging it out with Rowntree, Mackintoshes and Fry. And if Mars did well, Cadbury had a stake in their success by supplying their chocolate.

In addition to building a seemingly unassailable competitive position in the U.K., the profits flowing from the Bournville machine had simultaneously been funding a major shift in Cadbury's export strategy – the building of factories overseas.

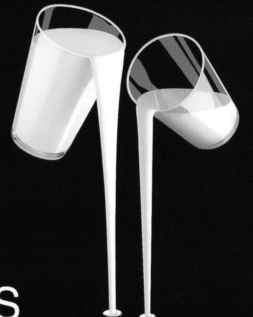

Chapter 8

OVERSEAS EXPANSION: PAINTING THE BRITISH EMPIRE PURPLE

Now more chocolate for 3ᵈ

Cadbury's DAIRY MILK CHOCOLATE

Here's wonderful news for lovers of Cadbury's Dairy Milk Chocolate everywhere! Now there's *more* in every 3d. bar, more chocolate with the smoothest, creamiest flavour you could hope to enjoy. And that means more nourishment, too, for remember, into every half pound goes a glass and a half of fresh full cream milk. So ask for the bigger 3d. Cadbury's Dairy Milk Chocolate bar today.

Shopkeepers! All 3d. Cadbury bars delivered to you since Jan. 2 are the new bigger size.

CADBURY'S DAIRY MILK CHOCOLATE

Cadbury had always been enthusiastic exporters. By 1900, exports were accounting for 10% of Bournville's production of cocoa and 22% of chocolate products [1] and by the outbreak of World War One, Cadbury's total exports had reached the level of half of the home trade. By far their biggest overseas market was Australia, which, in 1914, was accounting for over 50% of total exports, making it a sizeable business in its own right.

At this stage, Cadbury was not the least bit interested in opening factories overseas, having rebuffed a suggestion in 1911 from their lead man in Australia that a factory be built there. Cadbury had no desire to reduce the volumes going through the Bournville factory by relocating production to less efficient units elsewhere. But this export-only strategy required a radical rethink when Cadbury lost most of their export volumes during World War One.

The conflict initially had little impact on exports; in fact 1916 was a record year for Cadbury. But on February 28th, 1917, licenses for the export of cocoa and chocolate to all destinations were refused. As existing licenses were used up, Cadbury's export business reduced to a trickle. In 1918, Cadbury shipments to Australia were 13% the level of two years previously. This could have been just a temporary impact of the war from which the firm could quickly recover, but consumers in Cadbury's export markets did not have to go without cocoa and chocolate. Many local manufacturers, who had few of the restrictions placed on Cadbury, stepped into the breach and rapidly expanded their businesses to fill the void.

To make matters worse, local governments, including Australia, realised that this turn of events was good for local trade and employment, so they discouraged imports with the progressive imposition of tariffs. If Cadbury had remained a purely Bournville-based exporter, they would have been operating at a severe price disadvantage to local competitors, despite Bournville's ever-increasing efficiencies. Given the Board's over-riding belief that quality had to be accompanied by the best value, the only way they could see to regain their pre-war volumes was to set up manufacturing and sales operations inside the tariff barriers.

These events took place simultaneously with the Cadbury-Fry merger in the UK, and the Fry business had also seen much of its export volume disappear, so

---

[1] G.Jones, *Multinational Chocolate: Cadbury Overseas 1918–1939,* Business History, Vol. 27 (1985), pp59–75

one of the first tasks of the newly merged entity was to allocate overseas markets into 'spheres of interest', where the company who had been the strongest pre-war would take the lead in re-establishing the sales of both houses. On that basis, Fry were allocated Canada while Cadbury got Australia, where they immediately set about planning their re-entry strategy.

Australia

Cadbury recognised that the immediate combined sales of Cadbury and Fry were insufficient to support the costs of establishing a manufacturing and selling infrastructure. So another confectionery company, James Pascall Limited, was invited to participate in the venture – named Cadbury-Fry-Pascall Ltd. (CFP) – with their range of boiled sweets. This would not only enable a spreading of overheads, but would hopefully give the salesmen more influence with their customers.

The key decision then became the size and location of the factory itself. Cadbury, who were the dominant partner in the merged enterprise, brought to bear much of their thinking on how Bournville had operated. Their policy on expanding Bournville had been to erect buildings ahead of demand, invest in the most up-to-date machinery, and then run everything efficiently to drive down prices and create the demand. As a consequence, it was assumed that the Australian business would develop along similar lines, and the factory was designed to be much larger than even the pre-war volumes justified.

But Cadbury were to have difficulty in finding an Australian site for their proposed factory that would be as advantaged as Bournville, which was located in the middle of what had been the densest concentration of consumers

in the world. The population was widely flung across an entire continent. No matter which city was chosen, the majority of consumers would be hundreds, or thousands of miles away. This led Cadbury to prioritise ease of manufacture, rather than ease of market access, in their decision to set up near Hobart on the southern island of Tasmania. With a nearby port to receive the cocoa beans, local milk production, and the availability of cheap hydro-electric power, this seemed the ideal location. The cool climate meant that production could run smoothly year round without the need to refrigerate the key processes; a step that would have been essential had the plant been located on the mainland.

While the building of the factory went smoothly – being completed in 1921 – the building of an efficient and profitable business could hardly have gone worse. The new joint enterprise was commencing with nothing like the pre-war volumes of the three stakeholders, but with their miniscule post-tariff positions. As a consequence, the factory, which had been built with better times in mind, could not be run efficiently, sending product costs spiralling upwards. The factory location in Tasmania had also added extra distribution costs compared to the market-leading MacRobertson's, who were based on the mainland in Melbourne.

This combined cost disadvantage would prove to be a major millstone for many years.

The other half of the Cadbury *modus operandi* – the quality and appeal of the product range – also left a lot to be desired. Part of the horse-trading with Fry had involved a commitment to give their milk chocolate a two–year free run in Australia. Consequently, the first milk chocolate to roll off the Claremont production lines was Fry's Dutch Girl, soon followed by Fry's Belgravia, both inferior products made with dried, rather than fresh milk. As the two year term was about to expire, Cadbury vacillated over introducing Dairy Milk into Australia. Their new partner – Pascall – was also in the chocolate business in the U.K., so Cadbury had taken a view that they did not want to use the Dairy Milk recipe and machinery at Claremont in case the Pascall staff there were tempted to indulge in some industrial espionage. Cadbury held off re-introducing Dairy Milk into Australia until 1928, all the while

being hammered in the market by MacRobertson's.

MacRobertson's was no easy touch as a competitor, in fact it was the toughest that Cadbury had yet faced.[2] Driven by its charismatic founder, Macpherson Robertson, they were at the time the dominant force in the Australian confectionery market. 'Mac', as he was universally known (and hence the company name MacRobertson's), was a very different competitor to Cadbury's fellow Quakers in Fry and Rowntree. When his feckless father had left the family home, Mac had gone out to work at the age of nine as the family breadwinner. At fifteen, he secured his first chocolate industry experience, sweeping the floor in one of Melbourne's many small confectionery enterprises. Soon, he set up for himself, using the family bathroom to boil up sugar novelties, having purchased a used nail-can for 6d to act as his furnace. This nail-can would still be on his desk when he was Australia's richest man, having first seen off nearly a hundred competitors in Melbourne, and then more far-flung opposition in the other Australian states after the federation of the country in 1901. So he was not a man to be trifled with.

Robertson had been outraged when the Tasmanian government had bent over backwards to attract Cadbury.

Generous grants, the waiving of a tariff on Cadbury's imported machinery and even the funding of a railway from the port to the factory were, he loudly complained, a slap in the face for domestic taxpayers. As Australia's largest single taxpayer at the time, he was well qualified to make the point. But his complaints fell on deaf ears. Cadbury had to be confronted head on, which he was not slow to do, flooding the market with over 700 products.

Robertson had long been used to jousting with European manufacturers. Prior to the imposition of tariffs, he reckoned that upwards of 25 of them were trying to penetrate the Australian market. He also realised that he needed to upgrade his chocolate if he was to compete with them in the long term. So in 1916, he started up production of what he called his superfine chocolate, Old Gold. This dark chocolate was as good as anything being imported; no mean feat given that wartime restrictions meant that he had been forced to design all the machinery for himself.

MacRobertson's also had substantial cost advantages as it was by now a vertically integrated enterprise, owning the companies that produced its dried milk, glucose and packaging. When Cadbury initiated a Bournville-style

---

[2]   The following details on MacRobertson's have been taken from, Jill Robertson, *MacRobertson, The Chocolate King*, Lothian Books (Melbourne 2004)

price reduction in May 1924, they were to feel the full impact of the MacRobertson business model. Their price advantage lasted only 48 hours before MacRobertson's undercut them, leaving the Cadbury recovery plan in ruins. Not the kind of response they had become used to from Rowntree. However, a report by the new Bournville Board member responsible for export, Charles Gillett, reassured headquarters, *'we must expect a very fierce competitive struggle…If we are prepared to keep up our quality, and*

let no opportunity pass for getting sales, however small they may be, there is no doubt that we will get the turnover we require in the next few years.' Cheered up by this positive thinking, the Bournville Board generously allocated an extra advertising budget of £10,000 a year for three years.

The business would need every penny as the MacRobertson's machine continued churning out a succession of high quality new lines that were marketed with much flair and imagination. While Cadbury-Fry-Pascall (CFP) was struggling,

MacRobertson's Assorted Nut Milk CHOCOLATE

MacRobertson's was enjoying a golden period of booming sales and profits. But the rapidly improving economic conditions were floating all boats, and as CFP's problems were progressively ironed out, sales slowly increased, reaching the pre-war export level by 1926. But the burden of the high fixed costs of the factory, the high distribution costs and the low factory efficiencies meant the business was still making a loss. By this stage Cadbury had sunk over £650,000 into CFP. A small profit in the financial year ending June 1928 proved to be a false dawn as the business was hard hit by the onset of the Depression, with the hard-won sales falling away by almost half in the next two years, driving the business back to the brink, despite by then having the presence of the Dairy Milk brand.

So bad were market conditions that, in 1930, the Australian Government banned outright all imports of confectionery. This provided CFP with a lifeline as they were able to utilise spare factory and selling capacity in producing goods for British manufacturers now totally excluded from the market. Even Rowntree products at one stage were turned out by the Claremont factory, although this service was restricted to non-competing lines. Soon, 30% of company output consisted of products for other companies. Coupled with a prolonged holiday from paying any dividends to the British-based shareholding companies, CFP was able to keep on advertising and slowly building its consumer franchise.

1930 proved to be the turning point, but it had been a close run matter. Even by 1936, Cadbury in Bournville was owed over £500,000 by CFP; had written off their original investment

in the factory; spent £20,000 buying out Pascall to give peace of mind over the Dairy Milk secrets, and had received not one penny in dividends. Such a long term and deep-pocketed commitment had only been possible because Bournville was minting money throughout this period.

It would not be until after the Second World War that CFP would gain the upper hand over MacRobertson's. Cadbury, although they didn't like it, could afford to make a loss for years on end given the vast scale and profitability of Bournville while the business became established. It seemed that no matter what MacRobertson's did, CFP simply could not be killed off as long as they had an open chequebook. The other reason was that, although MacRobertson's had a vast range of products, they had never developed a really good milk chocolate Moulded bar to pre-empt Dairy Milk. This allowed CFP the opportunity to lay claim to the Australian palate for milk chocolate, from which flowed the success of their other lines.

By the early 1930's, the driven and charismatic founder of MacRobertson's reasoned that he had made his pile, and diverted his attention to other interests. After his death in 1945, MacRobertson's lost their vitality and CFP continued their ascendancy.

Canada

Fry had been ahead of Cadbury in developing exports to Canada, and had been Cadbury's main importer, so when Canada imposed tariffs on chocolate and confectionery in 1918, it was Fry who took the lead in responding. They pressed ahead into an ill-fated shotgun marriage with the Canadian offshoot of an American confectionery company, Lowney, and quickly commissioned a jointly-owned factory in Montreal. Lowney proved to be a hopeless partner and were ditched six years later as the business was by then chronically unprofitable.

Competition, which was already intense with many indigenous and U.S. firms in the market, became even fiercer when Rowntree purchased a local manufacturer. The continued losses of the Fry-run company, together with the danger of Rowntree stealing a march on an under-developed Cadbury franchise, prompted the Cadbury board to take a closer interest in what was going on in Canada. Paul Cadbury, the son of Barrow Cadbury, visited in 1927 and his report back exuded a similar optimism to that being expressed about CFP in Australia,

'Competition is fierce but only as regards price: as far as better class chocolate and confectionery are concerned, Canada is almost a virgin market. There is a very real demand…for the better class product associated with the English market. Rowntrees alone are reputed to have sold during the past year $1,500,000.'

In 1929, definitive plans were made to gear up for the manufacture of Dairy Milk at the Montreal factory, adopting the English 2d bar for sale at 5c. Cadbury's fears about Rowntree stealing a march by being first to introduce their milk chocolate bar had proved to be ill-founded. Even though Rowntree had indeed launched their York Milk Chocolate bar in 1927, the local management had cheapened the recipe and as a consequence, sealed the fate of York Milk. Given that both Rowntree and the current market leader, Neilson, did not use fresh milk in their process, Cadbury reasoned that

Dairy Milk would have a definitive advantage.

The successful launch of Dairy Milk soon precipitated a complete change in direction for the rest of the Canadian business. The Fry-run organisation had been reluctant to relegate the Fry name to that of Cadbury in their selling efforts. Fry's Cocoa was by far the dominant cocoa brand in the market – a position it still occupies – and the Cadbury name was seen purely as being an import brand. Cadbury had to resort to taking direct control of the Canadian business away

William Neilson Limited
TORONTO · CANADA

ONE OF THE LARGEST MAKERS OF ICE CREAM IN THE BRITISH EMPIRE AND ONE OF THE WORLD'S LARGEST MANUFACTURERS OF HIGH GRADE CHOCOLATES ●

from Fry's before it was too late. But, as in Australia, the Depression was to scupper any hopes of profitability for a few more years to come. Losses continued into the mid-1930s and spare manufacturing space was used for Pascall lines. Profitability was finally achieved by 1938 only to be disrupted for a further decade by the Second World War and its aftermath.

A foothold had been achieved, but in a market that had more than its fair share of local firms, the Cadbury position was far less well entrenched than it had become in Australia. At one stage, 15% of the entire net worth of the Cadbury business had been sunk into these two markets with little apparent hope on the horizon.

It is amazing that, although Cadbury had carried such losses for almost two decades in both Australia and Canada, it did not diminish the company's belief that lost export markets should be aggressively retaken by setting up operating companies inside tariff barriers.

But they had learned some painful lessons. Australia had shown that the UK model of vast manufacturing sites generating cost efficiencies could not be replicated as an entry strategy. The crucial role of Dairy Milk in re-establishing the status of the Cadbury name was also clear, as was the fact that Cadbury had been far too considerate to the sensitivities of Fry, and needed to take charge from day one. All these lessons were to be well applied in the next three export markets to throw up barriers: New Zealand, Ireland and South Africa.

New Zealand

Cadbury and Fry had followed their usual pattern in New Zealand of combining their selling agencies at the time of the parent companies merger in the UK. The combined agency had done well in restoring exports to New Zealand post World War One, but was floored by an increase in import duty from 6% up to 25% in 1928, which immediately reduced their sales by two-thirds. Cadbury began the search for a suitable site on which to build a factory, while simultaneously, a local manufacturer of chocolate and biscuits, R. Hudson & Company, were looking to expand their operations given the opportunity the import tax had presented them. A third party brought the two together with a view to forming a joint enterprise.

Cadbury were much impressed by the purpose-built Hudson factory in Dunedin, replete with its compliment of up-to-date and efficient chocolate moulding and enrobing lines. An agreement was duly signed on February 28th, 1930 to form Cadbury Fry Hudson Ltd., with Cadbury and Fry together holding the controlling interest. The new firm's remit was the manufacture and sale of the products of the three companies, but once again, got off to a sticky start due to the Depression.

There was also a sticky start between the managements of the parent companies, but Cadbury acted much faster than they had with the problems in

their Canadian venture, and sent a new man out in early 1931 to work with the Hudson family members running the company with the brief to patch things up. The other action taken much more quickly in New Zealand was the launching of Dairy Milk. Realising that the benefits of having the product spearheading their marketing efforts far outweighed the small risk of having their secrets stolen, plans were immediately put in place to import the top secret milk condensing equipment and Dairy Milk recipe into the Hudson factory. To improve efficiencies, the Cadbury board also agreed that Hudson's milk chocolate could be made using the same recipe and process up to the final stage where a slightly different flavour was added.

Although the Depression hit hard and the factory had to be put on a 4-day week, the contract manufacture of Pascall boiled sweets and some non-competing Rowntree lines helped keep the company stable. Cadbury also pumped in advertising money, something previously avoided by Hudson's, such that the company spend in 1930 was greater than Hudson's had spent since their inception 52 years previously.

Even though Cadbury Fry Hudson was operating in a much smaller market than Australia and Canada – New Zealand's population was only 1½ million at this point – the

company was profitable from the start, paying a dividend to its owners in its first year of operation. After a slight blip in 1931, the business continued to grow both sales and profits, even during the Second World War when the company concentrated all of its reduced sugar imports into maintaining the manufacture of Dairy Milk and their other moulded bars, cancelling many of their lesser known confectionery items. Being able to maintain a full supply of Dairy Milk to the market at a time when there were few alternatives available, the Cadbury brand, built upon Dairy Milk, consequently emerged from the conflict a lot stronger than it had entered it.

With a quality product range now focused fully on Dairy Milk, the New Zealand business was also able to generate some benefits of scale by gaining agreement from Bournville that it could take over the supply of many of Cadbury's Far Eastern export markets, and export Hudson's biscuits to almost any Cadbury territory apart from India. Cadbury Fry Hudson were then able to embark on a major upgrade to the factory, with a new factory block being completed in 1953 that was at the time the largest single factory building anywhere in the Southern Hemisphere.

Cadbury reaped the benefits of their speed in setting up in New Zealand, together with their entry strategy

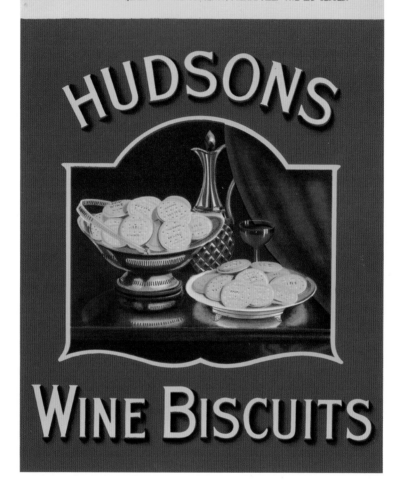

of combining with the strongest local player. With no major local competitors, a combined market share nearing 80%, and a relatively small consumer base, Cadbury were too well entrenched for any other of the major players to take a run at the market.

Ireland

A similar success story of establishing strong market shares while delivering profits from day 1 was to occur in another relatively small market, Ireland, where Cadbury had continued to manage its exports direct from Bournville after independence. The first import duty to hit confectionery came in 1924, which unnerved Rowntree more than it did Cadbury. While Cadbury could ride the storm because of their much lower unit costs, Rowntree, who were already losing money on their exports to Ireland, agreed to buy a local manufacturer of low-priced sweets to enable them to set up local production.

Cadbury were now concerned that Rowntree, once they began manufacturing their lines in Ireland, would be able to undercut them on price. But they stalled on taking action as the increasing economies at Bournville enabled them to keep their prices competitive. But an unexpected quadrupling of import duties in May 1932, together with a rather unique tax that applied 2d to each individual package, no matter how large or small, galvanised Cadbury into action, setting up a local joint company, Fry-Cadbury (Ireland) Ltd. in 1932.

Based on their learnings from both Australia and Canada, the company took two decisions that were to ensure the success of the new enterprise. Although Fry had developed the greater business in Ireland, where their Cocoa and Fry's Chocolate Cream reigned supreme, Cadbury, having learned from the Canadian debacle, were clear that the Cadbury brand would be the one pushed to the fore in the chocolate market, leaving cocoa to the Fry brand. As a result, Fry's milk chocolate

Proud moment!

Una, now a school prefect, takes charge at the crossing . . .

It doesn't seem so long since a very tiny Una once clutched *your* hand that first day to school. Now there's Pat and Terry and they're safe in Una's hands. My, don't they grow fast. And strong and sturdy! Fry's Cocoa certainly helps. It's so good for them and they love it. For a cup of Fry's is not only nourishing and sustaining. It's got that real chocolatey flavour all children enjoy. Remember: Fry's Cocoa builds the men and women of tomorrow. Give *your* children Fry's Cocoa—tonight!

Growing up on Fry's
—a cup of cocoa is a cup of food

FRY'S COCOA

bars and Bournville Cocoa were not reintroduced to the market, and the new company focused its advertising spend behind two lines: Dairy Milk and Fry's Cocoa. As demand for chocolate soared while the cocoa market stagnated, soon most of the advertising was building the Cadbury name.

Secondly, anxious to avoid building a massive factory to make small volumes of many Cadbury and Fry lines, which would have crippled the new business, the factory was only initially designed

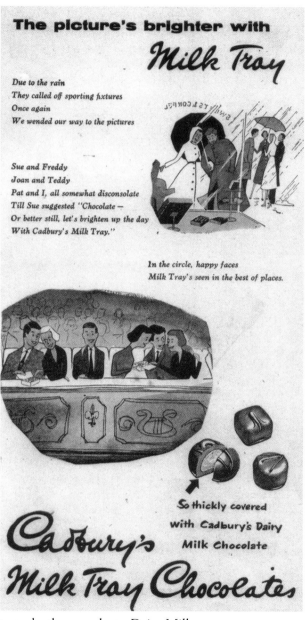

The picture's brighter with

Milk Tray

Due to the rain
They called off sporting fixtures
Once again
We wended our way to the pictures

Sue and Freddy
Joan and Teddy
Pat and I, all somewhat disconsolate
Till Sue suggested "Chocolate —
Or better still, let's brighten up the day
With Cadbury's Milk Tray."

In the circle, happy faces
Milk Tray's seen in the best of places.

So thickly covered
with Cadbury's Dairy
Milk Chocolate

Cadbury's
Milk Tray Chocolates

to make three products: Dairy Milk, Fry's Cocoa and Cadbury's Drinking Chocolate, and engaged only 18 employees, with the first bars of Irish-made Dairy Milk rolling off the production lines in 1933. All the other products considered suitable for sale in Ireland would be made by a local third-party manufacturer to Cadbury-Fry recipes. Obviously, such an approach reduced the profit Cadbury made per line as the contract manufacturer was taking his share, but the absence of huge overheads meant there was not the cost pressure to build sales ahead of consumer demand. Consequently, Fry-Cadbury (Ireland) Ltd. was able to extend its product range in an orderly fashion, rather than flooding the market with new lines to fill the factory.

The 1930's saw a succession of new lines that were planned with the consumer in mind, and with the Sales department able to give each sufficient focus and attention. As volumes increased and costs were well managed, in 1935 the company was able to reduce prices on its moulded bars and increase the weights of its Fry lines to turn the screw on the local Rowntree operation. In 1936, an Irish version of Milk Tray was launched, with the chocolates covered in thick Irish Dairy Milk chocolate. By 1938, volumes were increasing at an average rate of approximately 20% a year, necessitating the building of a second factory in Dublin while still maintaining the contract manufacturing arrangements. The company, after a small loss in its start-up year, was increasingly profitable.

Finally, Cadbury had found a way to grow a consumer franchise in an overseas company through their strategy of quality and value while making money in the process. By the time the last large Cadbury export market to raise tariff barriers – South Africa – did so in 1939, Cadbury had no trouble in immediately re-entering that market with an operation that was profitable from its first year, replacing an arrangement where Rowntree had made Cadbury lines there as a *quid pro quo* for Cadbury doing so for Rowntree in Australia.

Prior to the First World War, Cadbury had experienced no barriers to the building of their overseas sales. They had a simple model, sending travellers to the ends of the earth, and supplying product from a single factory, Bournville. One such traveller visited 22 countries across four continents in one epic two-year sales journey. Once the imposition of tariffs forced Cadbury to forgo their notion that Bournville could be their global supply base, they found themselves, somewhat against their better judgement, having to build stand-alone manufacturing, selling and distribution organisations from scratch. Not surprisingly, they began by using their U.K. experience as a template, but their Australian experience demonstrated that a production-led strategy could not succeed.

Fortunately, Cadbury's management style facilitated their overseas businesses acting with a lot of local autonomy to adapt to the very different market and competitive positions. Much emphasis was placed on exporting the company philosophy and processes rather than building unwieldy long-distance command and control systems. In August 1939, the Bournville Works Magazine was reporting on the setting up of the South African business, and stressed the importance of getting the right local management,

Every service at Bournville had to be duplicated at the overseas factory and operated on a simplified scale by a comparatively small staff, whose minds must be philosophical enough to discuss the local company's policy with Bournville at 6,000 miles distance, and yet versatile enough to deal with the local

> Tax Inspector, and settle the length of the girl's overalls….It was amazing how rapidly the Bournville tradition could be superimposed on local custom.

By managing through the local interpretation of overall company policy rather than following detailed dictates emanating from Bournville, each overseas business was able to be flexible and adaptable as circumstances demanded, although CFP in Australia was hampered by the cost burden of its overly-large factory for two decades. Decisions over product ranges, advertising campaigns and new lines were devolved to the local businesses, which became a critical success factor in the development of the strong Cadbury overseas markets. This local autonomy was crucial in building the leading market positions and the enduring local character of the Irish, South African, Australian and New Zealand businesses.

It is usually assumed that setting up companies in the old British Empire markets was a soft option for British companies such as Cadbury's, as opposed to seeking to enter, for example, Greece or Italy. But it was just common sense. All the markets Cadbury entered spoke English, and consumers there had long been aware of the Cadbury name and reputation, either from the local Cadbury importer or as immigrants from Britain. Why wouldn't Cadbury seek to exploit those advantages? But it was not a free ride. Cadbury were excluded from markets they had spent decades nurturing with little or no notice. The successful rebuilding by Cadbury of their positions was by no means assured, but was facilitated by prompt action as soon as they became at a disadvantage on price due to import tariffs. Other European chocolate firm's could have done exactly the same, but they did not. Cadbury got there first in re-establishing their presence.

The timing of Cadbury's moves turns out to have been critical. In manufacturing locally, Cadbury were shielded from other international competitors by the tariff barriers. Cadbury also had the advantages flowing from their timely rebuilding of Bournville. Building five new factories and setting up five new operations within the space of 13 years would not have been possible without the profits flowing from their U.K. success. Without the ability to write off investments, forgo dividends for years or even decades, and plough in extra advertising money, the operations in Australia and Canada would surely have failed.

In that period they were able to build very strong brand franchises, founded on the product superiority of Dairy Milk and the absence of a strong, local milk chocolate brand. Cadbury were able to define and own those nations' preference for chocolate taste. This then proved to be an almost insuperable barrier to entry for later arrivals after the tariff walls came down. Prospective market entrants faced a very strong incumbent Cadbury brand which consumers thought of as being local. Only in Canada did this formula fail to work, mainly because of the much more intensive competition from American firms.

It had been a long and expensive learning curve, but the benefits were more than sufficient reward. By 1939, Cadbury had overseas factory space over half that of the much enlarged Bournville, profitably manufacturing double the volume of the 1914 export peak, and sixteen times the export volume of 1918. The creation of

the Bournville machine had given Cadbury not only a dominant position in the U.K. market, but had also enabled the successful development of what would become even stronger and more profitable Cadbury brand franchises overseas. This was good news as things were beginning to change back in the home market.

DEVELOPMENT OF OVERSEAS FACTORIES AS A RESULT OF EXPORT RESTRICTIONS

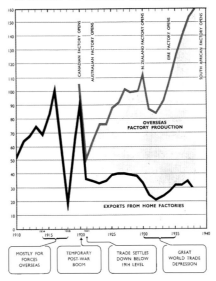

PART II – Summary

In Part I, we saw how selling better products had taken the company from the brink of ruin to being Britain's most successful confectionery manufacturer. But in doing so, they demonstrated the strategic weakness in relying on better products to drive long-term success. In each case, someone else had the best product until Cadbury came along with an even better one. Unless George Cadbury Jnr. and his team just happened to be the world's greatest confectioners, there was no reason why a competitor could not come along with an even better cocoa, milk chocolate bar and box of chocolates to trump Dairy Milk, Bournville Cocoa and Milk Tray.

The shift in Cadbury's strategy towards aligning their entire business model behind the delivery of quality and value protected them from having their products trumped. In creating a business model that made it uneconomical for competitors to challenge their brands head on, Cadbury were able to build leading positions for their brands relatively unhindered. Their brands did not remain as leaders in their respective fields because they were the absolute ultimate manifestation of the respective product ideas. They were to do so because competitors could see no way of making any money in attempting to topple them.

Cadbury had patiently built all the components of a business model that gave their brands a huge advantage versus their competitors. With the mechanisation of the factory in the 1920's and '30's, Cadbury were able to deliver a series of price cuts that intimidated their competitors and initiated dramatic market and business growth. Over a time-span of fifty years, the Cadbury business had become increasingly aligned behind its twin mantra of quality and value. To have substantially lower costs at a time when value was the main barrier to growth would have been sufficient. But to be able to establish benchmarks of product excellence simultaneously was a remarkable achievement. Even though Marketing had yet to be defined as a discipline at that point, Cadbury were demonstrating that Marketing should not be a functional business discipline, but a discipline for all business functions to pursue in tandem.

With protection from direct attack, and with the enormous profits rolling in, Cadbury were able to invest in building their brand name to a much greater extent than any of their competitors. They pursued this goal vigorously and with many imaginative initiatives. Cadbury were directly touching millions of U.K. consumers a year in ways that deeply endeared their name, further protecting their products from competitive pressures. They consciously decided to manage both their product range and their advertising to further enhance their efficiency-led approach. It is thought-provoking that one of the U.K.'s strongest consumer franchises was built by pursuing a strategy that revolved almost entirely around the efficient use of manufacturing assets. But at this stage, value was the trump card, and Cadbury played it to brilliant effect.

While their setting up of overseas businesses was prompted by the imposition of tariff barriers, Cadbury triumphed through the speed of their response and the financial muscle provided by the Bournville machine. This, coupled with their optimism and fortitude, enabled them to persevere in the most difficult circumstances imaginable in Australia. Circumstances that, in part had arisen because Cadbury had started off with the wrong business model there. The Bournville system of building large amounts of spare capacity that would then be filled via price cuts did not translate to a greenfield situation. Starting with low volumes meant that the factory was not a competitive weapon but a millstone around their necks. Pressure to cover the overheads demanded short-term quick fixes, rather than more considered approaches to building a business in an extremely tough competitive environment.

Canada was not much better, but the ventures in Ireland, New Zealand and South Africa ran much more smoothly as the company had demonstrated an ability to learn from their earlier mistakes. Another benefit the company gained was in choosing quite small markets such as Ireland, New Zealand and South Africa, where there was no incentive for competitors to try and muscle in on Cadbury's success. The markets simply were not big enough to make the fight worthwhile. Consequently, Cadbury were able to build much stronger competitive positions in those markets for far longer than would have otherwise been the case in the U.K.

Back in the U.K., The emergence of the Countline sector was a significant market shift. Rowntree adopted the approach more out of desperation than anything else. It was a last throw of the dice for a business under relentless competitive pressure. The emergence of Mars was a wild-card that could not have been foreseen at the time, and combined with Rowntree's change in strategy, gave the new sector an early significant stake in the market. If the Mars family relationships had been more cordial, and Forrest Mars had stayed working with his father in the U.S., the U.K. confectionery market could have evolved very differently.

So why did Cadbury not act differently and respond more vigorously to the emergence of Countlines? While it was by no means clear that lines such as Kit Kat Chocolate Crisp would ever amount to much, even though the Canadian market showed the potential of Countlines, Aero was certainly giving Cadbury pause for thought. Instead of the usual kind of threat, such as a Rowntree's Extra Creamy Milk that could be stifled at birth, here was a very different kind of competitor to Dairy Milk. It had a unique point of difference, strong advertising support, and consumers were buying it, so should Cadbury have quickly copied Rowntree's and Mars' approach?

But from Cadbury's perspective, such a route would have negated all the key advantages that they held. They would have been no more efficient in making Countlines than Rowntree, and less so than Mars, who soon had a lock on nougat-based lines. Bournville was simply not equipped to make anything much different to cocoa, Moulded bars and Assortments, and it could well have disrupted their finely tuned machine to have begun developing Countline products to be made there. The only realistic option would have been to see the Fry factory at Somerdale as the means of response. But since the two businesses were being run almost independently of each other, that was not a practical option. Equally, there were major risks on the branding side. The Cadbury name was a huge asset, so to go down a route that down-played the importance of the house name would have been wasting one of the most potent brand names the country had ever seen.

A generation earlier, Cadbury had risen to market dominance by latching onto new trends quickly. But the gigantic Bournville enterprise that grew out of the First World War, while having powered the business to undreamt-of heights, also limited Cadbury's flexibility should circumstances change. Many manufacturing businesses today are still imprisoned by the capabilities of their factories, even more are restricted by how they view their markets, as are many retailers and service providers. The more powerfully entrenched a dominant player becomes, the more they are tempted to solidify their status within their business model and see only continuations of current business conditions. The more successful you are, the more likely it is that your competitors will do something dramatically different. The more rigidly you view your market, the more likely it is that you will be outflanked.

Walmart were, and are, unbeatable on low prices delivered by a second-to-none logistics infrastructure; but Target's success has come from concentrating on products where price is less critical. Dell became unbeatable on made to order computers, yet suffered as their category changed, and have since reverted to selling computers through retail stores. More than ever before, building factories and business processes around current market conditions can quickly become a hindrance in times of change, as Cadbury were to find out.

Part III

DIFFICULT HEADWINDS

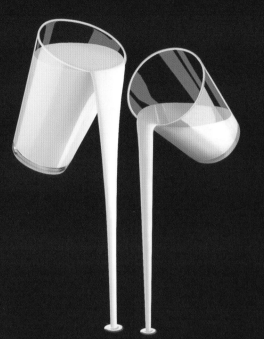

Chapter 9

IMPACT OF THE WAR

REDUCED PRICES
Half pound–2/-
Quarter pound–1/-
and 2 oz. for 6d
Cadbury's
DAIRY MILK
CHOCOLATE: 8 OZ
CADBURY'S MILK
FROM THE FACTORY IN A GARDEN!

Strategic Deep Freeze

While Cadbury had begun preparing for the next conflict as early as 1937 by reviewing their records of the last one, their planning would be nullified in October 1939 with the imposition of rationing of supplies to customers. Since raw materials were also allocated to manufacturers in proportion to their pre-war needs, both demand and supply were being regulated at reduced versions of the 1939 position. This, in effect, put the market into a state of suspended animation where consumer trends ceased to have any effect, as did the possibility of any competitive trends between manufacturers.

While Cadbury had dominated the pre-war chocolate market, there were plenty of other manufacturers still around who would have appreciated the fifteen year breathing space given them by rationing. The production of the nation's chocolate ration was divided up between 181 firms who were manufacturing more than two tons per week, but the impact of the blitz and large government orders meant that sometimes a firm would not be able to produce their own targets, in which case the balance would be made by another firm's factory with the label explaining that, for example, this Cadbury's bar was made by Nestlés.

To maximise production in this constrained environment, Cadbury took their efficiency skills to a new high, resulting in radical changes to the product range. The number of packings on the price list came down by almost 90% as the company concentrated production into lines where they had the greatest efficiencies. Since rationing was to last for fifteen years, selling what they could make would become standard practise for the company.

Another wartime necessity for Cadbury was the manipulation of product ingredients. The company had to take both the quantity and quality of raw materials made available, with the result that, within the 29 remaining lines, there had been some dramatic changes to the products themselves. A special wartime line named Economy Red Label Drinking Chocolate had been introduced in July 1940, being sweetened with a mixture of sugar and saccharin to conserve precious sugar supplies. Even with such ersatz products, the British consumer was well down the pecking order when it came to allocations. First were the Government with orders for the three armed services, then American armed forces, and even prisoners of war were given higher priority.

The government's ban in mid 1941 on the use of fresh milk for manufacturing purposes also condemned Cadbury's Dairy Milk to disappearing from the market;

the brand being cancelled in November that year once stocks of milk chocolate crumb had been exhausted. Although Dairy Milk would very occasionally reappear when there was a summer surplus of milk production, it was replaced in the reduced line-up by a completely new product called Ration Chocolate. This was made with dried skimmed milk powder and hence bore little relation to Dairy Milk's creamy taste. Almost as off-putting as the taste was the price; whereas the 2oz bar of Dairy Milk had sold for 2d in 1939, 2oz Ration Chocolate had risen to 3½d by 1945. The war was having a dramatic impact on Cadbury's ability to deliver on their twin mantra of quality and value.

Much of the factory had also been given over to war work. The sensitivities of the still dominant Quaker contingent on the Board were taken into account with the setting up of a subsidiary company to undertake the manufacture of aeroplane parts, jerricans, respirators and the filling of rockets. This employed 2,000 people at its peak, and the Allied war effort was to benefit from Cadbury's expertise in factory efficiencies. Soon after taking on the assembly of respirators, the

So now you
DRINK
the glass and
a half of Milk

It is some time since Cadburys had milk for their chocolate, and their supplies of Milk Chocolate are now exhausted. So Milk Chocolate, for the moment, must say ' Farewell.' The milk goes on your doorstep now — half-a-million pints a day of it to help your children's health !

ISSUED BY
CADBURYS
FROM BOURNVILLE — *the Factory in a Garden*

company suggested to the Government that conferences be set up with other firms doing similar work to share ideas. The net result was that the cost of assembling respirators came tumbling down. Cadbury had even offered to furnish a complete factory-building organisation to help the war effort, but the Government passed on that one.

By the end of the war, the Bournville annual output was little more than half its pre-war level, and mostly in products that were different to the ones upon which the company had built its pre-war reputation. Milk shortages continued well after the conflict; in 1948 the company was allocated only 4% of the milk quantity it had used in 1938. As a consequence, products using milk chocolate accounted for only 5% of Cadbury's U.K. sales. Moulded sales were almost a third of their pre-war level whereas sales of Assortments

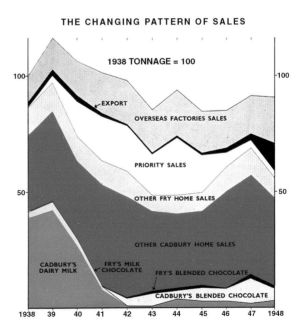

THE CHANGING PATTERN OF SALES

1938 TONNAGE = 100

EXPORT

OVERSEAS FACTORIES SALES

PRIORITY SALES

OTHER FRY HOME SALES

OTHER CADBURY HOME SALES

CADBURY'S DAIRY MILK

FRY'S MILK CHOCOLATE

FRY'S BLENDED CHOCOLATE

CADBURY'S BLENDED CHOCOLATE

1938 39 40 41 42 43 44 45 46 47 1948

and cocoa, which used very little milk, were 36% higher.

The total BC&C company was in better shape than its U.K. operation because the overseas factories had been relatively unaffected by supply shortages, and had geared up production during the War to meet massive Government orders in addition to their regular business. While they were booming, the U.K. business was completely constrained by the impact of rationing for what looked like the foreseeable future.

One ray of sunshine for Bournville was that there arose an opportunity to grow their export sales. This lay in the fact that the almost bankrupt British Government was heavily incentivising anything that could be sold for precious U.S. dollars. Generous rebates would be available on any sugar bought on the open market that was used in products exported to America.

Here lay the chance to restore some of Bournville's lost output.

United States

Cadbury had historically largely avoided having anything to do with the U.S. market. There were major logistical difficulties for anyone trying to establish a national presence in the U.S. The sheer size and scale of the market meant that only the giants could afford to have their own national sales force. Everyone else had to rely on an intricate web of wholesalers, distributors, brokers and the like, of whom there were thousands. It was difficult to ensure that products were getting the right kind of attention, and also something of a mystery as to where stock that went into the system was at any given time. Volume despatched and considered sold months ago could reappear at any moment, having languished in a warehouse somewhere down the line.

Cadbury's historical reticence had also been grounded in the fact that it was an exceptionally competitive environment. In addition to Hershey and Mars, there were some 1,600 other manufacturers who might not have had a significant national presence, but were strong in their own areas. But the prospect of earning dollar revenues, coupled with the exceptionally generous government allowances on the sugar used, meant that previous reservations had to be laid aside. So despite the shortages of raw materials for the home market, Cadbury set up their first U.S. operation, Cadbury-Fry (America) Inc. in 1948.

The initial product range was led by a 5c bar of Dairy Milk using milk chocolate crumb supplied by a new factory in Ireland, and was intended to go head-to-head with the Hershey Bar. Hershey had an unusual policy in the land of the hard sell of not running any advertising at all; a practice they would stick to, amazingly, until 1970. But in those post-War days they didn't need any. The Hershey Bar was an American icon of which Hershey was manufacturing stupendous quantities. Cadbury, on the other hand, had no choice but to advertise if they were to get any retailer support and consumer trial for their products. Beginning with a focus on the West Coast, business grew steadily. In 1950, turnover reached $624,000, which encouraged Bournville to contribute $100,000 to be spent in extra advertising.

Cadbury were soon encouraged by a piece of consumer research they commissioned in 1951. A survey of over 2,000 Americans across six cities seemed

full of good news. Measured against America's two largest chocolate brands – Hershey Bar and Hershey Almond – 60% of respondents preferred Dairy Milk, primarily for its creaminess. The only downside was that only 10% of people had heard of Cadbury, and only half of those knew their products were made in England. Supported by an almost national network of brokers, and with the $100,000 funding a national advertising campaign on ABC television and radio, all seemed set for a major success. The prospect of

eventually toppling the Hershey Bar sucked Cadbury into a major push. Fry Countline brands and Cadbury's Roses were added to the product line up with much optimism being expressed as to their potential.

However, the optimism was misplaced. In early 1952, much of the previous year's sales increase was still sitting unsold throughout the distribution channels. Getting brokers, sub-brokers and wholesalers to list the Cadbury products needed to be followed up by having feet on the ground working with these organisations, getting them to give higher priority to Cadbury lines among the many hundreds of other products on their lists, and booking regular orders. This essential follow-up had not been organised. Consequently, Dairy Milk was not getting into the one million 'Mom and Pop' stores that accounted for the bulk of Hershey's sales and profits. It was no use having a preferred product or an advertised product if it wasn't an available product.

To make matters worse, new products such as Roses and Fry Countlines had been a disaster,

'Fry lines were not competitive in weight or size with American domestic products and were not found acceptable to the American public'.

40,000 cases of Fry lines alone were languishing in the company warehouse, with little prospect of being sold to anyone. This was an early warning that the Fry range was not up to head-on competition with the likes of Mars. Reluctantly, the visiting Cadbury family member, John Cadbury – a son of William - agreed to slash prices in order to liquidate the stock, with the resulting $300,000 loss being assumed by Bournville. The losses of Cadbury-Fry (America) Inc.

in 1952 alone totalled $814,000, and the company could already see another $100,000 of losses on unsaleable Roses and Fry's stock, together with compensation payments to brokers.

This turn of events had unnerved Bournville, who sent over their own men to assume control of proceedings. The stock problems had damaged the reputation of the Cadbury U.S. selling organisation with the American trade, so the Cadbury team decided that a pared-down organisation, operating under the radar, was the best approach until the memories of mountains of unsold stock disappeared. The new management reported back to Head Office that,

'The only hope we can see in the future of improving the financial position of the American company is gradually, through experience, to build up trade in the U.S.A. in lines which we can sell on to the American market and which are not directly competitive'.

Cadbury's hopes of conquering the massive U.S. market, in particular the Hershey Bar, would have to be put on hold.

West Germany

Matters seemed to be progressing better in Cadbury's first step onto the European mainland. They had set up an agency in Hamburg in 1949 to see if an import business could be developed. However, to help the ruined indigenous manufacturers get back on their feet, an import tax of 40% was imposed by the West German government soon after. Cadbury by now were well practised at responding to tariff barriers, but this time took a new approach: arranging for a small, high-quality Bremen-based confectionery company, Hanseaten Schokoladen Werke, to make and sell Cadbury products under license. Establishing local production was also essential as, had the venture been a major success, Bournville's precious supplies of milk and sugar would have become too depleted.

Production commenced in 1954 of a small range of 50g and 100g moulded bars, with Germanic branding to help position the range as being locally produced. Cadbury's Vollmilch, Vollmilch-Nuss, Vollmilch-Mokka and Bournville Schokolade got off to a good start, driven by a growing sales force and widespread press, poster and radio advertising. Cadbury gradually built up a stake in their partner, setting up a joint company, Cadbury-Fry G.m.b.H., in 1960. Two years later, Cadbury bought out their German partner and took full ownership of the enterprise, which consisted of a sales office in Hamburg and a factory in Bremen. The imminent setting up of the Common Market, which excluded Britain, had prompted this move. Cadbury saw the opportunity to be inside the new trading community and their plan was to use their Bremen factory to supply not only West Germany but also sales offices they were setting up in France and the Netherlands.

But progress in the West German market was to be hamstrung by the issue of the preferred milk chocolate taste. The Hanseaten technical people had developed a superb powdered milk recipe that was as good as, if not better than anything made by the Swiss firms who had set the standard in pre-War Germany for how chocolate should taste. After taking full ownership, it was automatically assumed by Cadbury that the recipe should be changed over to Dairy Milk without the benefit of any market research to support the idea.

Plans were put in place to market the Dairy Milk recipe, initially using chocolate crumb imported from the UK and Ireland, with the aim of ultimately being produced in the Bremen factory, into which £2 million would soon be spent. Equipment was also purchased for the local manufacture of Flake, Buttons and Picnic – the German company being able to choose from both Cadbury's and Fry's product ranges. But the switch over to the Dairy Milk recipe proved to be a disaster. Germans had long been accustomed to the taste of chocolate made with powdered milk, and it had become their preferred taste. Indeed, consumers of the existing Cadbury milk powder product, which had now been on the market for fifteen years, preferred it as it was and did not take to the new Dairy Milk taste at all. To make matters worse, in order to cover the extra costs, the price of the new bar had been increased while competitors had responded by slashing theirs.

Caught in a triple whammy of higher costs, lower prices, and not being the preferred taste, the initiative was

doomed. The other new Cadbury brands had depended on a strong Dairy Milk as a means of building their own credibility on the back of the Cadbury name, and the hoped-for superior taste of the Dairy Milk chocolate; there were not the funds available to advertise them all separately. The business went into a terminal tailspin and, in May 1968, the Cadbury-Fry G.m.b.H board recommended to their parent that the venture be wound up.

Junge Leute Tempo, Schwung.

und natürlich CADBURY

Wie schön ist es, ein Vergnügen mit köstlicher Schokolade abzu-runden — mit CADBURY-Schokolade natürlich! Und jeder ist begeistert von dem besonders handlichen CADBURY-Format.

India

Cadbury's third post-war venture was much further afield. Although India had long been a Cadbury export market, trade had been completely disrupted by the War. In 1947, the Bombay branch of Cadbury-Fry (Export) Ltd. was up and running again, though having to source its products from the Australian business given the shortages of raw materials at Bournville. Following Indian independence in 1947, which again raised the spectre of tariff barriers, Cadbury moved quickly to set up a manufacturing operation in India.

Good health and good times go together

Drink up your Bournvita

Bournvita

The strategy was to satisfy the legal requirements for being an indigenous manufacturer while expending the minimum of capital in doing so. This was achieved by finding a disused silver refinery located in the heart of Bombay where cocoa and Bournvita, shipped in bulk, could be repacked. Most of the equipment came from Bournville and packing commenced in August, 1949.

But the Indian Government was soon putting pressure on Cadbury to make a firm commitment to full, local manufacturing. In February 1950, the Cadbury board agreed that:

1. The installation of a small re-moulding plant be proceeded with immediately.
2. That it is the intention as soon as feasible to have a factory in India manufacturing from the bean but allowing for the bulk of the chocolate production to be made from imported Dairy Milk crumb and to manufacture also Bournville Cocoa and Bournvita.
3. That Rowntree and Nestlé be informed of these intentions.

Nestlé responded with some interest in a joint venture, but Cadbury then decided to go it alone.

Following further pressure from the Government to give a firm timetable for the setting up of full chocolate manufacturing, the Cadbury Board in Bournville examined three possible options in July 1950:

- Full scale manufacture in India with a likely capital commitment of an eye-watering £500,000 – almost as much as had been sunk into Australia and Canada combined.
- The same scheme, but raising the bulk of the capital from Indian investors
- Complete abandonment of the Sub-continent, waving goodbye to the company's Indian trade and goodwill.

The Board reluctantly informed the Bombay office that the company would be pulling out. This grim news prompted their man in Bombay to have one more go at the Indian government, and, to relief all round, gained a licence to continue repacking and re-moulding with no further commitment to full manufacture.

But events in 1951 highlighted the difficulties in Cadbury's existing set-up. Import licenses were required for Cadbury to bring in their part-processed raw materials, but were extremely restricted due to shortages of foreign exchange. As a result, the company ran completely out of stock in June and remained so for the rest of the year. Sales for the year plummeted to £90,000 and hard won customers were not happy. 1952 saw the Indian Government changing their minds yet again and pressing for commitment to full manufacture. The vacillation was infectious as the Cadbury Board

first agreed to proceed, then in early 1953 changed their minds and again communicated to the Bombay office that they would be pulling out. Bombay pleaded for two years grace before passing on the news to the Indian Government, but were met half-way and given twelve months to prove their viability. Sales recovered to £225,000 as the staff in India rose to the challenge.

A senior manager was sent from Bournville to review the situation, and reported back to the Board that,

The Firm at present enjoys a very high reputation. India will soon have a population of 400 million. Provided we continue to sell a good quality product and make it under good conditions I am sure we can make a success in India.

Combined with the sales upturn, the report did the trick and the Cadbury Board finally agreed to make a go of their Indian business. The company offered to manufacture Bournville Cocoa and dark chocolate from scratch in India, but did not want to go to the expense of building milk processing and crumb factories, so still asked to mould bars using imported crumb, but the government proved stubborn. To resolve the impasse, Cadbury considered the nuclear option of producing a milk chocolate locally,

Your favourite

Cadbury's MILK CHOCOLATE

with the goodness of milk in every block.

but without the expense of building the milk processing and crumb manufacturing infrastructure. This would involve making a milk chocolate bar using dried milk powder.

The decision proved to be a turning point for their Indian business, and the go-ahead was given to proceed to full local manufacture of Bournville Cocoa, Bournvita, and the new milk chocolate bar. Local production of Bournvita commenced in April 1957 in the basement a larger factory that also served as the new Head Office. The import licence issue was also addressed

by the new factory gearing up for production of Cadbury's Drinking Chocolate, which Bournville agreed to import into the U.K., giving the Indian company import credits.

The sales agents set out to repay Cadbury's faith by showing what they could really do. Record sales of £380,000 in 1957 reached £1 million by 1960 and £2 million three years later, of which a healthy £400,000 was profit. Cadbury now had a fifth viable overseas business, all of which were located in British Commonwealth countries.

BACK AGAIN!

In Cadburys Dairy Milk Chocolate

FROM THE FACTORY IN A GARDEN

Post Rationing U.K. Boom

Cadbury had been able to focus on three major overseas markets precisely because the continuation of rationing gave them little to do in the U.K. The market did not finally emerge from its enforced Rip Van Winkle state until 1953, when full supplies to manufacturers of sugar and full-cream milk were finally resumed, and rationing of supplies to stores finally removed.

As retailers and wholesalers rushed to stock up, it was unclear to Cadbury just how much of their increased sales represented consumer demand and how much was the filling of the distribution pipelines.

After fifteen years of having been in suspended animation, Bournville was not in a fit state to meet this new demand. Its pre-war level of 8,000 employees was down to 3,000 and, as the Engineering Director reported in the March 1953 edition of the Works Magazine,

Our buildings were upside down, some of them in the hands of other firms. We had not only to clear up the mess, but to clear it up with some definitive target in view.

As it became clear that the definitive target was not a market of 6ozs per head per week, but a figure one third larger than that, it was apparent that the existing Bournville infrastructure would not be big enough to cope.

There were also changes in the market place to contend with; the main one being in the chocolate biscuits market. While Cadbury had been making chocolate biscuits since they patented the idea in 1891, they had never been a major focus for the company. As with other manufacturers, Cadbury's biscuits were sold loose in shops from 6lb returnable tins, but self-selection shops were appearing and demanding that biscuits be pre-packaged, however there was no space available at Bournville for the required new packaging machinery.

The extension of Bournville had been mooted as early as 1950 when a temporary de-rationing of chocolate the previous year had precipitated such a surge in demand that rationing was re-imposed almost immediately. This glimpse into the future had prompted Cadbury to apply to extend firstly Bournville and then Somerdale. At that time, companies had to apply for an Industrial Development Certificate, and in both cases Cadbury were turned down. The Labour Government's policy was to direct industrial development away from areas of high employment and into areas of high unemployment. Cadbury reluctantly set plans in place for a

Cadbury's
Milk Chocolate
WAFER
BISCUIT

Our 2d. Wafer Biscuits have had a wonderful sale over a long period of years. The new biscuits illustrated here are variations of these in a new mould and covered in milk chocolate.

2 D.
EACH

HALF TINS CONTAINING
10 DOZEN BISCUITS

APPROXIMATE SIZE OF BISCUIT

green-field development at Moreton, near Birkenhead.

By making such plans and committing the investment while rationing was still in place, Cadbury had shown much of their pre-war boldness. The Moreton factory had been designed to be focused on producing all of Cadbury's range of biscuits, and was able to take some of the space pressure off Bournville from where chocolate biscuit production had been removed. Opened on September 17th, 1954, this new capacity was very timely given the end of rationing a few months earlier. But Cadbury had not foreseen that the entire market would be one third larger, so it was immediately apparent that the £1¼ million factory was too

small: it had added only 7% floor space to that of the colossal Bournville site which once again was creaking at the seams. Company chairman Laurence Cadbury had announced in his opening speech that plans were in place to add two more duplicate buildings as soon as possible.

Even before the extensions were built, the most modern chocolate biscuit factory in the world at Moreton was soon churning out three million biscuits a day. The Moreton investment finally allowed Cadbury to have a good run at developing the market for biscuits either fully or half-covered in Dairy Milk chocolate – the idea they had patented over sixty years previously. Despite the fact that their patent had long since lapsed and allowed competitors in, by 1962, Cadbury chocolate biscuits sales had increased 17-fold from their pre-war level and were accounting for 11% of entire company sales.

But Moreton was never the ideal solution. The factory was originally supplied with chocolate made at Bournville and shipped up in a never-ending convoy of tankers, but the rocketing demand for chocolate biscuits soon made it more economical to build chocolate-making facilities at the new factory. There seemed to be a silver lining in that, since Moreton was built on a very large 100 acre site, had large, modern one-storey buildings, and was now self-sufficient from Bournville in chocolate-making, it would make sense to install there the latest modern machinery for the manufacture of Dairy Milk and Milk Tray. The Bournville pre-War buildings, which had been state-of-the-art in the 1920's, were not best suited to the long, continuous production machines being eyed by the engineers.

Through circumstances beyond its control, the Cadbury set-up in the U.K. was now fundamentally different than the one that had emerged from the First World War. Far from being a low-cost producer operating from one hugely efficient main factory, the company was now carrying the cost burden of three main producing factories, each with its own set of duplicated chocolate-making and management infrastructures. At its peak, Moreton was a mini-Bournville employing over 4,000 people, with many of the same employee benefits and facilities and had cost a whopping £6 million. The famed Cadbury low-cost model was beginning to crumble; a situation not helped by Moreton having a high level of industrial unrest where strikes or walkouts would occur over almost anything. There was even a strike against compulsory membership of the Cadbury Pension Scheme – widely acknowledged as one of the most generous in the country.

As all the new production lines were being installed at Moreton, there was no change happening at the Bournville site itself. This was to adversely affect the company in two ways: much of the machinery in Bournville was becoming dated and inefficient, as indeed was the outlook of the workforce and management, who were getting very used to things not changing. This meant that the culture was becoming conservative and the 'Bournville Experiment' gradually ceased to update itself, with many of the original investments becoming increasingly unproductive

costs. Education classes continued even though the raising of the school-leaving age had raised the education level of Cadbury trainees. The swimming baths were maintained despite most workers having indoor plumbing. Bournville still employed seamstresses for girls' gym uniforms and an army of gardeners, ladder-makers, window-cleaners and clock-winders.

The upshot was that the company was less and less in a position to deliver on the second leg of its pre-war strategy of quality and value. Cadbury's fixed cost problem was being compounded by much higher post-war prices of cocoa, which by then was trading at a level almost eight times that of 1940. The consequence was that the price of Dairy Milk was now three times the pre-war level – 6d for a 2oz bar – and Milk Tray prices were two and a half times. But it seemed to matter not. Consumers were increasingly affluent and the company was selling record volumes in the post-rationing consumption frenzy.

Chapter 10

SHIFTING SANDS: U.K. MARKET TRENDS GO AGAINST CADBURY

The Countlines
launched pre-war
by both Mars and
Rowntree were
faring just as well
as was the Cadbury
Moulded range
once the rationing
shackles had been
removed. Fry,
the Cinderella of
the Cadbury-Fry

combine, shared in this Countline surge,
even though it was not resourced to compete
head on with the resurrected Rowntree and
the aggressive Mars. In the mid 1950's,
Fry had set about replacing their range of
cheap generics with new Countlines such as
Walnut Bliss, Promise, Punch, Cokernut,
Tiffin, Five Centre and Picnic, to add to the
core of Chocolate Cream, Turkish Delight
and Crunchie. In contrast, the post-war
Cadbury product range was essentially that
of the late 1930s.

As indeed was Cadbury's approach to
advertising and sales promotion. Sand

MEET AT

The
Chocolate
House

FOR ELEVENSES,
LIGHT LUNCHES
OR BEFORE THE THEATRE
185 REGENT STREET

Yule Log

YOU'LL LOVE BAKING IT!
THEY'LL LOVE EATING IT!

"CADBURY'S BOURNVILLE COCOA ADDS RICHNESS TO
YOUR CHRISTMAS BAKING," SAYS SUSAN SINCLAIR

INGREDIENTS Sponge: 3 eggs, 3 oz. caster sugar, vanilla essence, 2½ oz. plain flour, 1 tblsp. Bournville Cocoa, 1 tblsp. warm water. Filling and icing: 4 oz. butter, 8 oz. icing sugar, 1 tblsp. Bournville Cocoa. Holly to decorate.
METHOD Grease and line a swiss roll tin approx. 12" × 9". Whisk the eggs, sugar and vanilla essence until thick, light and fluffy. Fold in the sieved flour and cocoa. Carefully add the warm water. Pour into the prepared tin. Bake in oven mark 6 or 400°F. for about 10 minutes.
When cooked, turn at once on to a piece of sugared greaseproof paper. Trim the edges of the sponge with a sharp knife and carefully roll up so that the greaseproof paper is rolled inside.

While the sponge is cooling, make up the butter cream by beating together the butter and icing sugar and adding a little milk or water if necessary to form a soft, dropping consistency. Divide this mixture. Blend the cocoa with a little boiling water. Mix well and allow to cool. Then beat the blended cocoa into one half of the butter cream, making chocolate cream. When the sponge is quite cool gently unroll and spread with the white butter cream. Re-roll and spread the chocolate cream over and around the outside. Draw a fork along the surface to give the effect of bark on a log. Dust with sieved icing sugar to represent snow.
Complete the decoration by adding a sprig of holly.

artists continued to wow the knotted hanky brigade; Demonstrators in their snappy purple dresses with gold trim sold millions of Cadbury drinks and handed out countless samples; Bournville's millionth post-war visitor won her own weight in Roses, which was then donated to St. Nicholas's Hospital in London; the latest Cadbury film, "The Bournville Story" won two Italian Oscars at the Turin Film Festival. The company also opened Chocolate Houses in places such as Regent Street in London, where people could indulge in a range of chocolate drinks, cakes and biscuits. In short, the post-war Bournville machine was largely indistinguishable from that of twenty years earlier.

Cadbury were still able to make improvements to their multiple touch-points model. The Cadbury cookery demonstrators, who had been providing more of an entertainment option for Women's Institute meetings than a brand-building tool, were reorganised in the late 1950's into a Home Economics Department. Cadbury were one of the first British food companies to adopt this idea, and soon gained a very good reputation in the world of women's magazines for their professionalism. With a dedicated kitchen facility on the Bournville site, they were able to draw upon the many resources of Bournville, such as

"I want Cadbury's .."

"Mr. Dim."
He laughs
over spilled
milk

Will he never learn the best
way to carry a glass-and-a-
half of milk?

"Family Favourites"

state-of-the-art design and photographic facilities to provide a top-class service. The public were soon writing in at the rate of 300,000 a year to get recipes from another pseudonymous employee, 'Susan Sinclair.'

The 30-Second Marvel

When commercial television began broadcasting in the London area on September 22nd, 1955, Cadbury had been quick off the mark with Drinking Chocolate being one of the first advertisements shown that evening. But Cadbury's transition to this new medium would not be smooth. Their early television advertisements had been rushed into production, and, along with those of most other pioneering television advertisers, showed some uncertainty as to how best to leverage the new medium:

Milk chocolate advertisements are humorous, suggesting the best ways of carrying a glass-and-a-half of milk; Milk Tray commercials consist of cartoons and incorporate a jingle. We are advertising Biscuits in a series of one-minute sketches featuring the famous trick cyclist, George Benson.

While struggling to adapt to a new medium was a problem for Cadbury, it was an understandable one. Many brands more recently strived for years to understand how best to use the new medium of the internet, with few having

Go on – spoil yourself!

Have a FRY'S CHOCOLATE CREAM

5 big pieces of Chocolate Cream *for only* 4d

had much real success. But making matters difficult for Cadbury was the impact television was having on the world of advertising in general. The arrival of television – the most powerful advertising medium the world had ever seen – greatly reduced the impact of the other media that had worked so well for Cadbury in the past and that had been resurrected after the War.

Equally as unfortunate for Cadbury was the fact that television was ideally suited to conveying a simple Countline selling point. Movement, sound and the focused attention of a nation of rapt viewers was a tailor-made environment for simple propositions such as "Have a Break – Have a Kit Kat", "Don't Forget the Fruit Gums, Mum", "Polo – the Mint with the Hole", "The Sweet you can eat between meals without ruining your appetite", "Chocolates? Maltesers!" and the like. These could be compellingly portrayed with a power many times greater than that possessed by all existing media, and were to turbo-charge the growth of the Countline sector.

For both Mars and Rowntree, the arrival of commercial television was manna from heaven. Both had a range of individual brands that needed a powerful and cost-effective medium to communicate their individual benefits and build their unique personalities. The Fry Countline range also benefited from the advertising revolution, using television to build on their previous press advertising campaigns for their Countline range. Cadbury, on the other hand, were not so well placed. Apart from Dairy Milk, Milk Tray and their cocoa beverages, they had a large product range of mostly small volume Moulded, Assortments and Biscuit lines that were neither sufficiently unique or of sufficient scale to be able to leverage the new marvel.

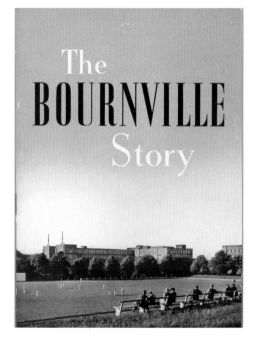

As Cadbury searched to translate their House brand/Dairy Milk/ product variants advertising model to the new medium, they targeted television for their 'prestige advertising' of the Cadbury name. When commercial television came to the Midlands a few months after London, Cadbury had the first spot, although not this time with a Drinking Chocolate spot, but with Paul Cadbury, introducing a cut-down version of their current film-unit offering, "The Bournville Story". Later that year, the company commissioned a series of 13 one-minute films, each describing in a travelogue style the harvesting of an ingredient used at Bournville. The series premiered on August 31st, 1957, when the entire interval of "Sunday Night at the London Palladium" was booked for Adrian Cadbury, a grandson of George and future chairman of the company, to be interviewed about the venture.

But despite such imaginative initiatives, the Countline tide could not be turned. Cadbury's Moulded sales, which had been the bedrock of the pre-war business, began to suffer under the pressure from the surging Mars and Rowntree brands. Cadbury tonnage sales for the year 1958 declined by 3% and in reviewing the previous ten years, the Chairman, Laurence Cadbury, clearly outlined the problem,

…we have a very large share of a contracting section of the market and we have a smaller share of the expanding section of the market.

As Cadbury's share of Countlines was a paltry 13% compared to their 64% in Moulded, Cadbury clearly had to rethink their approach of leaving Countlines to the Fry organisation.

Cadbury Moves Into Countlines

Cadbury conducted several major market research studies in 1959 to try and get to grips with Countlines. Their principal concern was how a range of Cadbury Countlines might impact the status of the Cadbury name. Cadbury had always seen Countlines as being of lesser stature than Moulded bars and were worried that in chasing volume, they might end up denigrating their hard-won reputation.

The news was encouraging. While the public agreed that Dairy Milk and its variants were a bit more special than the typical Countline, this was overshadowed by the feeling that the first duty of a manufacturer was to meet public demand. Much of the enjoyment of eating confectionery was in there being a wide variety of choice, and the consumer regarded most highly those who combined variety with quality. Since any Cadbury Countline would be automatically assumed to be of high quality, the door was open for Cadbury to increase its variety beyond its range of Moulded and Filled Blocks, which were seen as being rather 'samey' when compared to the competition's Countline brands.

In these same surveys, Cadbury dug deep in seeking to understand what made a good Countline, and whether they had any immediate candidates within their range that could, with a bit of tweaking, fit the bill. They discovered that, although the consumer didn't use such terminology, there were some very distinct differences between a Moulded bar and a Countline. While Moulded bars were segmented and could be eaten by oneself, easily shared or consumed over several sessions, a Countline was almost universally scoffed down in one sitting by the individual. Countlines were also much messier to eat, and thus tended to be a more solitary pleasure than Moulded bars, which could be discreetly eaten in public one chunk at a time.

In image terms, Countlines appealed more to the child in the adult whereas Moulded bars were seen as somewhat more sophisticated. This was reflected in the packaging designs which tended to be more colourful and cheerful than the somewhat more serious-looking Moulded bars. Advertising was brand-specific and only a tiny minority of Countlines were identified by their maker's names, each brand being assessed on its own merits.

Given that there were such significant differences between the two categories, with different usages and reasons for purchase, it would not have come as

a surprise that Cadbury did not have in their range a ready-made set of Countline blockbusters. Filled blocks, being segmented bars made on the Moulding manufacturing equipment, were categorised by the consumer as still being Moulded bars. Cadbury's Fudge, while having many Countline attributes, was too small to qualify and too sickly an eating experience to be much bigger than the existing size.

However, there was better news with Flake. It was seen as being a Countline, having a strong name and the right format, but with some obvious deficiencies. Firstly, its see-through packaging and reference to Dairy Milk was addressed in late 1959 by the change to a cheerful, bright yellow wrapper and the dropping of the Dairy Milk wording. Secondly was the absence of brand-specific advertising. That same year, television was already accounting for 64% of all chocolate advertising and was an essential component of building a Countline brand. Cadbury quickly developed a Flake advertising campaign that hit the sweet spot of a chocolate bar for solitary consumption by women. The advertising theme of "By yourself, enjoy yourself", with some rather suggestive visuals that resonated as being very bold and modern, was an immediate success.

However, one Countline brand was not going to be enough for Cadbury to get sufficient share of the seemingly inexorable growth coming from Countlines. Their problem was that Bournville did not have the manufacturing infrastructure to make products that were significantly different enough to their current offerings.

As a stop-gap, they did try to dress up one of their Caramel Filled Blocks as a Countline brand, naming it 'Extra', which served only to prove that their research had been correct.

The evidence was clear that Cadbury had to take on the Countline challenge in a much bigger way. The combined Cadbury-Fry sales in the U.K. had reached a peak in 1958 and from there on had begun to decline. Within that total, Fry had recorded a sales increase of 70% between 1953 and 1960 – the highest of any of the major houses, albeit off a relatively small base. Countlines were unequivocally seen as being the way forwards. Cadbury were still the dominant player in the chocolate market, with a share of 31%, together with another 9% from Fry. But the trends were ominous. In the space of just five years from 1957 to 1962, Countlines went from 26% of the chocolate market to 34%,

But developing some true Countline brands that could take on the likes of Kit Kat and Mars Bar would not be an overnight exercise. While the product development and engineering teams were coming to grips with their new brief, Cadbury encountered new problems on their core Moulded range.

A Challenger to Dairy Milk

In 1960, Cadbury's Dairy Milk had faced a new, direct competitor – its first since the early 1930's – that had come, not from Rowntree, but from Mars. After a test market in Northern Ireland under the brand name of Marabou, Mars had launched their now-renamed Galaxy chocolate bar in the autumn of 1960, supported by the biggest ever television advertising campaign for a U.K. chocolate bar. In response, Cadbury doubled their own advertising budget for Dairy Milk, using the strap line, 'The finest milk chocolate in the world –only 6d.', Mars having launched a larger bar priced at 9d.

Cadbury had been somewhat nonplussed that Mars would attack the leading brand in the market head-on, when the Mars strategy to date had been to build their own unique Countline brands. Mars, who in fact had long been nervous that Cadbury would bring their still powerful strengths to the Countline sector, had launched Galaxy to distract Cadbury from Countlines. Their reasoning that Cadbury would have to divert resources to defend Dairy Milk was correct, but they had the unexpected bonus of Cadbury's follow-up response going awry.

Seeing that the 9d price point had not killed Galaxy stone dead, Cadbury reasoned that they should be able to move their consumers away from the 6d bars into a larger size. Cadbury were keen to do this as they had become stuck at 6d – it having the advantage of being a single-coin purchase – but were seeing their profit margins being eroded by cost increases, particularly of cocoa. The 6d bar had now shrunk from its pre-war 2oz weight down to just over 1½oz in an effort to mitigate the spiralling cost of cocoa. The new Cadbury plan was to leapfrog Galaxy by launching a range of Dairy Milk, Fruit & Nut and Wholenut bars to retail at one shilling, and rely on the greater manufacturing efficiency to restore their profit margins.

All sales and marketing efforts were then put into making this the key size of the Dairy Milk brand. But it proved to be a bridge too far for the consumer. The replacement of the old 6d bar with the larger bar pretty much killed off the smaller bar without picking up much of the sale in the larger bar. Even though Cadbury never considered it as such, the 6d Dairy Milk bar, even after its weight emasculation, had been operating to some extent as a Countline: an impulse purchase more often than not consumed almost immediately as a pick-me-up. The 1/- bar, weighing 4oz, did not fulfil that role as it was too large; it could not be consumed in one go by all but the most hungry and it was ill-suited to an on-the-go consumption occasion. Mars Bar, which had bitten the bullet on price points and was priced at 7d, was much more suitable to an impulse eating occasion than a ¼lb block of chocolate priced at a shilling.

Changes in the Retail Trade

To add to Cadbury's woes at what had become a difficult time for them, they had also been struggling to come to grips with changes to their other pre-war competitive strength: their grip on the retail trade. As with their approach to advertising, Cadbury had emerged at the end of rationing with an identical approach for dealing with the retail trade to that of the pre-war period. And they could be forgiven for having done so: fifteen years of rationing had ossified British retailing just as much as it had the confectionery market. When everything was in short supply, and sales were driven by how many vouchers their customers possessed, there had been little incentive for retailers to adopt new methods of display and merchandising. Indeed a typical shop in the late 1940's would have borne a startling resemblance to John Cadbury's original shop on Bull Street. Yet once the shackles of rationing were removed, change came very quickly to confectionery retailing.

Mars had needed to challenge the status quo as they were cowed by the awesome power of the Cadbury distribution system and did not have the critical mass at that stage to be able to afford to match it. The solution lay in an aspect of American retailing with which Mars were already comfortable: letting someone else do most of the work. As we have already seen from Cadbury's first venture into the U.S. market, most of the donkey-work in getting products from factories to Mom and Pop stores was done by middlemen. Mars decided to go this route in the U.K. and as a consequence, embraced the emerging, but still largely inefficient Wholesale trade.

In this Mars got something of a free run. The market leader, Cadbury saw the Wholesaler as a competitor for the retailer's business, and one that would emasculate the Cadbury system if allowed to become established. Cadbury's advantage lay in their direct calling and delivery method. If Cadbury had embraced the Wholesaler, they would have to forego their main strength: their representatives being able to book big orders and fill retailers' stockrooms with Cadbury products. Wholesalers called on their customers much more frequently – it was one of their main selling points – and, as a result, the customer would not have to tie up his money with weeks' worth of Cadbury product. This 'stock pressure' made it much more difficult for Cadbury's competitors to get their products into shops.

But companies such as Mars and Cadbury's sister-company, Fry, were already pushing ahead in developing their sales through the Wholesaler. Fry would comb their sales force and offices to round up as many men as possible and blitz wholesale-serviced retailers, installing new displays and prompting the wholesaler to follow up and book larger orders. This Fry initiative, termed 'Operation Impact', highlighted a deeper shift that came out of the trend towards Wholesale: the critical importance of merchandising.

Handling the Products

The idea of merchandising was that products would be out on open display and ready for the consumer to pick up. With the advent of many Countline products from Mars, Rowntree and Mackintosh – all of which had been identically priced with 2oz Dairy Milk from their inception, and all heavily advertised – merchandising the display of product inside the shop would become the new category driver. Chocolate was increasingly an impulse purchase where the visibility and location in store could make the most difference to the amount purchased over time.

Within Cadbury, a continued reliance on their old selling methods was an increasing worry to Paul Cadbury, who had masterminded the company's hugely successful sales push of the 1920s,

Are we relying on 1939 techniques to face the problems? I am afraid some of us are. We feel we know all about it. Our battles between 1934 and 1939 were won on Quality, Value, Price Reductions, Intensive Selling and Advertising Campaigns, but

there are a host of other things, and these we shall develop to meet the new circumstances….I think you have got to realise, you chaps in the line – chaps on the road – that the answer to our problem is a word which has come into our vocabulary since 1939 – Merchandising!"

Merchandising was a revolutionary concept for the Cadbury Representatives to consider, and it flowed directly out of the rise of the wholesaler. Mars had realised from their American background that the two were, in fact, symbiotic. In going the Wholesale route, the job of the company representative shifted away from taking the order – that being done by the Wholesalers' Representatives – towards improving the position and prominence of the company's products within the store itself, which would improve sales and result in a bigger order for the Wholesaler the next time round. By contrast, under the Cadbury system of stock pressure, merchandising inside the shop had played little role. Cadbury had historically influenced the consumer to ask for their products through advertising, and the closest they usually got to directly influencing the purchase in the store was the window display.

But corner shops in the U.K. had not yet grasped the concept of merchandising. For fifteen years, confectionery had more often than not been under the counter, if available at all. When rationing ended, retailers had been uncertain how to display the vast quantities suddenly available to them while ensuring that their customers would not pilfer product. The solution came from some enterprising glass manufacturers who convinced most retailers to invest in glass cabinets. The products would be fully visible, but protected from the avaricious grasp of delinquent schoolboys. The retailer was happy that product would remain un-pilfered, but he was still not fully benefiting from impulse purchasing. However, since consumers were knocking down the doors in a post-rationing purchasing frenzy, it didn't seem to matter.

The Silent Salesman

The glass display cases in most stores (known as 'glass coffins' to frustrated Representatives) were a major barrier to the Mars company. By going through the Wholesale route, Mars could not influence the amount of their products sold to individual shops, so they needed to influence the sales out of the shop. But having the products entombed in the glass cabinets stymied Mars's ability to influence the quality and extent of the display. To overcome this major limitation in their route-to-market model, Mars offered to replace the glass coffins with their own, modern, open display units at no cost to the retailer.

Open display was a massive boon to the Countline brands which, with their brightly coloured packaging and bold brand names, were ideally suited to impulse purchasing. When combined with the impact of the 30-second television commercial, open display made further Countlines growth inevitable. Another problem for Cadbury was that any Mars display stand installed would have the Mars brands front and centre, with Cadbury brands marginalised at the sides. This began almost immediately to impact Cadbury's sales. A situation not helped by Fry's getting in on the act and producing their own version of the Mars display stand that gave much more prominence to the few Fry Countlines.

Cadbury had to respond to this seismic shift in the corner shop trade, through which went three-quarters of their sales. They hit back with

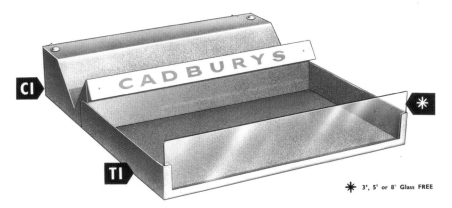

FREE

3', 5' or 8' Glass FREE

their own version of the open display concept, called 'The 3C Plan – Cadbury's Counter Conversion.' Sixty Cadbury Displaymen, hastily redeployed from window-dressing duties, were soon installing units in 500 shops a week around the country. Cadbury had been forced to move from a playing field heavily tilted in their favour to one where the competitors were ahead. By 1966, in shops called on by Cadbury Representatives, 43% would have a Mars unit displaying the products compared to 40% with a Cadbury one. This was a major reversal of the two firms' fortunes in what was still the primary retail channel for the sale of chocolate and had been historically completely dominated by Cadbury.

Struggling with the double whammy of the emergence of the Wholesaler and the arrival of open display would have been enough for Cadbury to cope with, but there was an even bigger shift underway in the retail trade that would adversely impact Cadbury: grocery chains.

The Rise of the Grocer

As U.K. consumers began to own cars and refrigerators *en masse*, the rise of the Grocery channel became inevitable, and would put pressure on the channel that was dominated by Cadbury, whose pre-war model had largely created the phenomenon of the specialist Confectioner/Tobacconist/Newsagent (CTN). This channel accounted for three-quarters of Cadbury's sales, and despite the incursions of Mars, Rowntree and Fry, it still represented a huge source of strength for Cadbury. But it was a retail channel that was past its peak.

What were Cadbury to do? Putting their weight behind the emerging Grocery channel would again possibly hasten their own demise. Cadbury would never gain such a dominant hold over Grocers as they exerted over the CTN's. Cadbury were snookered. They could not ignore the Grocer, but they were the worst-placed of

the main manufacturers to benefit from their rise. So Cadbury did business with the Grocers but gave them no special terms nor made any specialised packs, which of course did not earn them too much praise from the emerging retail giants.

In contrast, Rowntree had always been more friendly and responsive to Grocers, not least because they had been supplying Marks & Spencer with private-label products for years and had first-hand knowledge of the workings of that channel. Rowntree saw that the fortunes of Kit Kat could be greatly enhanced by becoming a part of the housewife's grocery shopping. As early as 1956, they produced a six-pack of the two-finger version specifically for Grocery stores.[1]

Cadbury's strategy was, wherever possible, to try and protect the beleaguered CTN trade. They were aided in this task by an initiative from the trade organisation for confectionery manufacturers, the British Cocoa, Chocolate and Confectionery Alliance who were keen, on behalf of all their members, to protect the existing Resale Price Maintenance regulations. These meant that a manufacturer could determine the retail selling price of their goods to the consumer, and legally refuse to supply any retailer who sold below the manufacturer's recommended selling price. This, of course, had been challenged by the Grocers, who had no intention of selling products at the same price as the smallest of corner shops. Their main advantage was their ability to sell cheaper, either through greater efficiencies or being able to strong-arm suppliers.

---

[1] Fitzgerald, *Rowntree and the Marketing Revolution*, p441

Cadbury, as the primary beneficiaries from the continued health of the CTN channel, contributed heavily to the industry initiative. However, the issue was lost and Resale Price Maintenance on confectionery was abolished. This was without doubt the least worst outcome for Cadbury in what had become an untenable situation: the prospect of delisting Tesco, Sainsbury and Fine Fare was too appalling to contemplate. But the CTN and Co-op trade appreciated that the industry, led largely by Cadbury, had gone to the wall for them, and that goodwill would be of benefit to Cadbury for years afterwards. The Grocers also understood why Cadbury had fought so hard, and bore no grudges beyond their continued frustration that Cadbury refused to do them any favours.

Cadbury's New Countline

While this had been going on, Cadbury had been making progress towards the goal of launching their own nougat-based Countline to challenge Mars Bar. The first attempt to do so, Bonus Bar, was launched in 1964, resembling a cross between a Mars Bar and a Milky Way. It was not a success, selling at around half the level of Flake. The inclusion of raisins, to differentiate it from Mars Bar, meant that it would never have the broad appeal of a Mars Bar.

Cadbury decided that a more direct, head-on assault was required, hoping that the power of the Cadbury name and the ability of the Cadbury sales force to flood the trade with product would be their trump cards, assuming the Mars Bar product offer could be matched. The outcome, Aztec, was launched in 1967 and was without doubt Cadbury's blockbuster event of the post-war period up to that point. Huge displays appeared virtually overnight in 100,000 shops, many flanked by a life-size cardboard Aztec warrior, supported by a major television advertising campaign filmed on the very steps of the Aztec temples of Teotihuacan.

Weighing in at a hefty 62.1 grams (nearly 2¼ ounces) and priced at 7d, Aztec was matching Mars on value for money, and the launch severely shook the Mars organisation. Their response was to flood the market with money off coupons for Mars Bars, restoring its value advantage. While this dented

a feast of a bar!

and it was judged that product acceptability had to be the key criterion. After all, Cadbury also had research that said people weren't really interested in who made any particular Countline.

But Aztec, although it got off to a spectacular start, was not the answer to Cadbury cracking the Countline market. Its advertising promised something new and exciting, but the product was too similar to a Mars Bar to live up to the claim. Cadbury would have to go back to the drawing board in their now unshakeable quest to broaden their portfolio into the booming Countline sector.

the progress made by Aztec, the ultimate downfall for the initiative lay in a conundrum Cadbury had wrestled with throughout the brand's development.

The key challenge had been to develop a product that was highly acceptable to Mars Bar consumers but that might also be optimally different enough to avoid consumer resentment at Cadbury stooping to produce a 'me-too'. Their research prior to the launch kept coming back to this issue: the closer the recipe was to Mars Bar, the higher it scored in blind taste tests, but the more negativity it generated when shown in branded form. Countless recipes were rejected as either being not good enough or not different enough. In the end, a decision had to be made,

Cadbury-Fry

Since Cadbury were now irrevocably in the Countline business, the anachronism of the continued sales and marketing independence of Cadbury and Fry could not be put off any longer. Marketers at Bournville had ignored Countlines for decades because "Fry do Countlines" and were now paying the price. The market for Countlines had grown by 30% during the 1960s, but Cadbury had been unable to move their share of it upwards. Any Fry claims to be the BC&C Countline experts were undermined by the fact that over the same period, their share of Countlines was in the process of declining from 24% to 17%.

There were also other issues. Cadbury and Fry Representatives fighting each other for prime display locations was wasteful and could no longer be justified given the rise of Mars in the CTN channel. Equally, Grocery chains couldn't understand why they had to see two Representatives when the products came on the same delivery van. The continued division between the two was now unjustifiable. The only possible solution was a full merger, which finally happened in 1967.

The 1960's were a tough decade for Cadbury in the U.K. Although overall sterling sales were just about maintained, inflation was eating into their real value such that Cadbury's U.K. confectionery sales of £40 million in 1962 were to decline in real terms by nearly 20% over the next eight years, and Dairy Milk, which accounted for 25% of total Cadbury profits, declined by over 30%. In a flat market for milk chocolate bars, Galaxy became established with a 10% share which came entirely at the expense of Dairy Milk, primarily because of the disaster that befell the 6d bar. However, it was not all bad news for the Cadbury Board. While their U.K. business had encountered several hefty bumps in the road, overseas things were progressing much more smoothly.

Chapter 11

OVERSEAS
PROGRESS

Cadbury's Chocolates

"It's the feeling, it's the caring; it's the giving, sweet feeling of joy..."

MILK CHOCOLATE
DOUBLE DECKER
5 star

Sometimes, Cadbury's can say it better than words

Bring home these moments

OBM/59

1981 Release

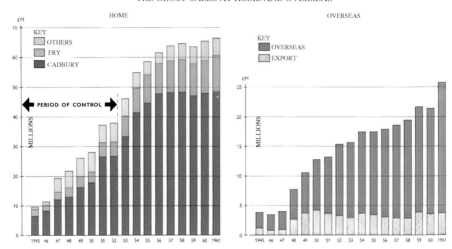

THE GROUP SALES AT HOME AND OVERSEAS

As early as 1960, it had become clear to Cadbury that the U.K. market was not going to continue to be the main driver of growth for the company. In fact, for the previous three years, all of the growth in the British Cocoa and Chocolate Company had been coming from the overseas divisions. The U.K., it was reasoned, already had the highest level of chocolate consumption in the world and not only was this unlikely to rise any further, it could well begin to decline. Also, in the U.K. market, competition was fiercest. Therefore, further progress in the U.K. would only come from an increasingly expensive battle for market share that would inevitably drive down profits.

That being the case, the company would have to rely on its overseas operations to keep driving the parent company forwards while it started to look for new sources of growth beyond its traditional product and geographic boundaries. The overseas businesses had always been managed at the local level, with Bournville's only say coming in the approval of board directors and major items of capital expenditure. This independence was to prove beneficial at a time when Cadbury in the U.K. was experiencing its own difficulties with circumstances that weren't really impacting the company overseas.

Ireland

The closest market to the U.K., Ireland, began to diverge from the U.K. quite significantly in the late 1960's in how it was approaching the chocolate category. Fry-Cadbury Ireland had the organisational advantage of always having been a merged business, so there was no blind spot as far as Countlines were concerned. While Cadbury and Fry in the U.K. competed for retail space, the two were embraced in one cohesive team in Ireland.

Also, as a much smaller business unit, Fry-Cadbury Ireland didn't suffer from the functional silos that had inevitably arisen at the much larger Bournville operation. There was no division between Sales and Marketing, which in Ireland were managed as one entity. This meant that there were no barriers to market strategy driving sales execution, market conditions driving pricing, and consumer insight driving the product range and the eating experience. This would result in some crucial differences that would make a radical difference to the Cadbury performance in Ireland compared to the U.K.

The Irish business, through their close connections with Fry's, saw immediately the value of the open display model being pioneered by the two organisations selling the most Countlines in the U.K., Mars and Fry. Fry-Cadbury managers in Ireland saw that this was no tactical shift in how to display products, but represented a fundamental strategic shift in how to drive forwards the category, and one's own share of it. The stock-loading model still had a role to play, but success would ultimately come to the organisation who could better sell the concept of displaying for impulse purchasing.

This is because it was rooted in the category truth that an important part of the pleasure associated with confectionery is the act of purchase. More often than not, the buyer starts with a vague sense that they want some chocolate, but leaves it to the display to help make up their mind on the particular product, savouring the various alternatives in their imagination. Equally, the display has a crucial role to play in stimulating the desire for chocolate in the first place. Demand for chocolate is elastic, in that impulse consumption could be triggered by an open and attractively laid out display. By controlling the display, and constantly improving it, a manufacturer's sales could be relied on to grow.

As the Irish economy improved in the early 1960's, the approach of the Irish business was not to build sales through price cuts, but to introduce much more variety into their Moulded, Filled Block and Countline ranges. This was another crucial difference to the approach taken in the U.K., where variety was seen more from the perspective of its negative impact on production efficiencies. Large runs of a limited range of best-sellers had always been the Bournville way, and indeed was the basis of Mars' success. But

Cadbury in Ireland, with their much smaller manufacturing set-up, did not have many economies of scale, so instead chose to implement the concept of variety through their much greater manufacturing flexibility.

Again, this played to a crucial category truth: that variety *per se*, was a consumer benefit in itself. Although consumers had differing motives for purchase, all responded positively to the display of variety and thought in terms of variety when buying confectionery. So a manufacturer who provided variety was meeting a key consumer need. New products are not necessarily bought because of any dissatisfaction with existing products, but because variety increases the opportunity to choose and the pleasure in doing so. In particular, Countlines were seen by the consumer as the growing and developing area of confectionery, and their brightly-coloured wrappers and jolly names made them a focus of the choosing experience.

Consequently, with a range of taste and textural experiences, such as Honey Crisp and Rum & Butter to compliment the core Dairy Milk, Fruit & Nut and Wholenut lines, flanked by a mixed range of Cadbury and Fry Countlines, Fry-Cadbury Ireland could claim to meet all of the consumers' needs for variety. While Mars were still restricted in their presence in Ireland through tariffs, Cadbury still had to work hard to keep competitors such as Rowntree and a local player, Urney Chocolates, at bay. With the widest range of products and a dominant lead in the development and placing of open displays (Rowntree lagging far behind on this front), Cadbury in Ireland were hugely advantaged.

As a result, the performance of Irish business during the years 1962–1968 could not have been more different to the U.K. While Cadbury and Fry in the U.K. had stagnant sales, those of the Irish business doubled. While the U.K. lost market share, the Irish business increased theirs from 41% to 52%. More crucially, by adding a breadth of variety to their product range that Bournville had largely avoided, coupled with a sales organisation whose priority was the prominent display of that range, Fry-Cadbury Ireland were able to keep the Moulded sector the predominant one in their market. It was not that Countlines *per se* were more relevant than Moulded, as Cadbury in the U.K. had come to believe, it was that both could meet consumers needs for variety. Moulded was still seen as the archetypal chocolate product, with Countlines as interesting variations.

The Irish business was also much more successful with their top-selling Dairy Milk bar, which the Irish company referred to as the '8 square bar', there being eight individual chunks. This had also been the format of the U.K.'s 6d bar prior to the ill-fated shift to the one shilling bar. Cadbury's 1959 Countline research findings in the U.K. had highlighted the strengths of the 8-square format, in that most consumers considered the number of segments, their size and thickness,

the 2 × 4 arrangement and the grooves between the segments to be ideal.

But as the Irish company was hit by the same rising costs of cocoa, they had initially followed the U.K. route of reducing the weight of Dairy Milk to maintain their own 6d price point and also their profit margins. But in 1968, having witnessed the train crash that had happened to the U.K. in their attempt to trade up the consumer from the 6d Dairy Milk to the Shilling size, they initiated a major change in direction which would further distance both their strategy and their sales results from those of the U.K.

In outlining their marketing plans for the years 1968–1971, Fry-Cadbury Ireland made clear what they thought was the way ahead,

The move from 6d to 7d is critical as regards our blocks and bars, which account for more than half our business. But far from being discouraged by the move to 7d, we look on it as a real opportunity to increase our profits and our sales. If we can persuade the public to maintain their unit purchases, we will achieve a value increase of as much as 17% on an important section of our business.

The plan to ease the consumer up in price point was both comprehensive and bold,

First, we are increasing all our lines from 6d to 7d and, because of our competitive strength…created a 7d world for chocolate lines and have left the 6d world behind. Secondly, for a limited period, we are increasing the weights of our Moulded range by amounts ranging from 8% to 20%, depending on the price increase, and we are using an "Extra Weight" campaign behind our vitally important Milk range to publicise this. By this means, we hope to ease the transition to the new prices, not only for Dairy Milk, but for our whole range.

The temporary weight changes achieved the objective of easing through the price increases, and over the next five years total Fry-Cadbury sales in Ireland doubled, as did profits.

The emerging supermarkets were encouraged to focus on what had been the 1/- bar which the consumer saw as a sharing bar, and hence the supermarkets saw as being ideal for their core shopper of mothers buying the family provisions. This size was offered with a broad variety of products, with innovative display solutions rather than discounting to drive consumer off-take. In both corner shops and grocery stores, variety and display would prove an effective barrier to entry for Fry-Cadbury Ireland's competitors. By 1974, the Irish business would have fifteen additional products in the Countline price bracket on their display, making competitor incursions even less likely.

New Zealand

Cadbury-Fry-Hudson in New Zealand was also not immune to the Countline phenomenon and cocoa price inflation. However, unlike the U.K. and Ireland, the biggest selling Dairy Milk line there was the large bar, retailing at 2/- or 2/6d. Cadbury-Fry-Hudson's Countline offer was limited to Fry's Chocolate Cream and a couple of popular unwrapped penny lines, Buzz Bar and Chocolate Fish. However, the Countline threat was seen very quickly and taken seriously as the large Cadbury bars were judged by the local management to be especially vulnerable to a switch to more impulse purchasing and on-the-go consumption.

Cadbury in New Zealand had also seen their Moulded sales suffer during the mid 1950's, this time under attack from Cadbury's long-forgotten adversary, Nestlé. Judging that a strong Cadbury Moulded range was the priority, Cadbury-Fry-Hudson adopted a similar strategy to Ireland, increasing the weight of their bars by 20%, supported by heavyweight advertising trumpeting, "*The thicker the block, the better the choc*". The lower profit margin was made up by a long overdue price increase on their range of cocoa products. There would be no restrictive 10% profit margin target for every single line as was the case at Bournville.

THE **THICKER** THE BLOCK....

THE **BETTER** THE CHOC!

CADBURY'S DAIRY MILK CHOCOLATE 2'6

Chocolate Blocks
are always
your best buy
in chocolate . . .

. . . more so today when Cadbury's
Chocolate Blocks are heavier and chunkier . . .
the best chocolate value in years!

CADBURY'S
CHOCOLATE BLOCKS

BETTER because they're **THICKER**

5154.12

The arrival of Mars Bars into New Zealand in the late 1950's, albeit in restricted quantities, galvanised the next leg of the strategy which was to quickly build a strong Countline range. Buzz Bar was upgraded, its marshmallow base given a strawberry flavour and pink colouring, and the toffee layer thickened, the whole bar being wrapped and re-christened 'Pinky'. The Crunchie recipe and process were borrowed from Fry in the U.K., the brand being launched under the Cadbury name. Picnic and Flake soon followed, the end result being that

Cadbury-Fry-Hudson gained leadership of the local Countline market in good time to be the main beneficiary of the introduction of television advertising into New Zealand in 1962.

Not content to rest on their laurels, and seeing the imminent relaxing of import controls, the New Zealand team learnt from the U.K. Aztec experience that once Mars Bar became established, it would prove impossible to dislodge, so it had to be pre-empted before it got a firm hold. Christened Moro, it soon became the leading Countline brand in New Zealand, and to this day has kept Mars Bar in the shadows. Cadbury-Fry-Hudson's dominant share of the market and Ireland-like grip of the displays were critical factors in Moro's success in addition to the product quality. By 1970, their share of the chocolate market had risen to a staggering 80%.

Australia

Cadbury-Fry-Pascall in Australia tackled the Countline threat in a different way. By the mid 1960's, their long-time foe, MacRobertsons had followed a strategy similar to that of Rowntree in the U.K. and largely foregone trying to tackle Cadbury head on with Moulded bars. As in New Zealand, Cadbury's biggest-selling size was the 4oz bar, and as in Ireland, Cadbury had cemented Moulded's dominance in the market and their own share of it by producing a wide range of variants, including such local favourites as Energy Bar, Scorched Almond, Grilled Almond, Cherry Rough, Candy Nut and Milk Punch.

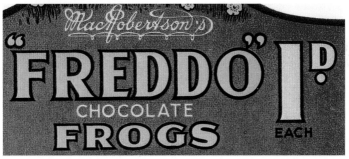

Thoroughly outgunned, MacRobertson's had got behind a variety of products such as Cherry Ripe (a coconut-based Countline), Freddo (a children's bar), Old Gold (a dark chocolate), together with snapping up the licence to import and in some cases manufacture under license the Mars brands. However, an ill-timed investment in building a new factory had plunged the business into a loss, and with the sons of Macpherson Robertson beginning to pine for an easier life, they sold out to Cadbury's in 1967.

This was a masterstroke by Cadbury-Fry-Pascall. Not only had C-F-P inherited MacRobertson's strong range of unique Countline brands, which complemented rather than directly competed with the Cadbury Moulded offer, C-F-P also were able to constrict Mars's route into the Australian market as they now owned the MacRobertson factory that was making Mars Bars and Maltesers under licence. Mars quickly expropriated their top-secret Mars Bar technology and recipe, but consented for the Cadbury-run business to keep making Maltesers.

The newly-merged company was now a very substantial enterprise in its own right, with a market share approaching 40% and sales half those in the U.K.

From such a strengthened base, the combined C-F-P/MacRobertson's sales were to increase by over 20% in the three years following acquisition as the Cadbury organisation brought their route-to-market strengths to bear on the MacRobertson lines which had been in long-term decline.

South Africa

The South African confectionery market had evolved quite differently to the other overseas locations in which Cadbury had put down roots. Rowntree, who had pre-dated Cadbury's presence there, had not been slow to develop the Countline category, having launched many Countline brands in the 1950's. In addition to the fruits of their R&D surge in 1930s Britain, such as Kit Kat and Smarties, they had also developed more Countlines locally, including a direct copy of the Mars Bar, called Big One. This approach not only created a vibrant Countline category in South Africa, but also, as had Cadbury's Moro in New Zealand, effectively deterred Mars from entering the market.

However, the Moulded category had not been steamrollered by this surge as, in addition to the Cadbury presence, South Africa was one of the rare markets outside of Continental Europe where Nestlé had been able to establish their Moulded range. There was also another local player, Beacon, who in 1982 diversified from sugar confectionery

firstly into supplying supermarkets with private label chocolate, and then into their own chocolate brands. Beacon had to be taken seriously as a threat due to their strong position in sugar confectionery which, with such a large proportion of the population having little disposable income, was far larger than the market for chocolate. Hence Cadbury, although the market leader, faced many competitive threats both to their Moulded heartland and their market share.

But Cadbury had their own strengths. Locally-focused, entrepreneurial management responding to local market conditions, a flexible factory producing a wide range of products and a merged Cadbury-Fry-Pascall product range had all contributed to a strong market position. Even the problematic Canada had a well-established and profitable Moulded range, but, apart from Crunchie, lacked any strong Countlines, and thus was more of a niche player in that crowded market.

India

The stimulus in India for Cadbury to develop its own range of Countlines was not competitor incursions but red tape. The Indian Government had placed restrictions on cocoa imports which prompted some creative thinking about how the business could continue to develop. Locally-grown cocoa would not be placed under the same restrictions, the only problem being that there was no cocoa-growing industry in India. So a retired cocoa planter from Malaya was commissioned by Cadbury to survey potential areas in the south of the country that might be suitable for cocoa cultivation.

The company immediately set about recreating their Gold Coast strategy of establishing a model plantation, complete with seedling nursery, to encourage local farmers to take up cocoa cultivation. But a plant which took five years to generate its first fruit was a tough sell, so Cadbury needed a compelling

story. Cocoa tree seedlings could be planted in-between existing trees in coconut plantations. Thus cocoa would utilise land presently doing nothing productive, with the added advantage that the tall coconut trees would provide ideal conditions for the shade-loving cocoa trees.

In a major difference to the West African cocoa industry, farmers would bring the unopened cocoa pods to local centres where Cadbury would exercise greater control over quality by conducting all the fermentation and drying of the beans themselves. Cadbury would also pay well above the world price for cocoa as a further incentive. The farmers were increasingly convinced, and by 1978, after Cadbury had distributed free of charge 5 million seedlings, 13,000 acres were under cultivation with Cadbury buying the vast majority of the output. While this wasn't enough to meet Cadbury's needs, they were able to procure import licenses from other companies to augment imports of their essential ingredients.

Two further ideas to circumvent the cocoa import restrictions proved to be crucial in the future success of Cadbury in India. The insight was simple: that a tin of Bournvita used far less cocoa than did a tin of cocoa. As Government regulations prohibited the importing of machinery from Bournville, Cadbury's Indian engineers, led by the company's first Indian board director, Mr. B. Unwala, took Bournville designs and were able to improve on them, reducing the production cycle while improving the quality. Promotional efforts were focused behind Bournvita, stressing its invigorating and healthy properties for children. By 1963, Bournvita accounted for over 55% of the entire company's sales, a proportion that had risen to two-thirds by 1966. The same year, Cadbury showed their confidence in the future of their Indian business by opening their first integrated and modern Moulded and Bournvita manufacturing facility in Thane on the outskirts of Mumbai.

The same need to be economical with the uncertain supplies of cocoa also led to the development of a range of Countlines; a box of Countlines using far less chocolate than a box of moulded milk chocolate bars. Although the company imported several product ideas for Countlines from the Fry business in the U.K., the local management focused mainly on developing their own. They did this for two reasons; firstly, the Indian climate could have a dramatic impact on the keeping qualities of chocolate products, so by developing their own, they would be able to engineer in climate suitability. Secondly, the Indian market had not yet been significantly penetrated by the companies who were having the most success with Countlines, Mars and Rowntree, so, in a strategy similar to that being used in New Zealand, Cadbury could pre-empt them by producing Cadbury versions of the best-selling Countlines in the U.K.

In 1969, the first new Countline product to be launched was a Smarties-type product called Cadbury's Gems. The main climatic problem to be overcome was that imported Smarties tended to crack in the heat and humidity. Gems were engineered to avoid this problem, using a process that remains secret to this day. Gems succeeded both as a product in its own right and also as a block to Smarties becoming a strong brand in India. Soon to follow in 1969 was a Mars Bar-type product called 5 Star. Gradually expanding from this base of

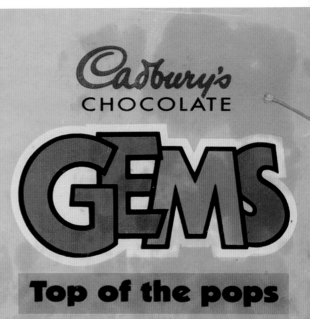

Top of the pops

proven product types, it would take only twelve years for Cadbury India's sales of chocolate products to overtake those of the highly successful Bournvita, which had continued to be successful, growing at double-digit rates.

Cadbury's Indian operation struggled for decades to manage a fast-growing business that was dependent on imported ingredients within a very restrictive set of government regulations, quotas and import licenses. Influencing the government in New Delhi was just as important as dealing with major wholesalers and distributors. Just when it seemed one barrier had been overcome, another would appear.

In 1971, Cadbury in the U.K. informed Cadbury India that they would no longer be importing Drinking Chocolate. This meant that the Indian business would lose priceless export credits which were being used to increase their imports of cocoa. However, seeing the impact this would have, the U.K. agreed for the first time that the Indian business could become an exporter of Cadbury-branded products into other markets previously serviced by the Bournville Export Department. The markets opened up to them were primarily ones that would benefit from India's expertise in the manufacture of temperature-tolerant products. Thus the Middle East, Equatorial Africa, Singapore, Bangladesh, Sri Lanka and Hong Kong soon began receiving shipments of Indian-produced cocoa, Drinking Chocolate, Bournvita and Countlines, with Five Star and Gems enjoying great success, particularly in the Middle East.

But it was only a part solution to the problem. Although the export sales provided scope for higher imports of raw materials, the increased volumes both at home and abroad meant that demand was growing just as fast as supply. The next bottleneck to hit the rapidly-growing enterprise was milk. To get around the issue, Cadbury purchased an 80 acre stud farm in Induri near Pune which they converted into their own dairy farm. The resourcefulness and flexibility of Cadbury India's managers was now being tested anew. By cross-breeding local cows with imported stock, Cadbury soon had a 300-head herd serviced by the company's prize bull, the Prince of Induri, and producing milk yields three times the national average. Cadbury were as keen to evangelise the benefits to local farmers as they had been with cocoa cultivation and were able to develop a viable local milk supply industry to meet their rapidly-growing needs.

Cadbury's overseas units had established extremely strong positions in all markets apart from Canada, where they remained a niche player in a very crowded field. Competitors had been pre-empted, sidelined or even

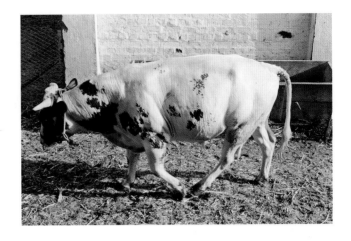

bought out. Such strong market positions, as had been the case in the U.K. between the Wars, gave the opportunity to cement the Cadbury brand reputation with consumers. Although the overseas businesses had a lot of local autonomy, the links with the Head office were very close. Most of the companies in the 60s and 70s were headed by life-long Cadbury men who had begun their careers at Bournville and been imbued with the brand ethos.

A part of that ethos was a firm belief in the importance of becoming very involved in the local economy and life which, when combined with strong local management and some very relevant local brands, meant that the Cadbury brand in each of these markets began to develop with a local flavour. While some of the Bournville products and strategies did not travel well, the Cadbury brand values did so extremely well. But, with very strong market shares in all countries bar Canada, it was becoming increasingly clear that the growth from the overseas companies could not continue on its current trajectory forever. Cadbury would soon have to enter a new phase in its development if it was not to gradually stagnate.

PART III – Summary

The difference in the post-war fortunes of Cadbury in the U.K., when compared to the almost runaway success in the overseas markets is remarkable. In the twenty-five years after the full relaxation of rationing controls, little went right for the Bournville management. 2oz Dairy Milk, the dominant product in the pre-war U.K. confectionery market, had virtually disappeared. The new Countlines failed to break through and sales were stagnant. While Cadbury were still the largest U.K. confectionery manufacturer, their market share was in decline and previously cowed competitors were confidently growing. Overseas however, the converse was the case. Dairy Milk was vibrant, new Countlines succeeded and both sales and market share were growing rapidly.

A key reason for this stark difference in fortunes is business model. Cadbury in the U.K. between the wars had been re-engineered from the ground up to provide the best quality and value, in particular with Moulded bars sold via CTN's, which was the predominant market of that period. It was able to do so precisely because the buildings, machines, methods of working, operating culture, innovation strategy, advertising methods and messages, distribution system and sales approach had been structured to work single-mindedly and cohesively towards that goal. But by definition, it was inflexible.

By the late 1960's the product range had become out of step with the times, the innovation capabilities found wanting and the sales force were struggling to come to grips with the seismic changes in U.K. retailing. The Cadbury Board were painfully aware of these issues, but the built-in rigidity of the Bournville model made change exceedingly difficult, especially as every change could easily, on the face of it, make Cadbury even weaker. Moving faster to the grocery trade would have accelerated the decline of Cadbury's CTN stronghold. Moving faster towards building a Countline range would have further weakened their Moulded stronghold. The moves were clearly necessary, but it was never the right time to do so aggressively.

These were daunting prospects, making the costs and risks seem almost insurmountable. But with the benefit of hindsight, the lesson is clear. When underlying changes in market conditions are both profound and inexorable, companies must grasp the nettle of change. The risk of staying put with a business model best suited to past conditions far outweighs any short term declines that such a change would inevitably entail.

The upshot for Cadbury was that, having led events up to this point in their history, they were now being led by them. The inflexibility of the business was a far cry from the days when Cocoa Essence itself would be sidelined by Bournville Cocoa; when building milk processing capacity to support the burgeoning sales of Dairy Milk; when Cadbury would be first to spring over tariff barriers and set up full-scale businesses overseas; when fortunes would be sunk into the Australian and Canadian businesses with no apparent hope in sight of ever seeing the money again. Their business model of the 1920s and 1930s, which had catapulted the business to undreamt-of heights, had then turned into something of a ball and chain.

The overseas businesses were never trapped in a business model prison because they never had the Bournville business model. They had survived, and then thrived, by being market-focused, adaptable and aggressive: traits that would stand them in good stead during periods of rapid change. Cadbury consumers in Australia, New Zealand, Ireland and South Africa stayed loyal because Cadbury was able to meet their evolving needs, whereas Cadbury in the U.K. was wedded physically, operationally and culturally to providing for their consumers' pre-war needs.

Yet the British consumer would have been hardly aware of the traumas impacting Cadbury in the U.K. In any normal business, such a depressing turnaround in business performance over such a prolonged period would cripple a company's consumer franchise. But the Cadbury brand reputation stayed remarkably intact through this period. Consumers weren't actively rejecting Cadbury; they were just increasingly shopping in stores in which the Cadbury presence was reduced, and buying into product categories where Cadbury had little participation. It is during this period that a large gap opened up between Cadbury's share of the consumers' minds and share of their wallets and purses.

While the Cadbury product range was becoming gradually less relevant to consumers, the brand name itself did not lose any of their respect, warmth and affection. This is partly because Cadbury were continuing to promote their name and reputation, even though the impact on the sales line was getting impossible to discern. Factory tours continued until the late 1960's. Schoolchildren, including this author, were still completing Cadbury educational projects on cocoa farming. Cadbury chocolate cookbooks were still selling hundreds of thousands of copies. The continued nurturing of the Cadbury brand would prove to be an excellent long-term investment. If all the problems could be fixed, their consumer franchise would still be there for them.

This is analogous to the problems endured by Marks & Spencer during the late 1990's. Their sales were slipping not because people didn't value them any more; it was because Marks & Spencer's product ranges were less relevant to their core audience. As this gap has been increasingly addressed, consumers have returned. This is because consumers will forgive a brand they love for messing things up occasionally. They will not forgive brands they never really bonded with in the first place, or brands that never seem to get things right again, such as the British motor industry. A strong, well-tended corporate brand provides a very effective breakwater against the shifting tides of short-term performance issues.

A strong corporate brand also provides growth opportunities in extending the reach of that brand into new categories and new geographies. This would be Cadbury's next major shift in strategy.

Part IV

THE PATH TO GLOBAL LEADERSHIP

Chapter 12

NEW CATEGORIES, NEW COUNTRIES: EXPANDING THE CADBURY BRAND FOOTPRINT

Confectionery Beyond Chocolate

Even as early as 1958, Cadbury had already begun thinking of diversifying beyond chocolate and cocoa as an option for further growth. In a speech that year, Paul Cadbury highlighted that the firm had already taken its first baby-step,

...and last year we introduced an important new line which had some non-chocolate confectionery units in it....my sales colleagues are thinking about other aspects of the market which are closely related to the section of the Food Trade in which we operate.

The important new product referred to was a new brand of Assortments called Lucky Numbers. This had been launched in response to Mackintosh's Quality Street. Mackintosh, a maker of fine caramels, had used well their merger with Norwich-based chocolate manufacturers, Caley's, in creating Quality Street, an appealing mixture of chocolate assortments and uncovered caramels. Lucky Numbers took the concept further with every single unit being a chewy sweet of some kind, some covered in chocolate and some not. The brand was a moderate success, selling at about half the rate of Cadbury's Roses, which had been launched prior to the Second World War.

Cadbury ventured further afield when they launched two new products, neither of which had any chocolate on at all. First out of the gate with a regional test in 1962 had been Trillions. A children's sugar confectionery line, the 5d bag of Trillions contained dozens of small fruit-flavoured chews, and was again supported well with both excellent distribution and displays together with television commercials. However, Trillions barely got off the ground, scuppered by the fact that Rowntree brought out Jelly Tots – a product preferred to Trillions – at much the same time, and also because Cadbury only gave the retail trade their usual chocolate profit margin as opposed to the higher one universally applied in the sugar confectionery category. The second product, Tops, which was launched in 1964, was a pack of boiled sweets that had soft centres, but fared just as badly.

Although both brands had the Cadbury name on, they had not been made at Bournville, but at the factory of the newest acquisition to the BC&C family made in 1964, their old partner in the Australian venture, Pascall Murray. The 31 products coming from the acquisition were given to the Fry sales force to sell, basically to keep them busy and put off the eventual Cadbury-Fry merger. However, the under-utilised Fry selling capabilities were put to good use with sales of Pascall Murray products increasing by 13% in the first year of ownership.

While the acquisition were not from the eclair Eclairs inferior with Dairy early searches for product synergies from the with Cadbury branded new sugar lines encouraging, more success would come rebranding in 1965 of a Pascall chocolate sweet. Renamed Cadbury's Chocolate – the company having replaced the chocolate used in the centre of the sweet Milk – it would be a valuable addition to the Cadbury portfolio in the U.K.; it soon becoming the mainstay of the Woolworth's Pick & Mix fixture. It would be even more valuable in overseas markets such as India and South Africa where, when sold as individual sweets, Chocolate Eclairs was able to take the taste of Cadbury chocolate to millions of emerging consumers who otherwise could not afford chocolate.

the sweets with the soft hearted centre

Cadbury's **tops** ASSORTED FRUITS

4d

Cadbury's **tops** MINT

Cadbury's **tops** LIQUORICE

Cadbury continued in their quest to diversify away from chocolate confectionery and cocoa beverages, realising that, while sugar confectionery acquisitions could add value, a much bigger opportunity lay in the emerging promised land of convenience foods sold through Grocers. The development of modern grocery stores in Britain signalled a sea-change in the British housewife's shopping habits and, as a consequence, the eating habits of the family, and Cadbury were not alone in seeing the vast potential that had been opened up. Rowntree were also looking to expand their grocery offering beyond their traditional jellies. Further afield, Associated British Foods were looking to expand from the heartland of sliced bread, and the likes of General Foods, Nestlé and Kraft were rapidly ramping up their British grocery operations.

Having Their Cake and Eating it

In 1961, Cadbury, not wishing to be left behind by their contemporaries, had set up a new company, Cadbury Foods Ltd., to focus on this opportunity. With the responsibility of developing new foods products for sale in the U.K. and overseas, its brief was to look well beyond the existing markets of chocolate and cocoa beverages. Cadbury's market research was on the button when it came to seeing that the future belonged to convenience foods. Most of the projects initiated by Cadbury Foods Ltd. would be targeted squarely at this need. The first manifestation of the new approach came in 1962 with pre-packaged cakes; Cadbury correctly divining that the modern housewife had both rapidly decreasing time and inclination to bake from scratch. Tests in the Nottingham and Derby areas proved successful and the company began gearing up for national production.

Aiming at the housewife purchase, Cadbury launched family-sized cakes such as a Butter Sponge, Rich Genoa, Iced Gateau and Chocolate Roll, all heavily branded with the Cadbury name to engender instant reassurance. As the business was expanded nationwide, sales doubled in 1964 and grew to a respectable £4.5 million by 1966: almost as big as their beverages plus biscuits businesses combined. But profits were harder to come by. An inefficient two-factory set-up, the need for a separate distribution system due to the relatively short shelf-life of cakes, together with intensive price competition from McVitie and Lyons meant the business was making a loss of £175,000.

The retail trade were also somewhat underwhelmed by Cadbury's product offering. A 1967 study quotes a general lack of enthusiasm in the retail trade for the Cadbury range of cakes. The missing ingredient was a unique and differentiated product, which Cadbury soon found in the Cadbury's Mini Roll. Being individually wrapped and sold a number to a box, they were fulfilling more of a snacking role rather than the formal family dessert need met by the large

cakes. In 1968, 85 million individual Cadbury Mini Rolls were sold, which accounted for over a quarter of Cadbury's total cake sales.

Grocery Products

During this period, the main market for Cadbury's cake lines had shifted rapidly from bakery stores to the grocery chains, which where already the main outlets for the company's cocoa beverages and range of biscuits. Cadbury were also seeing the apparent success of Rowntree's new grocery division which had been set up in 1962. At the same time as merging the Cadbury and Fry confectionery teams, the U.K. business was re-divided into separate Confectionery and Foods Divisions. Joining the range of cakes would be the company's biscuit and cocoa beverages lines, and the Foods Division would have its own separate factories, sales and marketing, market research, R&D and costing functions.

Cadbury's newly expanded Foods Division provided the ideal opportunity to address concerns of some new stakeholders in the company's future – shareholders – the company having been taken public in 1962 by then-Chairman, Paul Cadbury. The feedback from the new owners was that Cadbury Group Ltd (as BC&C Ltd was subsequently renamed) was too dependent on cocoa and chocolate confectionery, particularly as these were markets that

had stopped growing and in which Cadbury's performance was lacklustre. This was not news to Cadbury, who still viewed the U.K. confectionery market as being both maxed out and likely to become decreasingly profitable, and were already committed to a strategy of diversification.

But public ownership gave added impetus to the strategy that would entail a very different means of doing business from the past. A 1968 strategy paper began with the sentiment that,

The Foods Division inevitably bears the mark of its chocolate origin and our policy in a sense must be to live down the confectionery orientation and establish Cadbury in the eyes of the trade and the public as a purveyor of non-cocoa foods. In building the Foods Division we have two major tasks; one is to extend the range of lines from a relatively narrow base, and the other is to fashion a sales and distribution organisation appropriate to the selling of long shelf-life branded goods to the Grocery trade…Thus our trade margin and discount policies and our sales approach need altering substantially from the previously confectionery dominated pattern.

A completely new sales organisation was developed to focus almost entirely on the grocery trade, and much emphasis was placed into attracting the best and brightest Cadbury people into the Foods Division. It was seen as the future of the entire company. While being only one third the size of the Confectionery Division, it had the goal of achieving parity, and was given license to look at virtually any part of the packaged foods market where growth seemed likely.

Two Marvellous Smash Hits

They got off to a terrific start in that direction with a brand in a new product category that had been explored under the original Foods Group. It came from a technology developed in the U.S.; was very modern, innovative – the first of its kind in the U.K. – and at the heart of the consumer trend towards convenience. That was the instant milk brand, Marvel, which had been launched in test market in 1963, and had become available nationally during 1964. As Cadbury had been in the milk processing business since the turn of the 20th-century there was an excellent logistical fit, and the early sales were impressive, largely accounting for Cadbury's best year for nearly a decade, with total U.K. sales growing by 15%.

What is Marvel ?

Marvel is a new form of Non-fat Milk. Always ready to use, Marvel mixes instantly with cold water and has a wonderful fresh taste. Marvel is made from fresh milk by a special process which removes the water and fat and leaves all the rich body-building protein.

Marvel is compact and easy to handle, and is particularly convenient when making tea or coffee. It is so useful in an emergency, or when there are unexpected visitors.

Marvel is excellent for cooking wherever bottled milk would be used. It is so handy for the pudding you decide to make on the spur of the moment. For an extra milky flavour, just add more Marvel.

We hope you will try out these recipes for Marvel. No doubt you will discover many others for yourself.

The early success of Marvel had prompted the Foods Group to look further into the idea of 'instant'. The next big winner to emerge, which would be even more successful than Marvel, was the instant mashed potato brand, Smash. The launch was turbo-boosted by an iconic television

commercial that was voted by *Campaign* magazine as the best advertisement of the 20th-century and ITV's best ad ever.[1] The Home Economics Department focused on promoting these new lines, partly to overcome any lingering bad taste from consumers' war-time exposure to powdered milk and potato. But the new American technologies were light years ahead of those of twenty years earlier, and both brands quickly gained widespread consumer acceptance. Marvel gained a further fillip in 1965 when it was re-positioned as a low-fat aid to dieting.

[1] http://www.ipa.co.uk/news/news_archive/displayitem.cfm?itemid=1752; Accessed May 4th, 2007-05-04

Schhh. You Know who

Everyone knew the difficulties in launching successful new confectionery products, so to get two winners in a row reinforced with Cadbury that its strategy for its Foods Division was correct, and development work was started in the area of instant tea and in a non-milk creamer for coffee. However, as a stand-alone organisation, Cadbury Foods did not have the scale to give it critical mass with the large Grocery chains, and the bulk of its product range was still struggling for growth. The organisation had a major shake up when the Cadbury Group merged with Schweppes in 1969.

The Chairman of Schweppes, Lord Watkinson, in 1968 had approached the new Cadbury Chairman, Adrian Cadbury, who was already thinking of merger as a forward strategy for Cadbury Group Ltd. Adrian later reflected on how he had come to this conclusion,

The threats were clear enough, a static home market for confectionery, lower cost competitors in the confectionery trade like Mars, the abolition of Resale Price Maintenance and the growing power of the supermarkets, discriminatory taxation and increasing competition from large, international companies. Equally, we had great opportunity, which was that of broadening the market for Cadbury brands geographically... That required the concentration of effort behind major brands, the ability to give better value to the consumer and more in the way of financial resources than the Firm then possessed.... The combined company would have the resources to enter international markets, it would have three substantial product divisions – confectionery, drinks and foods (both businesses having diversified into foods) and the merging companies were complimentary geographically[2]

---

[2] Crosfield, p686

The combined turnover of the new merged entity, Cadbury Schweppes Ltd., was close to £250 million, which was big enough to qualify as a heavyweight, although still one third the size of Nestlé and one-fifth that of Unilever. Within the £250 million annual turnover, Cadbury sales were 50% higher than those of Schweppes, but years of cost increases meant that Cadbury was less profitable than its new partner.

In pursuing a strategy of diversification, Schweppes had gone the acquisition route and purchased a range of food businesses over the previous decade, including Chivers Jellies and Ty-Phoo Tea. In addition to those well-known brands, there were, however, a plethora of commodity-type products such as Hartley's tinned peas. Although the newly-combined Foods Division

was something of a rag-tag army, it was at least large enough to show up on the radar of every major Grocery chain with an annual turnover of £45 million – double the pre-merger total of the Cadbury Foods Division.

By the time of the Schweppes merger, a large proportion of Cadbury's total R&D investment had been going behind the Foods Division, but the early successes of Marvel and Smash would prove hard to replicate, and profits would be even more elusive. A deluge of new products were launched: Swiss Dessert, Appletree, Fine Brew instant tea, Angel Trumpets, Chillo, Snacksoup, Scanda Relish, Cheers, Stroodles and Soya Choice all came and went, sucking up a massive £5 million in test market advertising alone.

Takes the Biscuit

While all this innovation was going on, Cadbury's range of biscuits, which had been such a growth engine for the business post-war, had stalled. The boom in selections of chocolate biscuits served on a paper-doilied plate had begun a long-term and inexorable decline. The big shift in the market was the rise of what were called in the industry, Chocolate Biscuit Countlines (CBCL's). Individually wrapped and sold in large multipacks, brands like Club, Bandit, and Rowntree's Blue Riband had been joined by the two-finger multipacks of Kit Kat and a new product from Mars, Twix. This was the dynamic growth part of the biscuit market, being much more suitable for lunch-boxes and between-meal snacks, and was happening primarily in the grocery chains.

Prior to the confectionery and foods structure being established, the company had developed three brands which could potentially have played in the CBCL sector. The first had been the launch in 1956 of Cadbury's Snack, which was basically the repackaging into Countline format of four or six individual chocolate-covered biscuits from the paper doily range. While not being ideal for the snacking occasion – they were difficult to eat one-handed - Cadbury's lack of interest in the Grocery sector at the time ensured that Snack would remain a relatively small volume brand selling through corner shops, the product being seen as an expensive way to buy a handful of biscuits.

Four years later in 1960, the Cadbury Biscuits marketing team had developed a caramel and biscuit brand called Skippy, but the line did not break into the CBCL market, being primarily displayed with the rest of the Cadbury range in its corner shop stronghold.

The third effort got close to succeeding. Bar 6 was launched in 1964 as a direct competitor to Kit Kat. Despite the launch having to be delayed for six months because of the production line being sabotaged in yet another industrial dispute at Moreton, the Confectionery Division Representatives did their usual excellent job in getting distribution and display in every corner shop in the land. In a rare display of divisional harmony after the reorganisation in 1967, the Foods Division Account Managers were getting equally good availability and visibility for the multipack in Grocery chains.

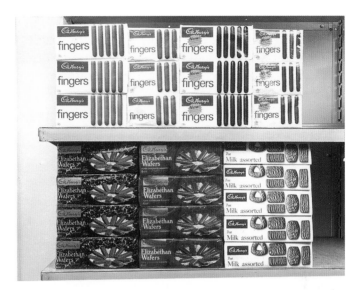

Cadbury's pre-launch research had indicated that Bar 6 could

be a winner; it was judged as every bit as good as Kit Kat, ideal for eating with a mid-morning tea/coffee or when watching television, and liked for its creamier and milkier tasting chocolate. Backed up by heavyweight advertising, at one stage Bar 6 was nearly matching Kit Kat's sales. But after such a promising start, Bar 6's fate would again be hampered by Cadbury's divisional structure. In the company's accounting terms, Bar 6 was considered a biscuit being made by the Foods Division and then transferred over to the Confectionery Division. The rules in place on such transactions meant that the Confectionery Division saw little of the profit that was coming from Bar 6 from 1967 onwards. As they had their own profit targets to meet, their attention soon turned to other new lines made in their own Bournville and Somerdale factories. Equally, the new Foods Division had little interest in promoting what was clearly a Cadbury chocolate line.

Bar 6's fate was sealed by a product quality problem. As the name suggests, Bar 6 had six individual segments, but Cadbury had not followed Rowntree's approach with Kit Kat of inserting a separate wafer into each segment; Bar 6 had one large wafer which straddled all six segments. Such a large wafer would sometimes warp, meaning that to ensure it remained covered in chocolate, it needed a deeper mould; this would then entail a greater usage of chocolate. As cocoa prices began to soar, cost pressures shaved away at the amount of chocolate which could be afforded, so Bar 6 would increasingly have an almost transparent covering of chocolate on the back, or, occasionally, a partly uncovered soft wafer.

In the U.K., neither the Cadbury Foods Division nor the Confectionery Division had effectively grasped the CBCL opportunity. The Confectionery Division was of the view that anything to do with biscuits or Grocery was in the Foods Division's remit, and CBCL's were both. The Foods Division had no interest in a chocolate sector; their brief was to develop a British version of General Foods or Kraft. So the structure of the business was to give it a blind spot for what would be one of the fastest-growing chocolate categories of the 1970's, just as the division a generation earlier between Cadbury and Fry had meant that the Countline opportunity would not be grasped at the most opportune time. In Ireland, where the much smaller scale meant that confectionery and foods remained part of the one cohesive entity, the company was to have much greater success in tackling the CBCL opportunity.
(See Chapter 14)

For an apparently conservative organisation, the entry into new food categories had been an extremely bold and imaginative move. Despite the new product failures, a questionable track record on generating profits and the missed opportunity of CBCL's, the formation of the Cadbury Foods Division contributed much to the reshaping of Cadbury in the U.K. It had a profound impact on Cadbury's overall relationship with the fast-growing Grocery trade, and also shifted consumer perceptions away from Cadbury being solely a name to be associated with chocolate. But for every positive association coming from such hugely successful brands as a Smash, Marvel or Coffee Compliment, there was a less complimentary one from a Soya Choice, Swiss Dessert or a Stroodle.

Building a foods business from scratch proved to be too big a challenge for Cadbury to conquer. While acquisitions might have proved a more successful route in taking on the established players, these had been ruled out by the disappointing share price for Cadbury in the early 1960s. The imposition of Purchase Tax on U.K. confectionery soon after Cadbury went public had depressed the share price, which would not have supported a bid for a good sized food company, so the company really had no choice if it was to pursue a strategy of diversification.

Foods Overseas

The Cadbury businesses that had local stock market listings after the Schweppes merger had additional incentive to diversify within their own markets. South Africa and Australia both acquired significant foods businesses which proved to be largely successful. But other diversifications developed from scratch in the overseas businesses failed to transform the local business's dependence on chocolate. Cadbury's Indian operation was hamstrung by Government regulations that limited both their cocoa imports and their production capacities, which made diversification even more attractive. But a venture into launching an apple juice concentrate brand was relatively short-lived.

The only real diversification success in India was one that again was tied to exporting to their U.K. parent at Bournville. Cadbury India successfully developed a process to manufacture a substitute for cocoa butter from the fruit of the Sal tree, which was the most important source of hardwood in the country. The only customer for this product was Cadbury in the U.K., who took to substituting a proportion of their cocoa butter when the price rose above certain levels. Although it was close in nature to cocoa butter, it was not identical and would come to an end several years later when Cadbury abandoned its substitution policy.

Go West

Experience was demonstrating that Cadbury was first and foremost a chocolate company, and the only viable way to reduce their dependence on the U.K. chocolate market was to ramp up their overseas operations, as had become apparent towards the time of the Schweppes merger. Although by the late 1960's the company had added to its original roster of overseas businesses with ventures in Nigeria, Kenya, and a joint venture in Rhodesia, to make a real shift in the global make-up of the Cadbury chocolate business, the seductive siren call of the gargantuan U.S. confectionery market could no longer be ignored.

Back in 1962, when the company had not needed to worry about such things as their global make-up of sales, the U.S. market had sat quite comfortably on Cadbury's 'too difficult' pile, as noted by the anonymous author of Cadbury's publication 'Industrial Challenge', *'To break into this market on a more substantial scale would be a speculative and expensive operation'*. However, by 1968, it was clear to the new Cadbury Group chairman, Adrian Cadbury that the nettle had to be grasped.

By that time, the U.S. operation had been pared down to the point that it amounted to two men and an office boy in New York. To beef things up, talented young Cadbury U.K. salesmen were seconded out to the

U.S. to do exactly what had failed to be done twenty years earlier: working with the wholesalers, jobbers and brokers to try once again and increase attention and effort behind the Cadbury range. Focusing on selected markets with a 5oz Moulded product range priced at 35c, the range was initially targeted at the specialist import sector.

It was a start. Presenting Cadbury as being the best of British chocolates, and with the range soon augmented by new lines such as Bar 6 and Snack, progress was being made, mainly in the large chains of food and drug stores serviced by the large food brokers who were already well-known to Cadbury's partner, Schweppes. But progress through the wholesalers and jobbers was still problematic. With huge price lists, these channels operated as order takers as opposed to sellers. And to take orders, there needed to be demand for Cadbury products from the small retailers, which did not yet exist.

Since Cadbury were also importing their products into the U.S., margins were tight, and restricted the amount that could be found for advertising. Producing locally would save trans-Atlantic transportation costs, which potentially could be used for building consumer demand. In 1974 Cadbury invested $10million building a factory in Hazleton, Pennsylvania. The timing seemed favourable. Hershey was no

longer the invulnerable behemoth it had once been. They were now number two in the market behind Mars, and the Hershey bar had finally gone up in price due to surging world prices for cocoa from 5c – a price point it had held with an ever-shrinking bar for sixty years – to 15c within the space of four years. If ever they could be taken head on, it was now.

But the core problem remained that Cadbury was still a niche player in a huge and very complex market. Having a local factory did nothing to build Cadbury's business in the all-important Mom and Pop stores, and their advertising spend was still puny by comparison with the market leaders – Hershey finally having embraced the concept. Hazleton was both expensive and inflexible, and really needed to be run round the clock to offer any advantage to the U.S. business. More volume was needed to improve efficiency and lower costs, and also the clout of some must-stock lines, which would enable greater access to the vast multitude of small stores.

Consequently, in 1978, Cadbury paid $58 million for the Peter Paul Candy Company, which had a 10% share of the market, built around three key sellers: Mounds, Almond Joy and York Peppermint Patties. These were brands with long and successful track records. Mounds, a dark chocolate covered coconut bar had

Peter Paul's different bites for different likes.

Nobody's quite the same.
Our Halloween Witch likes Mounds,
but the Ghost prefers No Jelly.
As for the Devil...only Almond Joy will do.
That's why Peter Paul makes
different bites for different likes.
Bite size candy bars in great big bags.
Sweeten up your Halloween season with
Mounds, Almond Joy, Caravelle, Power House
or No Jelly Bite Size candy bars.
The little treats that please even the gobbliest goblins.

been introduced in 1924, and had been copied by Mars in the U.K with Bounty. Cadbury merged their U.S. business with Peter Paul, creating Peter Paul Cadbury Inc., hoping that the much enhanced route to market capabilities brought by the much larger Peter Paul sales organisation would facilitate the rapid expansion of the Cadbury brands. Five of the Peter Paul old factories were closed with the volume being transferred mostly to the new Hazleton plant. To break into the massive sector of small stores, Cadbury introduced a range of 2oz 'Thick' bars, but with limited initial success.

Everything rode on a major relaunch of the Thick bars in 1984. Product specifications were upgraded: the Almond bar moved from chopped to whole almonds; Fruit & Nut was given 44% more almonds and 14% more raisins, and the advertising budget was tripled. A test market in Salt Lake City showed a sales increase of over 100%. But the advertising budget was still relatively small by U.S. standards. To make up the shortfall, an ambitious plan was put in place to push massive volumes into the wholesalers with generous discounts, hoping that the wholesalers would themselves use those discounts to push product out onto the street. The plan was a flop. Wholesalers sat on their discounts and their stock. As a consequence, orders completely dried up forcing

Cadbury to firstly halt production and then eventually take back much of the stock in a re-run of the 1952 scenario.

But this was a disaster on a much larger scale; the outcome was a financial meltdown. Profits from the U.S. business plummeted $42.5 million in 1985, plunging the business into loss. So great had been the catastrophe that it wiped out 25% of the entire profits of the Cadbury Schweppes worldwide organisation. New management were put in and achieved stability, but the U.S. business was barely profitable. To extricate itself, in 1988 Cadbury accepted a bid for $300 million from Hershey for the entire enterprise, together with its $30 million of debt and the rights to market Cadbury brands in the U.S.

From Cadbury's point of view, they got a good price for the business and a guaranteed ongoing income stream based on royalty payments on the Cadbury products, which by now included the successful Cadbury Creme Eggs. Equally, the deal for Hershey to market the Cadbury brands under license seemed to make sense. Hershey had already used this tactic before, persuading Rowntree in 1969 to let them have the U.S. rights to Kit Kat and Rolo. Under these arrangements, Kit Kat had become the first foreign bar in living memory to make a real impact on the

U.S. market. Maybe the same would happen with Cadbury. However, Kit Kat had filled a hole in the Hershey range while Dairy Milk and its associated lines competed head on. Although Hershey was happy to seek to grow the Cadbury brand, it would only be as a tightly controlled, niche player once again, primarily through the unique Creme Eggs.

Cadbury was not the first and would not be the last U.K. company to have to circle the wagons in the U.S. Marks & Spencer famously came unstuck in the retail arena, and very few food brands of British origin ever made much of an impression. The sale to Hershey was lauded for the financial gain, but mourned for what it meant for Cadbury's American dream. The Financial Times Lex column on March 23rd, 1988 summarised neatly,

It is impossible to view the Cadbury/Hershey arrangements with other than mixed feelings. The deal looks wonderful financially for Cadbury…But it also means an abandonment of the grand ambitions in the U.S. confectionery market. Cadbury is locking itself out as Rowntree did a decade or more ago, leaving Mars and Hershey

triumphant with market shares of over 40% apiece.

In attempting to extend their reach both into foods and into the U.S. confectionery market, Cadbury could not be accused of a lack of ambition. They had been bold responses to an over-reliance on a U.K. confectionery market in which Cadbury had clearly stalled. Either one would have been a huge undertaking for a company of Cadbury's size, with no guarantees of success at the end. Both were taking on companies many times their size in relatively unfamiliar environments. But both had failed in their ultimate objectives. The U.S. business failed absolutely and required major surgery to stem the red ink. The Foods Division did not reduce the overall dependence of the company profits on the U.K. confectionery market. While the Foods Division was still a decent-sized business, it was ultimately weighed down by too many undifferentiated products inherited from Schweppes and a spotty track record on innovation beyond Marvel and Smash.

The growth of the Cadbury part of Cadbury Schweppes would depend on re-energising their U.K. confectionery business unit, which was by far the largest individual operating unit within the merged entity. While their analysis was correct in assuming the

U.K. market would grow no further – chocolate consumption per head is not much different today than it was then – it was flawed in that there were still tremendous opportunities that would come from shifting consumer and retail trends within the chocolate market; opportunities that were being almost entirely snaffled up by Cadbury's competitors. It was a static market in size, but by no means moribund in dynamics. But if Cadbury was to benefit, there would have to be some major changes at Bournville.

Chapter 13

THE U.K.
TURNAROUND

Now chocolate
doesn't drop all over the place

NEW Cadbury's Curlywurly
CARAMEL COVERED
IN MILK CHOCOLATE

Because now there's a new Curly Wurly.
It's just as chewy as the old one, but it's
softer. So now they can bite straight through it.
So now the chocolate doesn't drop all
over the place. So it's better for them.
And it's better for you.

New Curly Wurly from
Cadbury

The turning around of Cadbury's U.K. Confectionery Division would not be through one magic bullet, but driven by four key events over nearly twenty years: the realignment from being supply-led to consumer-led; the focus on profit that came from the Schweppes merger; the reprioritisation of the Moulded category and the Dairy Milk brand; and the addressing of the Bournville cost base. Together, these would reverse the Cadbury decline and provide a springboard for future growth.

Putting Marketing into the Heart

While some changes were implemented in the early 1960's, it was not until the appointment of Adrian Cadbury as Chairman in 1965 that the Bournville structure became equipped for the latter part of the 20th-century. When Adrian became Chairman he was only 34 years old and the youngest family member of the Board. This was another bold move by the retiring chairman, Paul Cadbury, and a reflection of his understanding that the company needed a more modern approach.

One of Adrian's first initiatives was the appointment of McKinsey to conduct a full review of the business. They concentrated much of their effort into the Herculean task of realigning what had evolved as being largely a supply-focused organisation into one where the consumer and retail customer came first. Cadbury had already introduced the idea of Brand Management into their structure several years before, but had struggled to adapt the rest of the organisation to its presence, with the result that the Marketing Department was concentrating its efforts where there was least friction with the rest of the business – advertising.

McKinsey saw this as a major problem, and soon had the nascent Cadbury Marketing Department in their cross-hairs,

The brand strategies developed each year are a useful statement of marketing intent but, traditionally, they have been geared primarily to justify an advertising budget.

McKinsey were explicit that this state of affairs had to change, and that the role of the Product Manager had to be the focal point for overall product planning and coordination,

Product Managers have responsibility for planning the growth and profitability of their product groups and it is important both that they are supplied with the information that they need to discharge their responsibilities properly, and that managers in other functions come to view them as the focus of all discussions and decisions resulting in a significant change to their products.

Focus on the bottom Line

Following McKinsey, who had also recommended both the Cadbury-Fry consolidation and the setting up of the separate Foods Division, Cadbury now had a much better structure with which to begin the transition to being market-led. But one of the reasons behind McKinsey's criticisms of the Cadbury marketing department was cultural as well as structural: that the Cost Office saw profitability as their concern, and had evolved a work practice of being careful when it came to sharing detailed cost and profit data. This approach would be largely swept away by the merger in 1969 with Schweppes, who brought with them into the new company much more of a bottom-line culture.

Chairmanship of the newly-created Cadbury Schweppes had gone to the previous head of Schweppes, Lord Watkinson, with Adrian Cadbury moving on from running the Bournville operation to become Cadbury Schweppes Deputy Chairman and also Joint Managing Director, along with another Schweppes man, James Barker. Lord Watkinson was clear that, under his regime, the profitability would be central to the new culture,

My control is financial…using the Finance Committee of the Board as the controlling instrument to make sure that budgets and (Management By Objectives) targets are met.[1]

Lord Watkinson's numbers-driven focus was the turning point in eroding the power wielded at Bournville by the Cost Office, and facilitated the emergence of a fully-fledged Cadbury Marketing Department with true profit accountability. In case there was any doubt, every manager at Bournville was issued with a notice to adorn their office wall, quoting Lord Watkinson's mantra that, *The Name of the Game is Profit.*

Cadbury, who had struggled with increasing overheads and cocoa costs, needed to address their by-now convoluted and inefficient manufacturing set-up if they were to hope to regain competitiveness against the slick Mars organisation. All three key factories of Bournville, Somerdale and Moreton were making overlapping ranges of chocolate and food products, each factory having its own chocolate-making facilities. Sugar confectionery production was also split between Somerdale and Bournville. Implementing a plan that had been developed prior to the merger, cocoa-bean processing was centralised in one new factory at Chirk, near Birkenhead, Milk processing in an expanded Marlbrook factory, and each chocolate brand's production was centralised either in Bournville, Somerdale, or the Dublin factory.

---

[1] The Cadbury Schweppes Mix, *Management Today*, April 1970.

Out With the Old, In With the New

Lord Watkinson also did little to hide his impression that Cadbury needed a kick up the pants when it came to their track record on innovation. The Cadbury Head of Marketing initiated a crash programme of new products that would hopefully counter Lord Watkinson's view.

The area targeted was in giving Cadbury more stand-alone brands in its Moulded portfolio to benefit from the trend towards television-advertised, rifle-shot branding. Slow-selling venerable Moulded products such as Mild Dessert were replaced by new lines clearly positioned as individual brands, each with its own advertising campaign. Golden Crisp (a re-staging of Fry's Crunch), Old Jamaica, Velvet Blend, Special Recipe, Icebreaker, Country Style and Grand Seville were successively rolled out in the early 1970s. A range of children's Moulded bars were successfully launched in 1974 under the brand umbrella of 'Cadburyland'. The strategy seemed to be working as the decline in Cadbury's sales of Moulded products was reversed.

In the Countline portfolio, Lord Watkinson's prodding produced an even more dramatic response from a company that had historically struggled in the category. For the first time, a role was created specifically for new product development, with the incumbent being given the brief to launch twelve new products within the space of the next twelve months. While the timescale was not quite achieved, fourteen new lines would be test-marketed in 1970 and 1971. The Watkinson-inspired pressure on Cadbury's cost base meant that most of these products would be made on existing equipment, which limited the product creativity, and the rushed timescale meant that few would be based on identified gaps in the market.

However, despite the constraints, the deluge began well with Curly Wurly being launched nationally in 1970, a unique brand that is still around today. Efforts to use the largely redundant Aztec production line were less successful, with Supermousse, Amazin Raisin, Rumba and Welcome all coming and then soon disappearing. The most creative use of the equipment came with Perky Nana, a

banana-flavoured version of Milky Way launched in 1974, though the product was to become a success to this day in Cadbury's New Zealand operation. But even though most of the new products failed in the long term, Cadbury's sales of its Moulded and Countline ranges surged ahead between 1970 and 1974: Moulded by 25% and Countlines by a more sedate 6%.

Branding the Portfolio

In addition to the innovation, Cadbury were finally benefiting from the awesome power of television as they transitioned away from using the Cadbury name and the Dairy Milk brand as key supports for the rest of the range, towards a range of differentiated, individual brands. The process, led by Cadbury's new head of Marketing recruited from their advertising agency, had started with the graphical divergence of Fruit & Nut and Wholenut away from their Dairy Milk parent, and followed up with the development of individual advertising campaigns for each. Driven by two of the British confectionery industry's most famous advertising campaigns: *'Everyone's a Fruit & Nutcase'* and *'NUTS, whole ha-azel nuts, HA! Cadbury take 'em and they cover them in chocolate'*, sales of the two now individual brands increased by 73% between 1970 and 1974.

Successful brand-building was also coming in the Countline arena where Fry's Turkish Delight was wowing audiences with its *"Full of Eastern Promise"* commercials; Fry's Chocolate Cream was appealing to the more sophisticated ladies of leisure, and Fudge was reassuring Mum's that *'A finger of Fudge is just enough to give your kids a treat.'* Combined sales of the three brands grew by 10% during the 1970s. Not spectacular, but a real success in building some of Cadbury's long-established Countline brands. The star of the show, however, was Flake. Its campaign of *'By Yourself, Enjoy Yourself'* was turbo-charged by its evolution into, *'Only the crumbliest, flakiest chocolate, tastes like chocolate never tasted before'*. In a compelling demonstration of the power of television in driving good Countline brands, Flake sales almost quadrupled during the 1970's.

Another hit came with Cadbury's Creme Egg. Previously just one of many novelties available in the run-up to Easter, its fortunes were transformed by Cadbury's decision to re-introduce the brand immediately after New Year, and market it aggressively as a Countline until Easter, when it disappeared again. This novel marketing approach of restricting the brand's availability to three or four months created an annual frenzy among consumers that was termed within Cadbury as the 'Strawberry Syndrome.' The outcome over the 1970s was a tripling of Creme Egg sales, it becoming the largest selling confectionery product during the first quarter of the year. A consumer promotion to find twelve golden eggs buried around the country, Cadbury's Crème Egg Conundrum, drove interest in the brand to new heights.

There were also improvements in the area of innovation, which Cadbury now embraced as a concept – perhaps the single-biggest shift in mind-set from the pre-war model – while having learned the hard way to take a more measured approach. This would soon pay dividends with the successful launch in 1976 of three new Countline brands under the Cadbury name: Double Decker (which finally put a re-engineered Aztec plant to good use); Caramel – a re-staging of the old Caramello Filled Block, and Star Bar, a peanut-based product developed by their Irish company.

Cadbury had by now switched whole-heartedly to the idea of driving the portfolio at the individual brand level, and most of the historic activities used to promote the Cadbury name, such as factory tours, travelling films units and the like were quietly dropped. The awesome power of television

CRACK THE *Cadbury's* **creme egg mystery**
in your local shops now.

advertising in the 1960s and '70s was such that a single brand message, when portrayed creatively, could trump decades of consumers' personal, experiential interactions with a brand as strong as Cadbury. While it seemed

like Cadbury were moving to play on the Mars and Rowntree playing field, they had no choice. Television had changed all the rules.

Dairy Milk Languishes

While the crisis had passed at Bournville with a more realistic cost base and surging sales coming from the new branded approach, all was not well with the Dairy Milk brand itself. The advertising message of the last four decades – the Glass

Cadbury's DOUBLE DECKER 1p off REC. PRICE

NOUGATINE, CRISP RICE, CORNFLAKES AND RAISIN FILLED MILK CHOCOLATE

MILK CHOCOLATE CONTAINS VEGETABLE FAT. MILK SOLIDS 20% MINIMUM

and a Half – had been dropped in favour of more 'creative' approaches, one of which involved referring to the brand by its internal company acronym, C.D.M. (Cadbury's Dairy Milk). While the mid-1960s campaign of *'Award Yourself the C.D.M.'* won plaudits, some in the company questioned its wisdom. With a brand that benefited from the emotive power of the Cadbury name, the creamy taste connotations of the words 'Dairy Milk' and the compelling Glass and a Half visual, doing without all of these other than with the pack visuals

Award yourself the C.D.M.

again!

Bournville REPORTER

SPOTLIGHT ON COCOA centre pages

SEPTEMBER 1976   A CADBURY SCHWEPPES NEWSPAPER   VOL 8 No. 6

COCOA PRICE – NO CAUSE FOR PANIC

was a questionable tactic. Sales of Dairy Milk remained stagnant during the early 1970's as the rest of the Moulded portfolio surged ahead.

The first shock was a bout of hyper-inflation in the price of cocoa that tripled in the space of 18 months, from £700/tonne in mid-1975 to £2,000/tonne at the end of 1976. But Cadbury's cautious approach to the forward buying of cocoa had protected them to some extent during this period. Rowntree had not fared as well as some ill-advised speculation on the price had ended up costing them millions. The Chairman of Cadbury's U.K. Confectionery business had even prophesied during the surge that the increases could put chocolate into the luxury market,

For years the industry has taken for granted that cocoa beans could be bought at a price which allowed chocolate bars to be sold as an everyday purchase. But now we may be entering a new era.

However, a more encouraging message was prevailing in the September 1976 Works Magazine (now rechristened the Bournville Reporter) under the banner headline, '*Cocoa price – no cause for panic*',

(The) Confectionery Group Board has devised an action plan to overcome the problems. This is based on new products; products using less bean; and increasing the effectiveness of marketing and advertising expenditure.

Another part of the action plan involved the inevitable raising of prices; Cadbury being forced to put through two price increases of around 5% during 1976, followed by another 18% in January 1977.

Unfortunately, the same action plan also involved a reduction in the advertising budget. In 1976, Cadbury's share of total chocolate advertising had declined from its pre-cocoa inflation level of nearly half of all chocolate advertising down to less than a third as budgets were cut to prop up the bottom line. Mars, whose range consisted primarily of chocolate-covered nougatine bars, and Rowntree with their Countline approach and portfolio of strong sugar brands, were much less exposed to the rocketing price than was Cadbury with their large Moulded portfolio. This came at a bad time for Cadbury as their advertising spend was now being spread across far more brands due to their transitioning of their portfolio. This further reduced the amount available for Cadbury's number one brand, Dairy Milk.

The prophecy of doom on the fate of the chocolate category failed to materialise – volume dipped by 11% in 1975 and was back at pre-inflation levels by 1978 – but there were some dramatic shifts in consumer purchasing behaviour within the category itself resulting from the price shifts. The best value part of the chocolate market – Chocolate Biscuit Countlines – increased in volume by 62% between 1974 and 1978, while over the same period, the market for Moulded chocolate plummeted. Cadbury's Moulded decline during that period would be a cataclysmic 45%. Some of the decline would be the cancellation of many of the new products launched in the early 1970's, but Dairy Milk itself declined by 40% as it had simultaneously come under attack from another direct competitor.

The Yorkie Juggernaut

Rowntree had stunned Cadbury by launching Yorkie in 1976 during the thick of the cocoa price inflation. Yorkie, much to Rowntree's surprise and Cadbury's distress, was an instant runaway success that came almost entirely at the expense of Dairy Milk. By 1978, Yorkie's annual sales volume had reached a massive 13,000 tonnes[2] – double that achieved by any Cadbury new product since the War. Cadbury now had less than half of the Moulded category, one that Cadbury had invented and defined. The Dairy Milk brand had been the company's flagship for sixty years, so the blow to morale was even more powerful than the hit to the bottom line. But it had been a problem waiting to happen.

The Dairy Milk product itself had been changed to achieve cost savings to try and ameliorate the impact of the surging cocoa prices. In addition to

---

[2] http://www.nestle.co.uk/OurBrands/AboutOurBrands/ConfectioneryAndCakes/Yorkie.htm; Accessed July 25th, 2007

replacing some of the expensive cocoa butter with Sal fat from Cadbury India, a much bigger problem had resulted from an effort to maintain an impression of good apparent value as products weights were further shaved back. The surface area of the bar had been increased, resulting in a much thinner product. The complex matrix between quality, value and product eating characteristics was now out of kilter, a problem not helped by the advertising message having moved on to, *"One of today's great tastes"*, which it now increasingly wasn't.

Meanwhile, Yorkie was everything that Dairy Milk was not. Rowntree had seen the changes to Dairy Milk and ensured that Yorkie would decisively trump Dairy Milk on thickness: its shape giving Yorkie the bite and eating characteristics that people sought in a chocolate bar. Even Yorkie's advertising campaign was right on the money, featuring a beefy lorry driver who men wanted to be like, and women just wanted. With a product format and package borrowed from the Countline category, it made the ideal impulse purchase and made Dairy Milk seem old fashioned.

Cadbury quickly conducted in-depth market research to evaluate the threat, and were appalled at the results. While Dairy Milk was beating Yorkie on taste, it was being hammered on the attribute of offering a thick, solid bite. This was a critical feature rated as important by over 75% of all Moulded consumers, and the implication was clear,

The conclusion must be therefore that the precise, demonstrable benefit offered by the Yorkie bars is desired by a large proportion of the market.

The limiting factor to further movement away from the Cadbury brands would therefore appear to be simply one of trial for the Yorkie products.

In other words, it was only a matter of time before many more Dairy Milk consumers deserted the brand once they had got around to trying Yorkie, something that would inevitably happen as the Yorkie advertising was being recalled by three times as many people as was the insipid Dairy Milk campaign. This could signal the demise of Cadbury's pre-eminence in the U.K. chocolate market. If Dairy Milk lost its status as the leading brand of milk chocolate, then Cadbury itself would eventually crumble, no matter how many Countlines it launched. On the back of the Yorkie impact, in 1977 Cadbury lost leadership of the overall chocolate market to Rowntree for the first time since they had taken the honour from Fry in 1910.

Cadbury's response was both rapid and dramatic. As reported in the October 1977 edition of the Bournville Reporter, the rapidly-planned Dairy Milk relaunch would be Cadbury's biggest ever marketing initiative. Hosted by Eamonn Andrews who introduced the theme of 'Dairy Milk – This is Your Life', the assembled Cadbury sales force were reassured that,

The traditional standards that have made Cadbury's Dairy Milk the biggest selling Moulded chocolate brand in the U.K. are boldly reasserted in the massive relaunch of the £35 million range.

The incremental degradations to both product and packaging that had accumulated over many years were swept away. The optimum Dairy Milk recipe – a secret known only to four employees at any one time – was re-instated. The chasing of price points by weight manipulation was also decisively halted, with the product range being defined around fixed weights of 50, 75, 125 and 250 grams. The 50 gram bar, which equated to just over 1¾ ozs, came in a thick format, the chunk shape having been painstakingly engineered as the absolute optimum size and thickness in which to enjoy the restored Dairy Milk taste and texture.

The wrapper was strengthened and redesigned back to being predominantly Cadbury purple, with a prominent Dairy Milk logo and Glass and a Half icon. This had been researched against the existing design that downplayed the Dairy Milk name, which it beat decisively even when the existing design was transposed onto a chunky bar format. The 50 gram bars also came in

illusions that their jobs depended on 50 gram Dairy Milk being front and centre of the display in every shop they called on.

Just as importantly, the newly-developed brand advertising returned to the core brand basics. The famous Cilla Black was signed up to front a campaign that was all about Dairy Milk's creamy taste and the Glass and a Half. The advertisement generated the highest advertising awareness Cadbury had ever seen, and enhanced the brand image on the key dynamics of being a thick bar and good value for money. But most importantly, it helped stem the sales losses.

Although the bleeding was successfully stopped, the combined hammer blows of the 6d disaster and the Yorkie launch had reduced Cadbury's once mighty 2oz/50gram bar from being the market's best seller to not even being in the top ten. From now on the lead pack of Dairy Milk would be the new 200 gram bar, which had been introduced a year later in 1978 to

a display box that could be easily opened to showcase the rejuvenated brand right on the shopkeeper's counter. Long requested value promotions for the Wholesale trade were rolled out. Every member of the Cadbury sales force was left under no

replace the 250 gram bar in response to Galaxy having introduced a smaller bar to undercut the price of Dairy Milk's 250 gram. Cadbury's 200 gram bar became the annual subject of a price war every autumn between Tesco, Fine Fare, Sainsbury, with even Woolworth's joining in. While the retailers were making the slimmest of margins and giving the product prominent display positions, they were selling huge volumes, and it was soon accounting for over half of the total sales of Dairy Milk.

The grocery chains had also latched onto Cadbury's ranges of Easter Eggs and Christmas lines, recognising that when it came to a chocolate gift, the strength of the Cadbury name made their product ranges the most important to have in stock. But aside from 200 gram Dairy Milk and the seasonal ranges, there was not much in the Cadbury range for retailers to get excited about. The price inflation had seen Fruit & Nut, Wholenut and Bournville sales decline by 50% during the second half of the 1970s. Growth in Cadbury's Countlines during the same period would only make up a third of the volume lost on Moulded.

Tackling the Costs – Mk II

Stripping out the high market shares enjoyed by Cadbury in their Easter and Christmas seasonal programmes, their share in the year-round blocks and bars market was by the late 1970s inching down towards the psychologically crucial 20% mark. Although Double Decker was the fourth best-selling Countline in the market, Caramel and Star Bar had not been stellar successes as both offered relatively poor value for money: Caramel was the most expensively-priced Countline in the market. The cocoa price inflation had impacted Cadbury more than their competitors, but the underlying problem was that Cadbury were still uncompetitive because of their high cost base, despite the rationalisation of processes and brands within each factory.

This would finally be addressed head-on when the latest member of the Cadbury family to take the helm at Bournville, Adrian's brother Dominic, was appointed Managing Director of the U.K. Confectionery Division in 1980. In a speech delivered to every member of the Cadbury workforce, Dominic Cadbury laid bare the implications of the continued drift downwards: unless the share loss was reversed, the company would soon reach what he termed 'the Marketing Precipice',

From a cost point of view we were not competitive, and if we stayed that way, the sales force would not be able to maintain display parity, and sales would fall away, as if off a precipice.

The Cadbury sales team, with little successful ammunition over the years, had held onto more display space than the rate of sale of Cadbury's Moulded and Countline brands really merited. Selling the strong Cadbury seasonal ranges involved a lot of face-time with all the key customers, and the relationships forged in this environment stood the company in good stead. Cadbury had been able to convince retailers that each of the three big firms of Cadbury, Mars and the merged Rowntree Mackintosh was entitled to around 30% of the available space for the year-round business, leaving 10% for the minor

players. But, with a market share of only nearly 20% coming from products sold in 30% of the space, that argument was becoming less and less tenable. Cadbury were now extremely vulnerable: up to one-third of their display space could potentially be grabbed by their competitors. If that happened, the gradual volume seepage would turn into a tidal wave and the business could go into a terminal tailspin, irrespective of the strength of the Cadbury name.

Dominic Cadbury informed the workforce that major surgery on the cost side was essential,

We are in the business of making and selling branded confectionery in the U.K. That is where our skill, our name, our strength remains. Every activity that is not directly related to that must be challenged.

The sprawling Bournville site was still home to its own printing works for labels and box-making department. Another entire section of the site – Trades Street – housed dozens of different species of trades-people, from sheet-metal workers to carpenters, who had little to do with the making and selling of chocolate. Trade unionism, which had been encouraged in the early days, was also an issue. The Bournville site was host to 41 recognised unions while the Mars plant was union-free. But the political climate had changed sufficiently for Cadbury to tackle the unions.

In addition to a bloated payroll and too many ancillary activities, the main Bournville and Somerdale factories had become out-dated. The heart of the pre-war system, the use of the most modern and efficient machinery, was a long-distant memory. Cadbury's Factory Director described the factories as '*Monuments to industrial history rather than modern technology.*' If Mars were ever to be matched, Cadbury had to become far more efficient at making chocolate bars.

Dominic instituted the biggest revolution of Cadbury's U.K. factories since the rebuilding of Bournville in the 1920's. The number of production lines was decreased from 78 to 33 in a £110 million investment as ageing manufacturing lines were swept away to be replaced by gigantic, state-of-the-art chocolate production technology. And just as in the 1920's, that also meant a radical downsizing of the workforce. As Dominic later recalled,

The factories at Bournville and Somerdale were changed radically internally, even though they looked more or less the same from the outside. We reduced the number of employees by 40% fortunately by being able to take advantage of an age profile that made early retirement a pretty attractive option.[3]

Turnaround

Much of the savings were reinvested into improving the value for money being offered. Coupled with a beefing up of Cadbury's advertising and promotional budgets, the result was a reversal of Cadbury's long-term market share decline. In 1982 sales of all Cadbury's 22 key brands increased versus the previous year, which Dominic Cadbury attributed to the new strategy,

High productivity and good consumer value, widely advertised, add up to market success and growth in market share. This year we are going to become more price competitive. Priority will be given to improving value through weight increases and price reductions.

Crunchie was increased in size, Caramel was reduced in price to the going rate for Countlines, and both brands prospered. In April 1983, Cadbury announced a permanent reduction in the price of Double

---

[3] Crosfield, p695

Decker from 16p to 14p, aided by samples of an improved product recipe given out nationwide by the new brand mascot, Dougie the Double Decker dog. Coming at the same time as Mars Bar increasing its price from 16p to 17p, the initiative was a runaway success. To go head-to-head on product weight with Yorkie, Cadbury had also since replaced the 50 and 75 gram bars of Dairy Milk with a 60 gram bar which they then slashed the price of on a temporary basis from 24p to 19p with advertisements trumpeting,

'*Now with a Chunk off the Price.*' This move had been in order to put the key pack of Dairy Milk squarely in the Countline price bracket. Such a move was important as Countlines tended to have a younger buying age profile than traditional Moulded bars,

We wanted to tempt the regular Countline buyer to buy more of our chocolate at a price they could not ignore.

As well as galvanising Cadbury back behind Dairy Milk, Yorkie had also demonstrated to Cadbury that many of Countlines' clothes could be stolen and applied to bars made from nothing but chocolate. This then would allow Cadbury to play its trump card: that people loved the taste of Cadbury chocolate more than they did nougat, biscuit, wafer and other staples of the Countline products. Armed with this insight, Cadbury would roll out a series of new products which had chocolate as their core experience, but which played by Countline rules.

First out of the gate was a direct competitor to Rowntree's venerable Aero brand. Wispa, a much more finely aerated product, was launched into test market in the Tyne-Tees area in 1981 and was an immediate sensation. With consumer trial being driven by a stupendous Sales Force effort and a sensational advertising campaign, Cadbury's pilot production plant could not keep up. Shop owners would come to blows in Cash & Carry's over the few boxes of Wispa they could find. New deliveries sold out immediately.

The Cadbury Board rapidly decided to invest £12 million in a massive new production line and then withdrew the product from sale in Tyne-Tees, instructing their Sales Force to spread the rumour that, even though the product was a success, the technology was so complex that the line could not be manufactured profitably. Meanwhile, top-secret plans were put in place for a nationwide massive launch as soon as possible. Rowntree however, were not fooled by the story and managed to launch a chunky version of Aero which mimicked Wispa's shape in the meantime. Even so, when it came in 1983, the second Wispa launch was by far the biggest in Cadbury's history.

The brand was re-introduced into its original test market of the Tyne-Tees area. A sales conference was arranged on a Friday to 'announce a new Chocolate Biscuit Countline', and minutes into the deliberately dull and uninspiring presentation, the screen collapsed revealing a giant Wispa bar with the message, "*Wispa is Back*!!" sending the audience of Cadbury sales people into near hysteria. When the cheering had died down, it was announced that every retailer and wholesaler would receive an enormous delivery of Wispa the following Monday and everyone had to get on the phone immediately to ensure the order would be accepted. Over 70% of retailers had Wispa on display within 72 hours of the meeting. This formula was used to roll-out the brand to the rest of the U.K . and Wispa was soon one of the top-selling bars in the country, although the Aero response meant that the initial sales levels in the Tyne-Tees test market would not quite be replicated.

Cadbury chocolate was now competing hard in the Countline sector, Wispa having been followed up two years later with another all-chocolate Countline, Twirl, which had been developed by the Cadbury Ireland business. Twirl successfully combined an asset utilisation approach together with sound consumer insight to create a very successful new Countline brand, with minimal cannibalisation from the Flake brand whose technology Twirl predominantly used. This was closely followed by another all-chocolate brand using novel extrusion technology, Spira.

The corner had finally been turned for Cadbury's U.K. confectionery division, but much still remained to be done to restore their dominant position. While this turnaround had been going on, Cadbury's overseas operations had continued on their mostly successful trajectories.

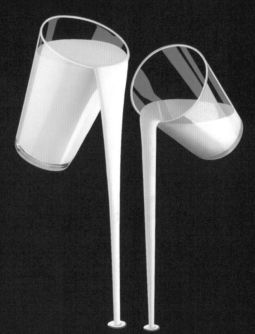

Chapter 14

THE OVERSEAS BUSINESSES GO FROM STRENGTH TO STRENGTH

Hindustan Cocoa Products Limited

Cadbury

Cadbury's DAIRY MILK MILK CHOCOLATE

37TH ANNUAL REPORT

The overall dependence of Cadbury on its U.K. business was not due to any lack of effort on behalf of the overseas management, but was a function of the absolute size of the British business. 50 million consumers with the highest per capita confectionery consumption in the world were, and still are, the basis of a huge business. While Cadbury's U.K. confectionery business had been undergoing its various traumas, matters had largely been progressing much better in the overseas companies, helping them further increase their share of Cadbury's overall confectionery sales.

Ireland

Across the Irish Sea, Fry-Cadbury Ireland, by now renamed Cadbury Ireland, had continued to build on its success of the 1960's and early '70's, even after Ireland's entry into the Common Market (EEC) in 1973 had swept away the remaining tariff barriers that had kept Mars out of the market. Indeed, by 1978, Cadbury's share of the Irish chocolate market was still an impressive 54% after five years of free trade. With 2,000 employees, a £60 million annual turnover (six times the level of a decade previously) and one of the biggest direct selling organisations in Ireland, Cadbury was now a substantial and successful entity. Not a bad return on the initial investment from Bournville in 1932 of £10,000, which a doubtful member of

the Cadbury Board had described as "...*might as well have been thrown into the River Liffey.*"

Cadbury Ireland had responded quickly and aggressively to the abolition of tariff barriers, recognising that, as a still small company by U.K. standards, it would be exposed to the hyper-efficiency of the Mars organisation. In a major change of direction, Cadbury saw that their range of locally-made products, which had by then expanded to some 90 lines, could not be competitively produced. Consequently, their local factory would be consolidated into an efficient unit which would focus on making the products they could produce in volume to generate sufficient economies of scale. The other products would be imported from Bournville or Somerdale, or failing that, dropped. As a *quid pro quo*, the Ireland site would take on the manufacture of a small number of lines for the U.K. market. Thus Flake, Chocolate Eclairs and, for a time, Buttons were made for both markets in Ireland; this gave their chocolate-making infrastructure the scale it needed to be highly cost-efficient.

Because of the tariff barriers, the Cadbury Ireland product range had been entirely locally-produced, a factor which the company had used to its marketing advantage, which thus made such dramatic changes to the

Irish product range a huge and risky decision. Dairy Milk, long promoted as being made with Irish full-cream milk, would still be produced locally, but many brands which featured lavish coatings of that same Dairy Milk, were now to be imported. Milk Tray was advertised as being "so thickly covered with Cadbury's Dairy Milk chocolate", as was the biscuit range and many other lines. Coupled with a Cadbury guarantee of satisfaction on every pack – Cadbury Ireland having been the first Irish food company to make such a claim – the importance of strong product values to the Irish success cannot be under-estimated.

Visits to Bournville and Moreton to examine the import options for products proved depressing as, by that time, years of shaving back had reduced the chocolate covering on UK-produced Milk Tray, and the coverings on Moreton biscuits had moved away from using the Dairy Milk recipe. There was the additional problem that, for a variety of reasons including differences in milk between the two countries, even their two Dairy Milk products tasted somewhat different. But marketing messages were adapted to the new circumstances, and local production was retained for products where the Irish Dairy Milk taste and quantity were a key part of the product benefit.

One such product was the hugely successful Sandwich Snack, which Ireland had developed and launched in 1966 to capitalise on the market being opened up by Jacob's Club. Snack from the very beginning had used the differences in chocolate covering between the two products as their main competitive weapon. Over the Cadbury was Dairy while Jacob's and also chocolate (ironically Department.) By 1978, Snack 70% of product weight Milk chocolate, were somewhat stingier using an inferior blended supplied by Cadbury's Contract Sales had overtaken Club and was the company's best-selling product through grocery stores, so it was imperative that local production was maintained.

Elsewhere in the product range, as the company had not been able to import Roses, it had developed its own version called Irish Rose, in which some of the units were distinctly different to the U.K. version that would now replace it. Locally-produced Countlines, such as Tonga and Swiss, which were short lifespan lines used as order-book openers with retailers, were now no longer possible. On the plus side, lines such as Picnic could now be imported into Ireland.

But Cadbury Ireland never pursued the headlong rush into developing a range of Countline brands as had occurred in the U.K. Even major U.K. Countline launches such as Aztec had been used in exactly the same way as Tonga and Swiss: to bring a bit of new news to the category rather than represent a wholesale switch of direction. 8-square Dairy Milk, together with a wide range of variants in the same format, stayed as the company's main competitor in the Countline arena as the company resolutely stuck to maintaining the lines at price parity with the big Countline brands, albeit by occasionally having to shave back the bar weights.

By avoiding the tactic of increasing the surface area of the bar and sticking with the 8-square shape, Cadbury in Ireland was not as vulnerable to the threat of Yorkie, which arrived in 1979. Even so, although Yorkie was facing a much more robust Dairy Milk brand than it had in the U.K., the Irish management team could take nothing for granted in their response. To head off the Yorkie threat, chunkier versions of Dairy Milk, Fruit & Nut and Wholenut were quickly rolled out in addition to the 8-square line-up. If people wanted chunky milk chocolate – there was a Cadbury offer. Seeing that Yorkie's U.K. franchise was predominantly male, Cadbury chose Chunky Wholenut to lead the advertising response, pre-empting Yorkie's position with commercials featuring, not a lorry driver, but a lumberjack .

At the same time as the Yorkie threat, Cadbury Ireland were also facing a much more aggressive Mars selling organisation who were rolling out major value initiatives – this time via bigger bars for the same price – on their key brands: Mars Bar, Marathon and Twix. Cadbury were now facing a pincer attack: Yorkie threatened to take share of the Moulded sector, and Mars threatened to reduce the size of the Moulded sector. To protect their core Moulded category, Cadbury rolled out a major strategic response to massively reinvest in Cadbury's Dairy Milk. Arguing that the best form of defence is attack, the weights of the 8-square range, which had been shaved in the era of cocoa inflation, were permanently increased by 30% to the old 2oz level with no increase in price. Supported by the organisation's biggest

ever advertising campaign, trumpeting the tag-line, *"Much more chocolate, much more taste"*, the Cadbury franchise not only survived the twin assault, but went from strength to strength.

By this time, Cadbury Ireland had finely tuned their commercial machine, with the Yorkie/Mars response being just one of many strong implementations of aligned Sales and Marketing strategies, supported by an absolute belief in the Cadbury brand, Dairy Milk's product values and the critical importance of display. Their re-investment in the Moulded range, coupled with a continual updating and refinement of the company's 'Salesmaker' display units, had worked to strengthen the Cadbury name and its ability to act as a masterbrand across the entire range. A succession of advertising tag-lines that prominently featured on every Cadbury display, such as, *"Cadbury – the perfect word for chocolate"*, and, *"The choice is yours. The taste is Cadbury"*, summed up the company's competitive key advantage.

The success of this approach was widely recognised by the Irish retail trade who, in 1978, nominated Cadbury Ireland as Ireland's Most Efficient Company. This award would be trumped three years later when Cadbury Ireland was voted by a judging panel of major retailers and wholesalers as "Manufacturer of the Year".

Another key difference between Cadbury's Irish and U.K. operations that emerged in the 1980's was Cadbury Ireland's proactive strategy of rapidly adopting any packaging or product format innovations that Mars would roll out in the U.K. Thus, Cadbury Ireland were using their efficient, but flexible factory to produce bags of small "Treat-size" units far earlier than was the case with the unwieldy Bournville or Somerdale. Such formats were then used to leverage Cadbury's strength in the existing seasonal markets of Easter and Christmas to develop a host of other seasonal purchase occasions for their brands. Halloween was built from nothing in 1987 to being the third largest confectionery seasonal market. Previously seen as a distinctly North American phenomenon, with the strength of the Cadbury name leading the way, the Irish public quickly adopted the idea of 'Trick or Treating'. No occasion was judged too insignificant to warrant a large display of Cadbury products. St. Patrick's Day, August Bank Holiday, the Whit weekend, and 'Back to School' would also be developed as confectionery opportunities by Cadbury.

The combination of always having an excuse for a large display, an appropriate product offer with which to fill it, and a very strong Cadbury brand franchise would keep competitors largely on the sidelines. Cadbury's market share in Ireland would remain above 50% throughout the 1980's and 1990's as the very strong Dairy Milk brand was complimented by the pure chocolate Countlines such as Wispa; locally developed Countline brands such as Twirl, Moro and

Chomp; and the stunning success in the Chocolate biscuit Countline sector of Cadbury's Snack.

North America

Elsewhere in the world of Cadbury, matters were progressing just as well with the exception of Canada, where the long-term failure to break through the problems of too many competitors, a very vibrant, long-established Countline sector, and an aggressive retail trade, had kept Cadbury's Canadian business only marginally profitable in the best of years. Consequently, coinciding with the sale of the U.S. operation to Hershey in 1986, the Canadian business was also sold to the owner of the market-leading local brand, Neilson, who merged the two together to create Neilson-Cadbury.

The U.K. still had an interest in proceedings, as they did in the U.S., because the Canadian owners were paying royalties, technology fees and also importing chocolate crumb from Cadbury Ireland. But such additional costs meant that the Canadian owners preferred to build their own Neilson Jersey Milk moulded brand, and thus Dairy Milk, and the Cadbury name, began to recede in importance. Similarly in the U.S., there would be no Kit Kat style growth for Dairy Milk under Hershey ownership, where the brand languished at much the same sales level it had achieved under Peter Paul Cadbury.

New Zealand

In the Southern Hemisphere, however, the three main Cadbury companies in New Zealand, Australia and South Africa were moving from strength to strength. The New Zealand business by the late 1960's had a broadly spread business and was market leader in every sector it competed in. In having such a dominant position of the confectionery market, Cadbury-Fry-Hudson had to look more aggressively than most Cadbury companies at diversification. Expansion from their core biscuit market into crackers was examined, as was entry into cakes, potato crisps and building a local Smash plant.

But by the early 1980's, the New Zealand business had realised that much could still be achieved in chocolate confectionery with a change of approach. Fearing a major entry into their market by Mars, who by then were well established in Australia thanks to their past collaboration with MacRobertson's, Cadbury-Fry-Hudson decided to adopt Mars' philosophy of putting asset turnover ahead of profit margin. Their Moro bar, which had had a free run in the absence of Mars, weighed only 48 grams, versus the Australian

Mars Bar that was a hefty 60 grams. So Moro was increased to match this with the change being supported by heavyweight advertising. The result was a near three-fold increase in sales, which then enabled the company to invest further in upgrading the production line, recovering their lost margin as the line became much more efficient. A similar approach was taken with their Moulded business, with equally impressive results.

But even with such local successes, there was the underlying problem that New Zealand, with a population in 1975 of only just over 3 million, was too small a market to sustain a fully independent Cadbury business. Ireland, which had a similar-sized population, had three benefits over New Zealand: firstly, a higher per capita consumption of chocolate; secondly, Cadbury Ireland becoming a manufacturer of product for the massive U.K. market; and thirdly, Cadbury Ireland's decision to rationalise their own production to their major lines and import the rest from the U.K. had reduced their costs. Closer arrangements between the Australian and New Zealand businesses were inevitable, and links were progressively forged during the 1980's. Gratifyingly for the company, this collaboration was managed such that it did not adversely impact the Cadbury market share or brand equity in New Zealand, where Cadbury is regularly voted the country's most trusted brand.

Australia

Following the Schweppes merger, Cadbury-Fry-Pascall had become the confectionery division of the newly-created Cadbury Schweppes Australia Ltd., a corporate entity that had local Australian shareholders in addition to the U.K.-based parent. While the MacRobertson acquisition had added a strong Countline business to Cadbury's Moulded heartland, and sales had performed strongly in the aftermath, Cadbury were still subject to many of the same market shifts that had hampered the U.K. business.

The cocoa price issue was nipped in the bud by the company deciding as early as 1971 to raise prices rather than reduce product weights, even though this meant moving their Countlines up from the attractive 10c price point. A 1972 marketing plan document summarised the outcome,

To date this year we have seen growth in those bars enjoying a strong consumer franchise built up over many years – Cherry Ripe, Crunchie and Flake – but have suffered a reversal in the weaker franchise bars…We have battled through a most difficult period, but consider it essential to establish the principle of price adjustment and trading up rather than perpetuate erosion of consumer values by remaining at round price modules.

Although the curse of product degradation had been successfully avoided, there were still further challenges in the mid-1970's as their confectionery business was coming under increasing pressure from the Nestlé/Mars pincer attack. Cadbury were holding on through their superior sales coverage and by price discounting in the grocery trade. But by fuelling a price advantage to the grocers, Cadbury were losing goodwill with the small retailer. They were in danger of accelerating a shift towards a trade sector where they were comparatively disadvantaged. However, this situation would be aggressively addressed when a new management team took over in the late 1970's. This changing of the guard would be a pivotal moment in the history of Cadbury in Australia.

The strategy implemented by the new team was both simple and effective, and would build the company's share of the chocolate market to over 70% by the mid-1980's. It was based on a small number of key principles

1. The basic recipes could not be changed. The factories had no authority to change any feature of the product, and they were required to meet stringent production, quality and operational targets.
2. Cost reductions would be achieved through increasing volume and improving efficiency. These were partly taken as profit and partly re-invested in sales and marketing.
3. The sales force were to be the most professional in Australia
4. The role of product innovation was to keep consumer interest in the category as high as possible throughout the year.

All of the above would be focused on the primary goal of increasing Moulded's share of the total confectionery market.

As had been the case in Ireland, Dairy Milk would be at the heart of everything the CSAL confectionery division did. A new advertising campaign for the brand in 1980 became legendary. Cadbury signed up a famous popular scientist, Professor Julius Sumner Miller to front advertisements for the Dairy Milk brand. Recreating the home-made physics experiments, which had made him a household name in North America and Australia, he creatively and memorably

demonstrated the benefits of Dairy Milk's natural ingredients. This campaign increased sales and the factory were able to justify investment in new production lines that would result in increased productivity and improved profit margins. As it had come as something of a shock to Cadbury's management to discover that MacRobertson's new factory had significantly lower costs than did Cadbury's Tasmanian site, the investment was sorely needed. As was happening at that time in Bournville, the influence of trade unions in the factory was also reduced, which greatly facilitated the necessary changes.

The innovation strategy was now in full swing where around 20 new lines (mostly Moulded bars) would be planned for each year, many with a life-expectancy of only a year or two. All would be presented to customers in readiness for the February–March start to the chocolate-selling season (December and January being too hot for retailers to consider large displays of chocolate.) Having bagged the prime spots, this space would then be used for Easter lines and then back to the new products for April and May. Price discounting was largely abandoned as a tactic, with impulse being stressed as the key to purchasing and display.

In February 1984, Cadbury launched a killer blow that would decisively switch the market back towards Moulded bars, and Cadbury in particular. Cadbury had been carrying over a year's forward cover of cocoa beans, which gave them a major advantage when the world price suddenly and unexpectedly increased. Their competitors, who had much less cover, would have to pay a much higher

price for the cocoa that would be used in the 1984 selling season. Cadbury took the decision to invest all of their good fortune into the product. Their 200 gram bars, which had been their best seller since being introduced in 1972, would be increased in size to 250 grams with no additional cost to the consumer for the entire year. Competitors were now faced with not only having to pay far more for their cocoa, but also being severely disadvantaged on value.

The outcome was dramatic. Not only did Cadbury gain share of the Moulded market, reducing Nestlé down to being an also-ran, but the Moulded sector also increased its share of the total

market at the expense of Countlines. Cadbury were now offering better value in their large bars than were most Countline brands, and with a large variety of products in the best display positions, all featuring the famous Dairy Milk

taste being demonstrated nightly by the eccentric
Professor, it was an unbeatable combination.
Having sold 13.6 million Moulded
blocks in 1979, the
number would
rise to 22.3
million by
1993.

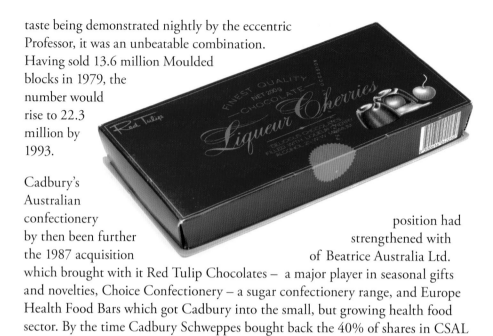

Cadbury's
Australian
confectionery   position had
by then been further   strengthened with
the 1987 acquisition   of Beatrice Australia Ltd.
which brought with it Red Tulip Chocolates – a major player in seasonal gifts
and novelties, Choice Confectionery – a sugar confectionery range, and Europe
Health Food Bars which got Cadbury into the small, but growing health food
sector. By the time Cadbury Schweppes bought back the 40% of shares in CSAL
that had been held by the public, the company was a hugely profitable concern
that would grow sales and profits for more than twenty years in a row. An
unimaginable position when compared to Cadbury's first 18 years in Australia
when they failed to turn a profit in every one of those years.

The Australian confectionery strategy also, as had happened in Ireland, resulted
in a major increase in the strength of the Cadbury brand name. By concentrating
on making Moulded, and within that, Dairy Milk, the centre of their strategy,
Cadbury were playing on home turf. While they still had launched some
Countlines to combat Mars, they never once considered de-focusing their
Moulded business. Their goal throughout was to make it more relevant to
Australian consumers than were Countlines.

South Africa

The market for confectionery in South Africa was anything but stable,
experiencing a dramatic series of peaks and troughs in response to the political
and economic turbulence in the country. Annual swings of 14% growth,
immediately followed by 7% declines made the market difficult to plan for, even
if the average trend over time was growth. A period of consistent growth arrived
in the late 1980s, mainly due to a surge in new products, but the competitive
scenario took a significant turn with the acquisition of Rowntree by Nestlé in
1988. The combination of Nestlé's Moulded range with the strong Rowntree

Countlines suddenly created a new competitor who was bigger than Cadbury. Plus, Beacon was by now making themselves a nuisance by launching their own Moulded range.

Although Cadbury had always had Countlines such as Crunchie in their range, it was clear that they would only be market leaders by competing much harder in that sector. A range of new Cadbury Countlines were developed in the space of a few years, including Lunch Bar, Snacker, P.S. Bar and Astros with the result that, along with proven favourites such as Crunchie and Flake, by 1995, Cadbury was snapping at the heels of Nestlé for leadership of the Countline sector, which was almost double the size of Moulded. Cadbury was using the Chocolate Eclairs brand to compete in the Sugar category and added to that with the purchase

of South Africa's leading bubble gum brand, Chappies. Both these brands, due to being sold by the individual sweet at low price points, were able to reach much deeper into the poorer parts of the population than was Dairy Milk, whose price point was at this time restricting it largely to the wealthier individual.

By 1995 Cadbury had wrested leadership of the chocolate market away from Nestlé and built a strong number two position in the combined chocolate and sugar markets behind

Beacon. But future success would not so much reside in fighting over share of the existing market, but by being the fastest to develop the lower-income markets in the new political climate. Although the company had increasingly been building distribution in the Townships and directing advertising to emerging market media, this was then complimented by producing much smaller Moulded bars to reach more affordable price points. Cadbury would further build its position in the South African market by drawing on both the learnings and the product range of the acknowledged experts in the world of Cadbury on developing lower-income markets – India.

India

In 1978, Cadbury had reduced their shareholding in their Indian business down to 40% to comply with government regulations that overseas-owned companies be 'Indian-ised'. Many consumer goods companies as a result closed down their Indian operations, not being willing to relinquish full ownership. Indeed, Coca Cola pulled out as they could not countenance the prospect of perhaps having to reveal their top-secret formula to company outsiders. Cadbury had worked too hard at developing their presence in India to back out now and willingly complied. However, the arrangement

tested resolve at both ends. The Indian business – renamed Hindustan Cocoa Products Ltd. – was starved of technical know how, and Cadbury in the U.K. received very little profit. But the local shareholders knew full well that the value of their investment depended entirely on the continued building of the Cadbury brand name in India.

Although Bournvita and the local Countlines were increasing sales, the great leap forward came in 1984 when the powder-based milk chocolate was replaced by Dairy Milk. This had been made possible by the spectacular success of Operation Flood, a nationwide scheme to boost Indian milk production and consumption. With greatly expanded supplies of fresh milk, Cadbury was able to both get out of running their own dairy farm, which was developed into a modern chocolate factory, and finally bring Dairy Milk to the market. The production of Dairy Milk involved little extra capital as spare Bournvita capacity could be used for crumb-making, (Bournvita having been developed in 1930s Bournville as an asset-utilisation exercise using the crumb process.)

Unlike as had been the case in Cadbury's post-War German venture, where the replacement of a milk-powder-based product by Dairy Milk had failed, Dairy Milk was immediately embraced by the Indian

consumer who found the fresh milk message to be a powerful motivator on the new medium of television advertising. The 1985 annual report of Hindustan Cocoa Products sums up the impact,

...the new launch of this improved product met with such instant success that you will be pleased to know that today consumers are demanding "Cadbury's Dairy Milk." Similarly a major programme for packaging design changes was also undertaken resulting in a whole range of attractively packaged and presented Cadbury products which are very prominent and visible on shop shelves in the market place today.

Aided by the launch of Dairy Milk and the rolling out of the company's first open display equipment – the Sheet Metal Dispenser – for the newly-presented range, the rather sedate growth rate of the business was turbo-charged with sales trebling in the next six years. The broad range of Cadbury-branded Countlines kept emerging local competitors at bay, and also restricted the impact of Nestlé's entry into the market in the late 1980s.

But in the early 1990s the business stagnated as growth in the company's two leading brands of Bournvita and Dairy Milk ground to a halt. Bournvita had been afflicted by a disastrous product innovation of 'Added Glucose' which created a massive product quality problem where the contents of the entire pack would, under certain conditions, solidify. This would take years to overcome, but the health and wellness thought would not be lost in that a key selling point for Bournvita today is its new vitamin and mineral enriched formula.

With Dairy Milk, the only problem was that the existing market seemed to have reached its limit. Up to that point in India, chocolate had been seen as an occasional treat for children. For Cadbury India (as it had now been renamed once again) to keep growing, it had to make chocolate a legitimate category for adults. The signs were promising – Indians have a very sweet tooth – so the barriers were more attitudinal. The answer came with spectacular effect when Cadbury launched a new advertising campaign for Dairy Milk in 1994. Known as 'The Real Taste of Life', the campaign captured moments when people shook off convention and broke free revealing their real selves, demonstrating that Dairy Milk was not only for kids but for the kid in everyone. The most memorable advertisement in the campaign, when the famous model Shimona dances onto a cricket pitch at a key moment, was awarded India's advertising campaign of the century.

Aided by other initiatives such as a range of smaller-sized products at the attractive 5 Rupee price point, a slew of new products and a much greater sales coverage – over a million stores – the Cadbury India business trebled again between 1994 and 1999. The chocolate category had been moved from occasional indulgence for children to impulse snacking for all ages, and the Cadbury brand is increasingly reaching down into the less affluent mass of Indian consumers. Despite a significant presence of the key Mars brands in addition to those of Nestlé, Cadbury's market share stands at over 70%, with their sales having doubled again between 1999 and 2006.

But the strength of the Cadbury brand in India was given the stiffest

test imaginable in 2003 when the company was engulfed in a crisis. In October that year, a handful of the 30 million bars of Dairy Milk bought every month in India were found to be infested with insect grubs. This, unfortunately, is an occupational hazard in the chocolate industry, especially in warm climates, and is almost always caused by poor storage conditions in retail outlets. But the issue got an enormous level of media coverage, which had an immediate and dramatic impact on sales of Cadbury's products.

For the first three-quarters of 2003, Cadbury's sales had been running at a 16% increase versus the previous year; in the last quarter, sales were 24% down. Consumer research indicated major shifts in consumer sentiments among those who were aware of the media hullabaloo versus those who weren't. Of the blissfully unaware, over 80% of them agreed with the statements that they would buy Cadbury products for their children, whereas for those aware of the issue, only 40% of people agreed.

This, not unnaturally, prompted a major response by the company. The top-selling 5 Rupee bar of Dairy Milk was given an extra layer of sealed packaging, with other sizes having their foil heat-sealed. A 'Purity sealed' graphic was developed and placed prominently on all packaging,

advertisements and display materials. In addition to the usual panoply of media desks, press briefings, direct mail to mothers' organisations and the like aiming to clarify the facts and restore faith, the trump card was a new advertising campaign that tackled the issue head-on.

Bollywood superstar, Amitabh Bachchan, was signed up to be Cadbury's spokesman on the issue. Known throughout India simply as 'Big B', Amitabh had enormous credibility with the Indian public, a fact that was central to the advertisement. Speaking direct to camera, Amitabh emphasised that he would not risk his credibility for the sake of an advertisement, and had been round the Cadbury factory to see for himself,

So, when Cadbury officials approached me to talk to you on their behalf, I hesitated, even though I love Cadbury chocolates. I asked them a question: "After this, will I ever get a good night's sleep?" In answer, they took me to their factory and showed me their international technology, their strict quality controls and double-protection packaging. These days, I sleep very well at night…

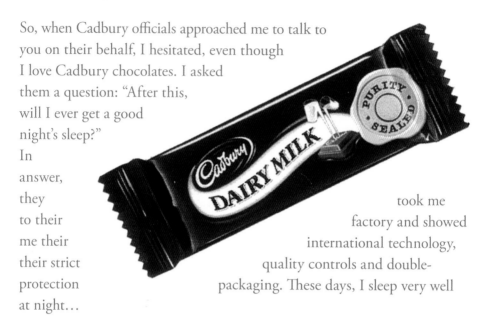

The outcome of the combined initiatives was a dramatic recovery. With confidence fully restored, Cadbury sales in India stabilised in 2004 and in 2005 sales shot up by 17%, such that in September that year their market share touched a ten-year high of 73%. As early as the year 2000, India had surpassed Australia as the second-largest market in the world for sales of Cadbury's Dairy Milk. With the law of large numbers on its side, it surely can only be a matter of time before it overtakes the U.K.

The overseas companies, with the exception of Canada, succeeded in the four crucial tasks that faced them in the latter quarter of the 20th-century:

- Maintaining Dairy Milk as by far the pre-eminent brand in the Moulded sector;
- Keeping the Moulded sector relevant and contemporary, and at the heart of the confectionery market;
- Building a presence across the whole range of product categories
- Keeping the Cadbury brand strong and dynamic, and a key part of their marketing and selling success.

Cadbury's decentralised approach to the management of the various companies was a significant strength during this period. As the U.K. was still by far the largest Cadbury operation, any approach to a more centralised style would have been U.K.-centric and thus completely unsuited to the problems, opportunities and local capabilities in the other markets. Largely because of its unique pre-war business model, the Bournville operation was the outlier in the Cadbury group. In addition, there was no thought in those days to regional or global sourcing strategies: each business unit had its own factory and was fully self-supporting, so brand portfolios and recipes could be tweaked to suit the local markets with no loss of manufacturing efficiencies. This did result in some differences between markets in the taste and packaging design of Dairy Milk in the earlier years, but these were progressively ironed out. The important commonality was the role Dairy Milk played as the bedrock of the Cadbury name, reputation and market success.

Cadbury's continued success in their overseas markets also demonstrated that the Cadbury brand was not solely a U.K. phenomenon. The failures to establish the brand in Germany and America were now fading memories. As the business had entered the late 1980's, extending into new territories and also new categories had risen again to the top of the agenda.

Chapter 15

EXTENDING THE GEOGRAPHIC AND CATEGORY FOOTPRINTS

Cadbury®™

怡口莲 原味

牛奶巧克力夹心太妃糖
Milk Chocolate Filled Toffee

净含量: 200克

Despite the ill-fated ventures in post-War Germany and America, Cadbury had never really stopped looking to expand overseas, and had been gradually extending into new countries on an opportunistic basis, sometimes as a consequence of their tropical ventures into opening up new cocoa-growing areas.

Early Emerging Markets

A project in the mid-1950's to explore the potential for cocoa-growing in Nigeria had led to the setting up in 1965 of a new company, Cadbury Nigeria Ltd. to handle local manufacturing, in addition to selling imported lines such as Bournvita from India. Bournvita soon became the dominant food drink in the country, and a new factory was built in 1967 near Lagos to meet the demand. The enduring success of Bournvita in Nigeria – it is still Cadbury's largest-selling brand in the entire African continent – owed much to its rather unique brand positioning there. In the U.K., it had always been sold as being essential to a good night's sleep, whereas in Nigeria, in stark contrast, Bournvita promised boundless energy and endurance.

Further locally produced products were added to the range, but none would be chocolate bars due to the perceived inhospitality of the climate. Tomapep was a spicy, tomato-based mix for addition to stews, and was soon joined by Tom-Tom, a cough-sweet that became Nigeria's top-selling confectionery product. The Smash technology was even used to launch a line of instant yams, called Poundo Yam. Goody Bar – a chewy toffee bar with no chocolate covering – was the closest the product range came to a line that would have been recognisable to Bournville until Nigeria's launch of Cadbury's Chocolate Eclairs in the 1970's.

Eclairs proved itself the ideal product to introduce low-income consumers in hot climates to the taste of chocolate, being temperature tolerant, individually wrapped and thus able to be sold by the piece.

Following the relative success enjoyed by the rather unique Nigerian

operation, it was soon followed by the establishment of broadly similar operations in Kenya and Ghana, together with a joint venture in Rhodesia with local player, Crystal Candy. But outside of Africa, a more traditional approach to building the Cadbury brand involving the local manufacture and sale of Dairy Milk and other Moulded lines was still seen as the best way to go. The economic development of Malaysia in the years following its independence in 1973 had prompted Cadbury to set up a stand-alone business there – the first multi-national chocolate player to do so – again following their local knowledge gained from the cocoa industry. A small factory was built in the city of Shah Alam, close to the capital, Kuala Lumpur, in the late 1970s making milk chocolate using a low-cost technology to make a milk powder recipe chocolate.

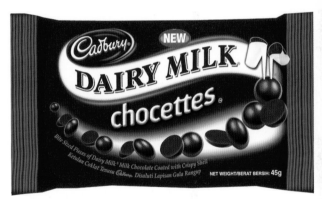

The key to being able to produce Dairy Milk chocolate locally in emerging markets lay in the development of a new chocolate crumb/milk chocolate-making process that required much less up-front cost. The science and technological innovation to enable such a move eventually came together in the 1980s. This low-cost chocolate-making technology meant that small factories could be established at acceptable cost, which would give an infant business

time to grow organically, without the incessant pressure of having to fill an expensive factory to cover the overheads.

This new crumb-making technology was introduced into the Malaysian factory in 1987 and enabled Cadbury to develop the largest product range of any manufacturer in Malaysia. The new Dairy Milk moulded range was introduced, along with Chocettes (chocolate-covered pieces), and the temperature-tolerant Chocolate Eclairs, which, together with their existing chocolate-covered wafer brand called Zip, enabled Cadbury to participate in all key sectors of the market. Along with Cadbury having bought out their distributor in 1983 and establishing their own direct sales force, the ground was now set.

With a substantial local middle class target market to aim at, serviced by a good infrastructure of air-conditioned supermarkets, Cadbury has subsequently built up a market-leading position in Malaysia, being some 2.5 times bigger than the nearest competitor, Nestlé. However, not all such ventures were equally successful. Cadbury Indonesia, established in 1986, struggled building a chocolate business based on Moulded bars due to there being virtually no middle-class section of the population. Wealthy consumers would buy imported Swiss chocolates, while the vast majority of relatively impoverished inhabitants would buy cheap, low-quality local products. The Cadbury chocolate business in Indonesia almost continually lost modest sums, and chocolate production ceased there in 2007, the market then being supplied by imports.

Cadbury's expansionist ambitions would remain relatively modest until 1988, when they embarked on a new path of growth through acquisition. The strategy was three-fold: to acquire new overseas chocolate businesses; to opportunistically establish new Cadbury businesses; and to get serious about their participation in the sugar confectionery category. All three routes would be explored virtually simultaneously in what was a major change of direction for the company. The fragmented global confectionery market was ripe for consolidation, and Cadbury Schweppes was determined that their confectionery interests should be leading that process.

The Acquisition Trail

Any strategy to acquire new chocolate companies of sufficient size would inevitably involve the European continent, where the category was most developed. This time though, the lessons of the German and American ventures would be well remembered. It was by now clear that there were different local tastes for chocolate around the world, the three major ones being Cadbury in the British Commonwealth, Hershey in North America, and the Swiss/German/Belgian type in Europe and South America. This being the case, Cadbury looked for companies with existing strengths within confectionery rather than mere vehicles to try and propagate the Dairy Milk brand.

The first major acquisition was of the number 3 chocolate player in France, and one with as long and as proud a heritage as Cadbury, Chocolat Poulain, which was purchased for £100 million. This was a big acquisition for Cadbury and sent a clear signal of their major change in direction. Although Cadbury senior managers were sent over to Poulain's two factories in Blois to search for suitable Poulain products that could be launched in the U.K., and the Poulain management reviewed the

Cadbury range for potential launch in France, there were few sales synergies to be exploited. The acquisition of a Spanish chocolate company a year later in 1989, Chocolates Hueso would also be run largely as it had been prior to Cadbury's ownership, and was further evidence that the goal of building Cadbury as a consumer brand in Western European markets would be a difficult task.

Sugar

Although the company had some interests in Sugar confectionery with the U.K. acquisition of Pascall Murray in 1964, and Australia's purchase of Choice Confectionery that had come with the Red Tulip deal, these had been more tactical than strategic. But the continued concentration of confectionery sales into the large Grocery chains had changed the equation.

As early as the 1960's Cadbury in the U.K. had found it increasingly difficult to exercise control over displays in the summer months when warm weather depressed sales of chocolate, especially Moulded bars. Mars had made great play of the summer sales potential of their range of Spangles and Opal Fruits brands, as had Rowntree with Fruit Gums, Fruit Pastilles and Jelly Tots, and even Mackintosh with Tootie Frooties. This dynamic was exacerbated over time by the increasingly powerful grocery chains who treated all confectionery as one category, and thought nothing of shifting space from chocolate to sugar confectionery to chewing gum and back again. To have more influence over how these decisions were made, it had become vital for Cadbury to develop strength across the whole confectionery fixture rather than just in chocolate.

Cadbury's abortive attempts to brand sugar products such as Trillions and Tops had convinced them to keep the Cadbury name well away from the category in future. A 1975 document co-written by Dominic Cadbury made the point clearly,

We should avoid the trap of believing that the Cadbury name of itself will secure a branded franchise for us in the sugar confectionery market...diversification into sugar to be successful needs to be via unique branded lines that can stand up in their own right without depending on the Cadbury name.

in the North of England, followed by the much bigger purchases in March 1989 of Bassett Foods and, six months later, the Trebor Group, merging the two in the following year to form Trebor Bassett Ltd. Cadbury decided to run this new operation completely separately from the Bournville chocolate side, and it would be a much more mobile organisation with little of the Bournville red tape to slow things down.

The range of famous brands acquired by this move was impressive. Bassett's Liquorice Allsorts, Bassett's Jelly Babies, Trebor Mints, Trebor Extra Strong Mints, Maynard's Wine Gums and Sharp's Toffee were all best-selling lines across the country. In 1996, further acquisitions brought the Keiller, Craven's of York, Barker & Dobson and Butterkist brand names into the group. However, with the gems came thousands of not-so-famous products such as Coconut Mushrooms

This advice would be followed when Cadbury came to look for a suitable approach to substantially enlarging their sugar confectionery participation.

The U.K. sugar confectionery market had many players, most of whom had wide ranges of cheap, unbranded lines. But within the morass were some very strong brands spread around the various manufacturers. Cadbury saw the opportunity in being the consolidator of this fragmented industry, and accumulating most of the strong sugar brands not owned by Mars or Rowntree Mackintosh. The first step was the 1988 purchase of Lion Confectionery, a regional manufacturer based

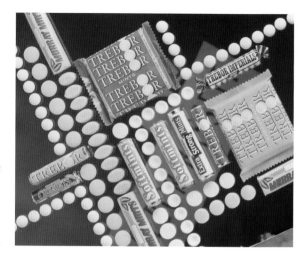

and the like. These, along with many private label packs, would be hived off in 1999 into a separate, low-cost organisation, Monkhill Confectionery.

The strategy of moving into the sugar category would also be used around the world to strengthen existing market positions. Cadbury in New Zealand took the momentous step in 1990 of exchanging its Hudson biscuit business for Beatrice Foods' Griffin's sugar confectionery operation. This swap was emotionally difficult as Cadbury had been teamed up with Hudson's for almost seventy years. But logically the move made much sense and greatly strengthened the ability of the New Zealand company to influence their key customers.

Middle East

Simultaneously with acquiring chocolate and sugar confectionery businesses, Cadbury were still setting up new Cadbury chocolate businesses where circumstances seemed promising. The next such venture in Egypt came as a consequence of the re-opening of Middle-Eastern markets to Cadbury, from which they had been boycotted as a result of Schweppes

operating a subsidiary in Israel. Working with local importer, Kuwait Foods, Cadbury initially addressed this opportunity via a major export drive of Bournville and Cadbury Ireland produced lines. Indeed, so successful was the initiative that Cadbury received the Queen's Award for Export for the only time in their history.

When Kuwait Foods suggested in the late 1980's that Cadbury join with them in setting up a joint enterprise manufacturing and supplying the Egyptian market, Cadbury readily signed on for a 35% share of the new company. A factory was designed, built and operated to Cadbury specifications, and began production of Dairy Milk, Dairy Milk Krisp, and Dairy Milk Hazelnut in 49 gram bars. However, even with a relatively low-cost factory, the extremely low disposable income of the average Egyptian meant that the Cadbury products were only affordable to the very top end of the market. With a target market of expats and the rich elite buying through the relatively small number of air-conditioned shops, the business struggled to get off the ground.

To rectify the situation, a range of much smaller Moulded bars was launched that would be cheap enough to be of relevance to the vast armada of street kiosks, who were selling much smaller and cheaper locally-produced chocolate bars. In addition, production of Chocolate Eclairs was ramped up as this was a line that was much more temperature tolerant (the kiosks not being air conditioned), and could also be sold singly at very low price points. As a consequence, the business moved back into profit, albeit marginally so.

Salvation lay in the 1997 acquisition of a strong local player, Bim-Bim, who was the market leader, and dominant in the kiosk trade. Since the acquisition, Cadbury Egypt has used Bim-Bim's distribution strength and low-cost production facilities to market the Cadbury brand to Egypt's emerging middle class. Smaller product sizes – down to a 13 gram bar – hitting key price points are introducing the Cadbury brand in an affordable manner. The Bim-Bim acquisition gave the Cadbury brand the critical components of affordability and availability; the revised product range corrected the required balance between quality, value and competitive advantage; all supported by awareness-building advertising which positioned the Cadbury brand as a more relevant, but still aspirational brand built on a platform of quality.

The Americas

Cadbury's first venture into South America came in 1993 with the acquisition of Argentina's leading chewing gum business, Stani. As Stani already had a range of sugar confectionery products, it seemed that the addition of a Cadbury chocolate range would create a confectionery

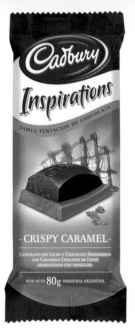

powerhouse company with strengths in all three key sectors. The excellent Stani sales and distribution capabilities could be used to rapidly build a retail profile for the Cadbury brand, whose products would be manufactured from a Cadbury-designed chocolate factory bolted onto the existing Stani facility.

The usual Moulded bar range was rolled out, but encountered a similar mixture of the problems Cadbury was simultaneously encountering in Egypt. While Argentina also had a large street kiosk trade servicing a largely un-affluent consumer base, just to compound matters, in the large, air-conditioned supermarket serving the affluent shopper Cadbury were facing two well-entrenched competitors in Nestlé and, in particular, Suchard's Milka. With an established Milka brand positioning based entirely on alpine milk, Cadbury's Dairy Milk was not able to establish itself on its milk credentials. Although the Stani business in total continued to thrive, even in the most difficult of economic conditions, the Cadbury brand has still yet to become fully established in Argentina.

Cadbury's purchase of Trebor in 1989 had, by default, brought them back into the Canadian market with Trebor's Canadian subsidiary. This was added to in 1995 with the purchase of a local manufacturer, Allen Candy. Re-entry into the Canadian chocolate market would come a year later when Cadbury bought back the by-now merged Neilson-Cadbury. But even with the scale advantage of being market leader, albeit marginally so, profits would be as hard to come by in the Canadian chocolate category as they had been throughout the history of Cadbury's Canadian involvement.

Eastern Europe

The sudden and unexpected collapse of the Communist regimes in the early 1990's provided an opportunity on a massive scale for all Western consumer goods companies that simply could not be ignored. Cadbury quickly evaluated the options, discarding Russia as being not politically stable enough to set up a manufacturing operation, and markets such as Hungary or Czechoslovakia which did not represent a big enough potential. By far the best option seemed to be Poland; with a large population of around 40 million, it was a significant confectionery market and also had the most advanced liberal legislation amongst the former Communist countries to attract foreign businesses.

Cadbury reviewed the entry options of possible acquisitions or joint ventures, but ended up rejecting both in favour of a Cadbury start-up. Local Polish firms, such as Wedel and Goplana, had been starved of investment for decades, so rather than take on a huge reconstruction task, Cadbury took the decision in 1993 to establish their own factory and selling organisation. £20 million was committed to the building of a new factory near the city of Wroclaw in south west Poland. Spearheaded by three brands, Dairy Milk, Chocolate Eclairs and Picnic, Cadbury were hitting the main sectors of the Polish market; Moulded blocks reigned supreme with nearly half the market, and Countline wafer-based bars had a quarter. In a rapidly-growing market, Cadbury achieved modest success, primarily with teenage consumers, and was making a profit by its third year of operation having taken an 8% market share.

But the new company was on shaky ground. Dairy Milk had failed to establish its taste credentials against the local brand leader, Wedel, who had a long tradition in Poland and had established a preferred taste that was much less milky and sweet than Dairy Milk. For the minority of consumers who preferred a milkier taste, Cadbury was again facing an entrenched Milka brand that already owned the milk credentials. Worse still, Cadbury couldn't even take the low price position, that having been grabbed by another new entrant into the Polish market, Stollwerck, whose entry strategy was to slash their prices for their vast range of Moulded bars and had shot to leadership of the Moulded category within two years. The Moulded category was overcrowded and Dairy Milk was unable to break into being even one of the six best-selling milk Moulded bars. Cadbury were a niche player in the market. More scale and a change in direction were needed.

In 1998, the opportunity arose to purchase Wedel from its first post-communist owners, PepsiCo, who had taken on the reconstruction burden. Wedel were no second-tier player, as had been Peter Paul in America, but had a much more impressive 23% share of the market. This raised a much larger question mark over the future of the Cadbury brand in Poland. Having acquired Wedel, it seemed pointless continuing trying to build the Cadbury name. Wedel was in many ways the Cadbury of Poland with an exceptionally strong bond with Polish consumers. Consequently, the decision was taken to de-prioritise the Cadbury brands and utilise both factories in further developing Wedel; a situation that continues with success to this day.

The Wild East

If Poland had been difficult, Cadbury's next Eastern European venture would prove far tougher. Following the collapse of communism, a local distributor had approached Cadbury and begun importing Cadbury brands into Russia in 1992. Soon the importer was taking all Cadbury could produce and pleading for more. This success was being driven by a seemingly seismic shift in the Russian confectionery market. By 1994, half of all sales were accounted for by imported brands. The impending erection

of tariff barriers, plus the news that Mars were planning to build a Russian factory, prompted Cadbury to put together a joint venture with the distributor who would provide the sales capability for a 30% stake and Cadbury, with 70%, would build a factory in Chudova, mid-way between Moscow and St. Petersburg, of sufficient size to take a serious run at the market with locally produced products.

But Russia was by then earning its status as the new Wild West. The original premise for building a local factory – avoiding tariff barriers – proved to be a burden rather than a benefit. Endemic corruption meant that importers, for a suitable bribe, could avoid the tariffs altogether, while locally-based operations such as Cadbury were hit with swingeing taxes. In

addition, the volume projections had proved wildly exaggerated. Imported western chocolate bars had been bought up in bulk by currency speculators, meaning that much product was locked up in the system, rather than having sold through to the consumer. Cadbury's 1997 sales were less than a quarter of the initial projections.

The company was then hit by the 1998 Rouble crisis when the factory was closed for weeks on end. Cadbury responded by fast-tracking new products from the Chudovo factory more in tune with local preferences for dark chocolate and pralines that had begun to reassert themselves in the market – the Russian love affair with Western brands had proved to be a passing fling. Beginning with a focus on 100g Moulded bars in more premium packaging styles, there soon followed dark chocolate variants of Picnic and Wispa, a "Russian range" of Moulded tablets named Zolotoi Fond, with a locally developed milk-dark chocolate recipe blend that tested extremely well with consumers.

But this was not addressing the core problem: Cadbury was a sub-scale business saddled with high fixed costs and the equally burdensome costs of trying to build national distribution, which together sucked funds away from brand-building investments. Without these millstones, Cadbury could have been a profitable niche player with meaningful participation in Moscow and St. Petersburg and access to the rest of the country via distributors. In a replay of the Peter Paul Cadbury problems, Cadbury Schweppes in 1998 reported a £68 million exceptional charge against profits relating to the writing down of their Russian assets.

But the Russian business was not closed down or sold off. Progress was being made, albeit from a much lower base, and the business broke even for the first time in 2001. Although it had been a rocky road, Cadbury managers reminded themselves that this milestone had been achieved in less than a third of the time it had taken Cadbury to get out of the red in Australia. The situation was eased further when Cadbury Schweppes acquired in 2002 a European-based chewing gum company, Dandy who had significant sales in Russia; the combination creating a much more viable business.

China

The most recent emerging market in Asia to get its own Cadbury local infrastructure is China. Opened in 1995, the factory and selling organisation were set up and run by Cadbury Australia, with the obligatory

joint venture partner providing much of the land and infrastructure. This again was not a smooth start up. Hampered by a lack of reliable market data, sales volumes in the first three years were well below initial targets, and the business was losing over £10 million a year.

While Dairy Milk spearheaded the range, breakeven would be reached in 2000 primarily through the growth of Chocolate Eclairs (by now renamed Choclairs.) This caramel product with chocolate on the inside was proving to be an ideal vehicle for establishing a Cadbury presence in developing markets. Volume of Choclairs increased a hundred-fold in three years to become Cadbury China's largest selling line. It was also a product that had no direct competitor in the line up of Mars, who had got to China before Cadbury and established a strong leadership position in the market. The acquisition in 2000 of local chewing gum company, Wuxi-Leaf, added scale to the Cadbury operation and again eased the time pressure on building the Cadbury name.

Cadbury's Global Position

Since sending their first traveller to Ireland, Cadbury has been working at the internationalisation of their brand for very nearly a century and a half. By 1997, the confectionery arm of Cadbury Schweppes was the fifth-largest confectionery company in the world. Cadbury is the leading chocolate brand in two continents – Australia and Africa; a sub-continent – India, and a host of ex-Empire countries – the U.K., Ireland, Malaysia, Singapore, and New Zealand, and is still

competing hard in Canada. The footholds in China, Russia and to a lesser extent Argentina must be viewed as long-term investments for the future, as explained by Dominic Cadbury,

If we fool ourselves by thinking "We could still be in the market in 10 or 20 years' time when we don't have a competitive manufacturing base, or we're not in the growth markets in the world – India, China, Russia – then we're not going to be there long-term."[1]

However, not all seeds sprout: Western Europe and most of the Americas remain *terra incognita* for the Cadbury chocolate brand. It was apparent that the Cadbury brand would remain a largely British Commonwealth phenomenon. Cadbury failed to become established in these areas for two reasons. Firstly, by the time Cadbury seriously entered the European and American markets, local and-or regional chocolate taste preferences were already deeply entrenched. Secondly, Cadbury's entry strategy of building factories to make Dairy Milk chocolate saddled the start-ups with large fixed asset bases that dominated the local company's profitability, leading to too much haste and not enough investment in developing their route to market and sufficient consumer demand. This contrasts with their inter-war experiences where chocolate preferences were up for grabs and the only way to keep building overseas markets was to build local factories.

In switching to an acquisition strategy, Cadbury tried strenuously to buy very large or international chocolate brands, but most were, and are, beyond the reach of acquisition because of family ownership or, in Hershey's case, trust ownership. As a result, Cadbury bought what was available, local chocolate brands such as Poulain and Wedel; although it did mean that Cadbury's global chocolate position was built on a more fragmented base than would have been ideal. There were far fewer barriers to entry in foreign markets in the sugar category, where the 'First Mover' advantage of defined taste preferences doesn't exist. But sugar confectionery is a very fragmented category and, with few major brands, good profit margins can be hard to come by without large scale. Hence, it was unlikely that chocolate and sugar alone could fulfil Cadbury Schweppes' global ambition to become the world's number one player. That would come with entry into the chewing gum category, which has big brands, high growth and good margins. When combined with chocolate and sugar, a company could approach the big retailers with genuine total confectionery category solutions.

---

[1] *Business Solutions* (West Midlands edition), Issue 13, Feb/Mar 2004

Cadbury saw at first hand how attractive the gum category was with their acquisition of Stani in Argentina, which prompted the search for other opportunities to expand their gum presence. Cadbury bought the leading gum brands in France, Turkey, Northern and Eastern Europe, and China; all the while courting the owners of the world's number 2 gum player, Adams. When their eight-year pursuit of Adams paid off in 2003, Cadbury Schweppes became the number 1 confectionery company in the world – a situation that would have staggered John Cadbury in his Bull Street shop.

However, back in the heartland of the Cadbury brand itself, the 'First Mover' in chocolate markets was not an invulnerable position. If the incumbent fell asleep at the wheel for long enough, disaster could ensue. Hershey had ceded a dominant position in the U.S. market to Mars, only gaining it back via the acquisition of the Peter Paul Cadbury brands. Cadbury in the U.K. was veering towards the ditch until steered back. Having been awoken to the danger, the Cadbury U.K. position would regain much of its former glory by a renewed focus on its enduring strengths in that market: the Cadbury brand and Dairy Milk chocolate.

Chapter 16

U.K. RESURGENCE: CONTEMPORISING THE CADBURY STRENGTHS

Back to the Core

With the transformation of the U.K. factories and cost base in the early 1980s, the time was ripe for Cadbury to put Dairy Milk and the Moulded category back into the heart of their thinking. The recovery of the Moulded sector and Cadbury's share within it was seen as vital to re-invigorating the Cadbury U.K. business. Yorkie had shown that the Moulded category could be grown, even in the face of intense competition from Countlines. In reality, prior to Yorkie, Cadbury had long since given up hope that the Countline tide could ever be turned. They had been stunned to see a major competitor launch a brand into what they considered to be a moribund sector of the market.

The factory investment programme and the accompanying core brand focus meant that the Moulded launches of the early 1970s, such as Old Jamaica, Grand Seville and the like, had been cancelled by 1980, with production now focused on the bare minimum core range of Dairy Milk, Fruit & Nut, Whole Nut and Bournville dark chocolate. The resulting manufacturing efficiencies were ploughed into advertising to drive up demand for the remaining lines. In

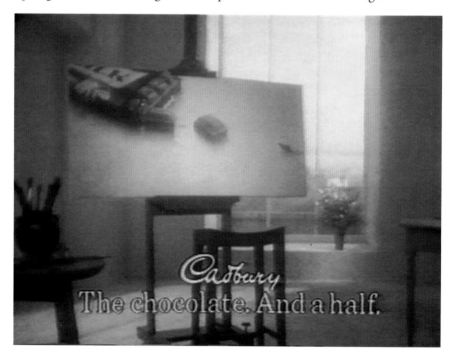

March 1981, a new advertisement for Dairy Milk got right back to the brand's core values: *'Only the Glass and a Half gives you the Taste and a Half that makes Cadbury's Dairy Milk the Chocolate and a Half.'* To make the ad, Cadbury had made what at the time was the world's biggest chocolate bar, weighing in at 72lbs, that had been filmed in slow-motion close-ups to accentuate the deliciousness.

This campaign signalled a new-found confidence in the taste appeal of Dairy Milk chocolate. Cadbury ran a press coupon offer entitled 'It's Your Choice', where the money-off coupon could be clipped one way to give 5p off a bar of Dairy Milk, or clipped another way to give the same discount off 'any other bar of chocolate', expressing confidence that consumers would make the right choice. Which they did – over 90% of the coupons redeemed were for a bar of Dairy Milk. Driven by Dairy Milk, Cadbury gained five share points of the Moulded category in the first half of 1981, with Dominic Cadbury telling the workforce,

Because Cadbury's Dairy Milk has a significance across our entire range, it is reassuring to see our share improve markedly.

The Purple Spine

This significance of Dairy Milk would be leveraged the same year as Cadbury took the momentous decision to put an end to the 1960s notion that Fruit & Nut and Whole Nut should be packaged, marketed and advertised as distinct brands. The previously very divergent packaging designs of Dairy Milk, Fruit & Nut and Whole Nut were dropped, with a new design system being developed that worked across all three. When displayed side-by-side, there could be no mistaking that they were a family, rather than a set of separate brands.

This was the first real step back towards a marketing model that had been at the heart of Cadbury's historical success, and was being brought back into service due to shifts in the world of media. The power of television had already begun to wane while, perversely, it was becoming increasingly expensive. Many packaged goods brands were being priced out by massive growth in the advertising of banks, building societies and automobiles, who were driving up the price of airtime well ahead of inflation. Being able to leverage the Dairy Milk brand in this way was an advantage available to neither Rowntree nor Mars who, when they stopped advertising a second-tier brand, had nothing to fall back on. Cadbury found that, despite the two brands losing their advertising, sales of Fruit & Nut and Wholenut

increased. As individual brands, their packaging had been adding to the visual noise on the display, but as a family with Dairy Milk, now stood out as a 'Purple Spine' running down the centre of every Cadbury display.

The new-found confidence also flowed through to the hyper-competitive range of Family bars that were still the subject of an annual autumnal price war between the major grocery chains. The Cadbury range of 200 gram Dairy Milk and 150 gram Fruit & Nut and Whole Nut were relaunched, each 50 grams heavier and with a proportionate price increase. The result, somewhat counter-intuitively, was an increase in the number of bars sold. This success demonstrated that impulse consumption was not just a dynamic of the corner shop, but operated equally well in the home: the more consumers bought and took home, the more they ate.

This played to a core strength of Dairy Milk: that consumers would eat more Dairy Milk in one sitting than they would competitors' chocolates. This was codified in the Cadbury business with the term *'More-ishness'*. Cadbury's use of fresh, rather than powdered milk, and their unique crumb process, created a combination of flavour and texture that could be enjoyed for longer before the consumer became satiated. Galaxy had attempted to match this effect but, in attempting to still be differentiated from Dairy Milk still had something of the mouth-feel of the continental milk chocolates. Rowntree had always stuck to their own process and taste profile.

But, while Cadbury were gaining share of Moulded, the category was not sharing in the success of the chocolate market, which had by now recovered from the cocoa inflation shock, growing by 20% in the first three years of the 1980s. Moulded's static volumes, which came principally from the decline of Yorkie, contrasted with dynamic growth in the Countline and Chocolate Biscuit Countline sectors, which together were now over four-times the size of the Moulded category. Cadbury's other heartland of Assortments was also doing badly, so if Cadbury were to regain market leadership, they had to find ways to energise the categories in which they had strong market shares.

The best way to expand a Moulded category, as had been demonstrated in Cadbury's overseas markets, was to offer variety and value. In the efficiency focus of the early 1980's, all of the Moulded lines deemed 'non-core' had been cancelled when it seemed that the new efficient production lines at Bournville would be unable to handle a large variety of products.

However, several years of operating experience with the new technology gave Cadbury the confidence to re-introduce in 1987 many old favourites under the banner of 'Cadbury Classics.' Thus, Golden Crisp, Grand Seville and Old Jamaica rose once again from the grave, joined by even older favourites such as Ginger, Apricot & Almond, Turkish and Walnut & Orange.

Cadbury were also rejuvenating their Assortment brands and seasonal ranges. 1987 also saw Roses overtake Quality Street to become the country's largest Assortments brand – an amazing turnaround from when Roses had nearly been

Cadbury news

A Cadbury Schweppes Newspaper

November 1981   P   No. 1

Volume 1 Number 1 and our aims ...

...s Number One of ... newspaper whose ... quite simply, is to ... employees in touch ... the Cadbury con-... business. ... is significant. A ... and deter-... sional identity is ... as a result of ... investment in the ... tion plan, and ... toughest trading situ-... the company has ever

... that Cadbury ... operates as one big ... rather than an ... of separate ... and operations, ... playing its part in ... It is important ... same information

CDM TAKES BIGGER BITE OF MOULDED MARKET

CADBURY CHOCOLATE BARS TOOK AN EXTRA FIVE PER CENT SHARE OF THE MOULDED CONFECTIONERY MARKET IN THE FIRST HALF OF THIS YEAR, REPORTS MANAGING DIRECTOR DOMINIC CADBURY.

He told *News:* "Because some Bournville production with plans to achieve an

discontinued in the 1960's after a botched packaging change had virtually killed the brand franchise. That same year, both the Moulded and Assortments categories grew faster than Countlines for the first time since the rise of Countlines in the 1950s. During the latter half of the 1980's, with a succession of Cadbury-branded innovations, the Cadbury Christmas programme increased in sales by 20% and its market-leading range of Easter Eggs shot up by 50%. Seasonal ranges provided the perfect medium to focus much more on the Cadbury brand equity rather than on the individual product brands, and the success demonstrated the power that still resided in the Cadbury name.

But even with strong performances in rejuvenated market sectors, Cadbury were still neck and neck with Rowntree and Mars in the total market. Cadbury were unable to regain a substantial lead because of the continued growth in market sectors or pack types in which Cadbury had missed out on during their times of crisis in the 1960s and '70s. By 1988, the chocolate Biscuit Countline sector had grown to a massive £500 million with Cadbury barely getting a sniff of it. Conversely, in Ireland, Cadbury's Snack was the leading product in the sector and a primary reason why the company held a market share of 50% there. Similarly, Cadbury in the U.K. had been slow to produce new pack types for the grocery trade and, as a consequence trailed badly in both multipacks and bags of bite-size products. Since Grocers now held 35% of the entire chocolate market, this was a major hindrance.

To grow aggressively in these sectors would require enormous discounts with no guarantee that they would not be matched or even trumped by competitors. For Cadbury to regain a healthy lead in the market profitably, it had to find ways to

increase sales of its existing brands in the massive market for single Countline bars. To do that, it had to harness the latent power of the Cadbury name in that category.

Cadbury Means Chocolate

While the Cadbury name was a huge advantage on a Moulded bar, Easter Egg, box of chocolates or a Christmas tree decoration, it was not really doing much for Cadbury's Countlines. The Cadbury name had never been considered a key selling point of Countlines, which of course it had not been during the sector's heydays of the 1960s and '70s, when good distribution and a television advertisement could virtually guarantee success for a decent product. The Cadbury logo was invariably small and came in a rainbow of different colours, having been designed to fit in with the unique colour scheme of each Countline brand. There was also the added problem that, with the Cadbury name prominent on brands such as Marvel and Smash, it was becoming unclear as to what it stood for beyond a guarantee of good quality.

But, it was reasoned, the values associated with Cadbury in the Moulded, Assortments and Seasonal sectors could work to the benefit of their Countlines if there was complete clarity as to what Cadbury stood for and the name was clearly and consistently visible on all their brands. Cadbury research had highlighted that a substantial proportion of the population thought they were buying Cadbury products when, in fact, they weren't: upwards of a quarter of consumers thought that Mars Bar and Kit Kat were made by Cadbury.

The first move to address this came as an indirect result of one of the first decisions Dominic Cadbury took when he was appointed Chief Executive of Cadbury Schweppes in 1985. The focus of Cadbury Schweppes would be reduced down to confectionery and soft drinks with the sale of their Jeyes operation and the problematic Foods Division, both to management buyouts. At the same time, a similar focus was decreed for the Cadbury name which would now no longer be used on any product that did not contain chocolate or cocoa; it thus being dropped from Marvel and Smash.

Consequently, a consistent Cadbury logo was designed to be featured on all packs. With the Cadbury signature on a purple 'swatch', there would be a clarity and consistency that had been lacking. Every television commercial would end with an equally consistent device where it would appear as if the bottom corner of the screen was being ripped back to reveal the Cadbury signature forming in chocolate. Cadbury display equipment was redesigned with a brighter shade of purple for greater branding of the Cadbury name in-store. While these changes did not create an instantaneous and 100% accurate awareness of which brands were Cadbury's, it was a big step in the right direction. This was to evolve later into a more appetising visual of the Glass and a Half pouring into the Cadbury signature on a chocolate chunk.

There were also dynamics occurring with the market for Countlines that Cadbury could use to its advantage. Although the biggest Mars Bar

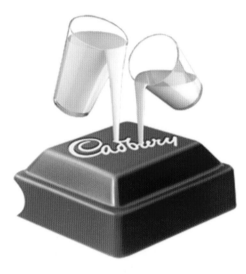

played by the more filling Countlines was being eroded by offerings from other categories and changes in eating habits. Having a Mars Bar for lunch – whether working, resting or playing – was no longer seen by everyone as a perfectly acceptable choice of diet.

Conversely, the Countlines that offered a more indulgent eating experience as an occasional treat, which was a category virtually invented by Cadbury with brands such as Flake and Crunchie, were doing well. The Cadbury name, and Cadbury chocolate, wrapped around a range of products that offered taste, value, pleasure and eating satisfaction was proving to be a potent combination

ever had been a success, similar follow-ups on other brands had struggled to gain a permanent foothold. The core issue was that the meal substitute role

and helped drive consistent gains in Cadbury's sales, market share and profits.

But it was not all plain sailing. Cadbury were perhaps guilty of taking the thinking too far that chocolate could become the primary ingredient of so many different brands. In addition to the Countline size of Dairy Milk, there was Flake, Wispa, Twirl and Spira, all consisting of nothing other than chocolate. Equally, Cadbury's next great effort to conquer the Chocolate Biscuit Countline sector, with the launch of Time Out in 1992, following its successful development and launch in Ireland, was based on the premise of adding a rich layer of Flake between the wafers. The outcome was a reasonably successful brand, but one that was still at the indulgent end of the scale and that left Kit Kat and Twix relatively untouched. But, although boundaries existed to how far the role of Cadbury's chocolate could be pushed, overall it was a very successful reversion to one of the company's core strengths.

The Purple Envelope

As the Cadbury name was now doing much more of the heavy lifting in driving sales, the company could not just rely on its historical strength. When drawing more water from the well of 'Cadburyness', there was a responsibility to top the well up. Cadbury commissioned two pieces of

research, the results of which gave a huge stimulus to Cadbury returning to updated versions of their experiential and presence marketing strategies of the past. An annual piece of research on Britain's most respected brands still showed Cadbury, together with Marks & Spencer, way ahead of the pack, but a key trend was the continued rise up the charts of retail brands such as Sainsbury and Tesco. This, it was hypothesised, came as a result of the prolonged and personal contact the consumer had with these brands in the stores.

Another piece of research on consumer loyalty by age group highlighted that older consumers in general were more likely to buy Cadbury, and that people who had been on one of the old factory tours were much more likely to, even twenty years after the tours had ended. But in the updated Bournville, it was no longer practical to have thousands of people wandering around the factory every day: modern safety and hygiene requirements ruled that out. But a return to the personal, in-depth interaction with Cadbury could play a key role in re-establishing the brand's strength in the U.K. Consequently, in 1988, planning commenced on using part of the Bournville site to build a major visitor attraction.

Opened in the autumn of 1990 and having cost £6 million to build, Cadbury World was a major step into the unknown for the company. Initial estimates that it would attract 250,000 visitors a year were blown out of the water as more than 350,000 crammed in during the first full year of operation. However, it was not without its teething troubles. Not having been designed for that number, busy days could see queues of 2–3 hours to get in. While people accept such prolonged waits in the vast open spaces and warm Florida sunshine of Walt Disney World, they were somewhat less tolerant when standing in the drizzle on a factory site in Birmingham.

But a turnaround plan was quickly put in place before too much damage could be done to the Cadbury reputation – the very thing Cadbury World was supposed to be enhancing. With Cadbury World back on an even keel – annual visitor numbers increased to 420,000, the number of complaints had been reduced by 97% and the finances were close to breaking

even – a longer-term plan was put in place to keep upgrading the exhibition, including a walkway through part of Cadbury's venerable 1930's Chocolate Block which housed Moulded bar production. Now that the concept was proving a success, Australia followed up by redeveloping their long-standing factory tours to encompass more of a multi-faceted Cadbury World experience, as did Cadbury New Zealand.

Cadbury World was the most radical element of a much broader presence marketing strategy. Increasing restrictions on the ability of cigarette companies to advertise their products meant they were going to

be banned from using the vast acreage of shop-front signage to advertise their brands. Cadbury moved quickly to step into the void and were soon signing up thousands of retailers to have their shop-fronts decked out in purple Cadbury signs. This was the old enamel sign strategy magnified a hundred-fold in terms of the visual impact that could now be achieved, coupled with a more purposeful linking of the colour purple with the Cadbury name. Cadbury sponsorships of sporting arenas, theatres and most of the annual pantomimes run around the country added to a huge uplift in the visibility of the Cadbury name.

Surrounding the Consumer with Cadbury

To add to the strategy of enveloping the consumer with Cadbury messages and experiences, Cadbury began to think about how the Cadbury presence could not only be increased in peoples' leisure time but in their shopping baskets and larders.

Their very first venture into a non-confectionery category – Cadbury cakes – had never made any money while Cadbury ran it themselves, and had been sold off in 1982 to a specialist manufacturer and distributor, Manor Bakeries, under a licensing arrangement. The result had been beneficial to both parties. Manor Bakeries had another string to their bow – they also owned the Mr. Kipling and Lyons cakes brands – and Cadbury were profiting from the royalties accruing from Manor Bakeries use of the Cadbury name. The cake range, led by Cadbury's Mini Rolls, had thrived, especially when being joined by new lines such as Flake Cakes and Mini Egg Nests.

After the management buy-out of the rest of the Foods Division, Cadbury also had a similar arrangement with their cocoa beverages and chocolate biscuits, both being sold under license. The new owners of the biscuit range were equally as successful as had been Manor Bakeries with the cakes. Led by the unique Cadbury's Fingers, the range of biscuits was adding another splash of purple into the typical grocery store. There was also a strong Cadbury presence in yet another grocery store aisle, that of hot beverages, with Cadbury's Cocoa and Drinking Chocolate. Both these categories, which had become staid under the latter years of the Foods Division, had benefited from the focus and attention given to them by their new owner.

But there were other product categories in which chocolate was a desirable ingredient, and hence Cadbury could enter as a highly credible brand name, but without the need for the company themselves to build new infrastructures to service. Cadbury's research into their brand name was highlighting that categories such as frozen cakes, toppings, chilled desserts and ice cream would be ideally suited to a Cadbury presence.

Cadbury's first serious licensing venture into a completely new category had been pioneered by their New Zealand operation who, with an 80% market share of chocolate, had more reason than most to see if their strong brands could work in other categories. Working with a local ice cream manufacturer, Crunchie, Moro and Dairy Milk were successfully launched as premium ice cream products. Cadbury Australia immediately followed suit, approaching Streets, who were the Unilever ice cream company in Australia, and already being supplied with chocolate-flavoured coatings by Cadbury Australia's industrial division. But the initiative stumbled as Street's passed on the idea presented by Cadbury of a vanilla ice cream on a stick covered in a thick layer of chocolate with the unique Cadbury flavour. Undaunted, Cadbury found a new supplier, PB Foods Ltd., who could see the potential for a premium ice cream branded as Dairy Milk. In 1994, supported by an absolute commitment to build the market by Australia's number 3 ice cream player, a range of over 20 of Cadbury Australia's brands were launched in ice cream format. Street's would subsequently follow suit without Cadbury branding

and develop the brand that was to become a global hit for Unilever: Magnum.

Cadbury U.K. had also been quick off the mark in following up New Zealand's initiative, and had licensed their brands for development into ice cream products to Unilever's Walls subsidiary in 1991. However, Walls, as the number 1 player in the U.K. ice cream market, did not fully commit behind developing the Cadbury franchise in ice cream, not least because they felt its success might come at the expense of their leading brands such as Magnum and Cornetto. Consequently, Cadbury switched licensee in 1998 to Frederick's, a predominantly private label supplier, reasoning that they would have a good infrastructure and trade contacts, but would make the Cadbury brand their number one focus, which they did.

Similarly, Cadbury's first venture into franchising chilled desserts began with St Ivel in 1992, subsequently moving to Müller in 2002. A Cadbury Cream Liqueur with brandy also hit the shelves but would not succeed in toppling the long-established Bailey's.

Cadbury's U.K. franchising activities became a very successful part of their overall business strategy. By 1998, there were 120 Cadbury branded franchise products spread across 10 different food markets. Cadbury-branded products could be found in 18 of the 32 aisles in the average supermarket. The combined retail sales of the franchised products were over £200 million, nearly 20% of Cadbury's

U.K. confectionery sales. Each franchisee fully appreciated the pulling power of the Cadbury name and did an excellent job in designing packaging which shouted the Cadbury design architecture of purple and the Cadbury signature. The Cadbury name was now more visible to the consumer than it had ever been in the golden inter-war years; their strategy of multiple touch points having come full circle.

The Return of 'Prestige' Cadbury Advertising

There was also a seismic change in Cadbury's television advertising strategy. The continued inflationary increases in the cost of television advertising had made Cadbury's advertising of seventeen different brands impossible to continue with.

The budget was being spread so thin, the danger was that none would achieve sufficient air-time to really break through. The first stage of the solution came in 1996 when Cadbury diverted a substantial portion of their media spend to become the first-ever sponsor of Britain's long-running and immensely popular soap opera, Coronation Street.

The total cost of the initiative to Cadbury was a staggering £10 million, but the potential value was spelled out by an article in *The Sunday Telegraph* newspaper,

For the next 12 months all the goings-on at the Rovers Return will be neatly wrapped at both ends and in the middle with the confectionery giant's familiar icons – the Glass and a Half of full cream milk, the swirling Cadbury's logo and its distinctive purple livery. It is the biggest programme sponsorship ever seen on British television and ensures that Coronation Street's 18m fans will be unlikely to sit down to their thrice-weekly fix without thinking about chocolate. [1]

[1] *The Sunday Telegraph*, September 8th 1996, pp B5-6

The £10 million annual investment was nearly 50% more than that of the confectionery brand with the highest individual advertising budget, Kit Kat, but to have bought the equivalent airtime in Coronation Street's commercial breaks would probably have cost double the amount. So successful was the arrangement that it would continue for over ten years.

Back on Top

The early 1990's also saw Cadbury put further support and focus behind their Moulded range and the Dairy

Milk brand. An incursion into the U.K. market by Suchard's Milka brand was decisively beaten off as Cadbury quadrupled their Dairy Milk advertising budget in a swift and aggressive defence of their heartland. The 1kg block idea was borrowed from Australia, and in 1995 and 1996, the Cadbury Moulded range more than doubled in size as new product ideas, such as Black Forest, Swiss Chalet, Cappuccino and Double Fudge Dream were borrowed from other Cadbury operations.

The strategy was to offer variety by what was, in effect, a controlled obsolescence programme, a concept that had been working so well for Cadbury in Australia. The moving in and out of new flavours and recipes played on the consumer's search for, and enjoyment of, variety; trust in Cadbury as a brand; bringing news and excitement to the Moulded category, and a strong desire by Cadbury to hold onto their hard-won shelf-space as some of the lines were withdrawn from the market.

By 1995, after three years of increases in volume, advertising spend, profits and market share, Cadbury had regained clear leadership of the U.K. chocolate market with a 29% share, leaving the newly-merged Nestlé -Rowntree and Mars trailing in their wake with 25% and 21% shares respectively. In the ten years between 1985 and 1995, Cadbury's U.K. tonnage sales increased by 50%, more than double the rate of the market. They had four of the top ten best-selling Countlines while still ruling the Moulded sector. By 1998, Cadbury's share of the total chocolate market would be back over the 30% mark.

Playing on Home Turf

Cadbury's focus on their core strengths, updated to the 1990's, had proved to be a decisive move. In contrast, the Mars Countline brands were becalmed; hit by the double-whammy of changes in eating habits and the relative decline of the pulling power of television advertising. Mars were now enviously eyeing Cadbury's strength in indulgent products and seasonal ranges in a complete reversal of what had happened in the 1960s when Cadbury had pined for gut-busting Countlines.

Mars transformed their habits of a lifetime and rolled out increasing numbers of new brands, all targeted at Cadbury's indulgent strengths, Galaxy Caramel was put up against Cadbury's Caramel; Galaxy Ripple against Flake; and to muscle

in on the Roses territory came Celebrations. Cadbury would not sit back and under-estimate the Mars threat. Aggressive price promotions and advertising plans were rolled out on Caramel and Flake. Cadbury rushed out their own version of the Celebrations concept – which was a selection of twist-wrapped small versions of major brands – called Cadbury's Miniature Heroes. All this activity stimulated the market into further growth, but it had decisively tilted the battle back onto Cadbury's home turf of indulgence. Cadbury now held the incumbent's advantages and easily shrugged off the Mars efforts to dislodge them.

The Final Pieces of the Jigsaw

A key change in how Cadbury looked at its own business came in the late 1990's when Cadbury Schweppes adopted a managing for shareholder value philosophy under the direction of the Chief Executive, John Sunderland. Such was the importance attached to this shift that John visited every major and many minor business units to communicate it personally to the company's senior managers. This entailed a much more rigorous, fact-driven approach to the identification of gaps, evaluation of opportunities and decision-making. Cadbury's U.K. chocolate division, as the largest confectionery business unit in the Cadbury Schweppes group, put a high level of resource into ensuring that 'Managing For Value' became the new operating mantra.

One clearly-identified opportunity was that Cadbury needed to return to its long-lost position as the industry's leading sales organisation, rather than still tacitly accepting the 30:30:30:10 split of display space that had worked to the company's favour in the late 1970's. During the 1980s, the economics of servicing small independent retailers with direct deliveries had changed, and Cadbury actively reduced the number of independent retailers it took orders from, the slack being picked up by the now much more proficient Wholesale and Cash & Carry sectors. Cadbury had sought to maintain its ability to influence the display in those shops with a separate Cadbury sales force that carried stock in the car and could sometimes take an order on the wholesaler's behalf. But the reality was that, as the number of directly-serviced accounts reduced, so had the size of the Cadbury sales force.

Reinvestment in feet on the street had begun in the mid-1990s, but the real step change came as a consequence of the merger in the U.K. of Cadbury with Trebor Bassett in 2001. The newly created Cadbury Trebor Bassett (CTB) was a clear leader of the British confectionery market, with annual sales of £1 billion and nearly 29% share of the combined chocolate and sugar confectionery markets, compared with 22% for Mars and 18% for Nestlé-Rowntree.

Most crucially, and unusually in a merger situation, the new 600-strong sales force was larger than had been the two separate ones and was by far the largest in the confectionery industry. The CTB sales force was now calling on 80% of the U.K.'s 6,000 grocery outlets and 60% of the 87,000 independent outlets – the best level of coverage they had had since the Second World War – and making a substantial step-change in the availability and display of Cadbury, Trebor and Bassett brands.

In the major grocery chains, the new sales team was able to affect a complete break from the past and build a completely new relationship for Cadbury. The grocery sector was critical to success as by now it accounted for nearly half of the £4 billion confectionery market, so Cadbury Trebor Bassett heavily resourced new Trade Marketing and individual Customer Marketing teams. Within three years, CTB had achieved Category Captaincy or Preferred Supplier status with over 35% of grocery customers – up from 6% at the time of the merger. This was the real benefit of combining the market leaders in both chocolate and sugar confectionery into one industry behemoth.

At the store level, CTB's focus was on "the last fifty yards". Investments in pre-merchandised display units, shelf-ready packaging and mobile "Impact Teams" made sure that their products were on display, all the time, and in the best positions. In 2004, the impact of CTB's dynamic approach with the grocery trade was highlighted when the company won the *Grocer* magazine's Gold Award. It had been a long haul to achieve this position from the dark days of the 1960's when Cadbury were on the brink of refusing to supply the likes of Tesco because of their price-cutting.

A Broader Dairy Milk Brand

The impact of this retail strength would be turbo-charged by further mobilising of the consumer pulling-power of the Dairy Milk brand. A review in the mid-1990s of Cadbury's global brand portfolio had produced the sobering statistic that they were marketing more than a hundred brands, including twenty that were all essentially a wafer covered in chocolate. The review concluded that,

Cadbury's product variety is a strong competitive advantage as consumers desire a variety of confectionery experiences, and variety drives trial and consumption. However, Cadbury's brand variety is a competitive disadvantage because marketing efforts become fragmented and difficult to focus, and, in some cases, Cadbury brands are competing more with each other than they are with competitors.

In 2002, the main global Cadbury markets agreed to the radical step of substantially reducing the number of brands the company would actively market and advertise. Rather than just cancel brands from the portfolio – history had shown that the lost volume was never recovered from the remaining lines – brands would be reincarnated as variants of the Dairy Milk brand. Thus Wispa became Dairy Milk Bubbly; Caramel became Dairy Milk Caramel, and so on. This was again returning full circle to where Cadbury had started off. With a greater emphasis on the Cadbury signature, purple and Glass and a Half, the Cadbury range was unmistakable on the shelf and paved the way for Cadbury in the U.K. to return to the kind of display dominance that had characterised their inter-war successes.

The impact of expanding the breadth of the Dairy Milk brand, combined with what was now clearly the best sales force in the industry, was substantial. The brand in the U.K. grew by 14% and then 22% in consecutive years. By 2004, Dairy Milk had annual sales in the U.K. of £324 million; dwarfing Galaxy at £79 million and Yorkie at £23 million. It is difficult to believe that Cadbury once feared Yorkie could steal Dairy Milk's crown.

This strength of the expanded Dairy Milk brand also transformed the fortunes of the U.K. Moulded category, which by 2004, was nearly double its low point of two decades previously. The once feared Countline category had ceased to eat away at Cadbury's heartland. That same year, Cadbury's share of the U.K. chocolate market reached its highest level for over thirty years: a clear demonstration that the brand health in the U.K. had been fully restored.

Part V

OVERVIEW

Chapter 17

THE CADBURY BRAND: A PERSONAL VIEW

BETTER BUSINESS

MAURICE·C·
WILLIAMS

BOURNVILLE 1928

Thanks to its strength in the three main global categories of chocolate, sugar confectionery and chewing gum, Cadbury Schweppes is the world's leading confectionery company. But it is chocolate with which the Cadbury name is indelibly associated in the minds of consumers. Around the world, Cadbury chocolate has never been more ubiquitous than it is today. It has the greatest reach, consumer awareness, and sales presence than at any time in its history. As we have seen, Cadbury has not managed to conquer the entire globe as the definitive brand of chocolate – but then neither has anyone else. There are global product brands, such as Mars Bar, but no definitive global chocolate house name.

However, in the markets where Cadbury have been able to successfully take root, they have managed it mostly with spectacular effect. Consumers in Cadbury's main overseas markets believe that Cadbury is not only the definitive chocolate brand, but a brand that is indigenous to their own country.

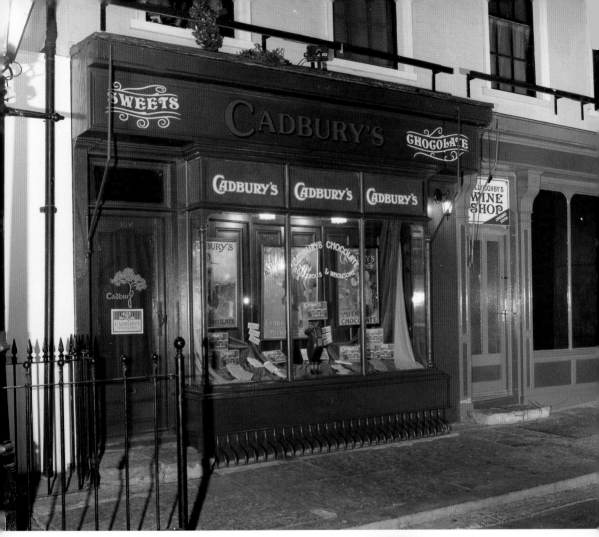

In both Australia and New Zealand, Cadbury is regularly voted as being the most trusted brand in the country. In 1997, on the fiftieth anniversary of Cadbury setting up their Indian company, Cadbury was voted by consumers as being the country's top brand in a major poll run by the Indian *Economic Times*. No other single chocolate house name has managed to achieve such close bonds with so many consumers around the globe. Cadbury, a brand that originated at the dawn of mass consumerism, is a brand of the masses.

So what are the ingredients that have taken the Cadbury name from a shop front in Birmingham on to billions of chocolate bars; cakes; biscuits; hot beverages; desserts; ice creams and the like, consumed every year around the world? I believe there are four core elements that have contributed to the building of the Cadbury brand as we know it today:

- Market-defining product brands: Cocoa Essence and Dairy Milk.
- A capacity for reinvention.
- A part of consumers' lives, throughout their lives.
- A unique combination of business strategies and corporate values.

Market-Defining Brands: Cocoa Essence and Dairy Milk

For the first quarter-century of their existence, Cadbury were indistinguishable from many of their competitors. For the next half century they were absolutely defined by Cocoa Essence. Without Cocoa Essence, none of us today would have

heard of the Cadbury name. It saved the Cadbury Brothers' struggling enterprise barely before it had got off the ground.

Cadbury's Cocoa Essence was certainly an early pioneer as a branded product, pre-dating such luminaries as Royal Baking Powder (1873), Heinz Tomato Ketchup (1875), Colgate Dental Cream (1877), P&G's Ivory soap (1879), Lever's Sunlight Soap (1884), Del Monte (1891), Maxwell House Coffee (1892), and Campbell's soup (1897). But being first out of the blocks was not the secret of its success.

Neither was the notion of betting on the concept of quality. In the mid-late 19th-century, many early branded products focused on product quality in order to differentiate themselves from substandard alternatives. Just as George and Richard Cadbury aimed to match the best continental cocoas, William Lever's Sunlight Soap sought to emulate the oil-based Castile soaps of the wealthy elite. Equally, the notion of avoiding product adulteration was also a popular tactic in many product categories. Henry Heinz packed his pickles in clear jars, as opposed to the normal opaque vessels; this being to demonstrate the product as being free of the twigs, leaves and other assorted foliage used by his less quality-conscious competitors to pad out their offerings. P&G's brand leader, Ivory, was advertised for decades as being over 99 percent pure.

What made Cadbury's Cocoa Essence such a success for the company, and so critical to the building of the Cadbury brand itself, was the fact that, having been first in the U.K. with the idea of a pure cocoa, the company ceaselessly campaigned for the idea of product purity itself. While their advertisements for Cocoa Essence never missed an opportunity to point out the alleged dangers of adulterants, it was the combination of George Cadbury's passionate advocacy against adulterants, together with the company's extremely bold move to cancel their non-pure cocoa lines, that helped make purity the defining characteristic of the emerging mass market for cocoa.

TAKE CARE

when drinking Cocoa to have the pure article only, as many so-called "Pure" Cocoas contain added matter that is not only unnecessary, but often positively harmful.

CADBURY'S COCOA

ABSOLUTELY PURE, therefore BEST.

REFRESHING—NOURISHING—INVIGORATING.

The *LANCET (May 27th, 1899)* says :

"The statement that Cadbury's Cocoa is an absolutely pure article cannot be controverted in view of the results of analysis which, in our hands, this excellent article of food has yielded."

When asking for Cocoa, insist on having **CADBURY'S**—sold only in Packets and Tins—as other Cocoas are sometimes substituted for the sake of extra profit.

On receipt of Post Card *giving name and address, and mentioning* "The Graphic."

A FREE SAMPLE

of Cocoa will be sent by CADBURY BROTHERS, Limited, Bournville, near Birmingham.

As newly-moneyed consumers were looking for guidance on how to spend their wages, the Cadbury name acted as a lighthouse, guiding them to think about purity when buying their cocoa. And as Cocoa Essence completely owned the concept of purity, it was inevitable that it would become the market's leading brand. The morphing of the brand name in the company's advertisements, from Cadbury's Cocoa Essence to Cadbury's Cocoa, sealed the deal in the consumers' minds in terms of building a distinctive and relevant profile for the Cadbury brand name.

For a company to achieve such a feat once is rare, but to do so twice is remarkable. In the last 100 years, Cadbury's fate has hinged primarily on

the performance of its leading brand, Dairy Milk. Dairy Milk has held the position of being the company's largest brand since 1914 and is currently enjoying its highest ever sales, having increased a further 7% globally in 2005.

Cadbury's Dairy Milk became the U.K.'s leading chocolate brand by standing for quality and value. Cadbury initially defined quality as being related to the nutritional benefits of the milk. As Dairy Milk had taken ownership of these benefits through their product name, recipe, production process, logistics strategy and advertising message, they were leading the debate in consumers' minds. The Dairy Milk product itself was better tasting than anything else on the market. There was a compelling reason to buy it, and a compelling reason to keep buying it.

But the position was not invulnerable. Milk, per se, was not a defendable benefit. Any competitor could, in theory, add more milk, fortified milk, low fat milk or creamier milk to trump Dairy Milk. So Cadbury protected Dairy Milk's position, and in the process increased the market size several-fold, through a highly aggressive value strategy. Constant price cuts crushed all chance of a significant competitive response. At a time when affordability was the key barrier to consumption, the Cadbury business model provided the lowest prices and the highest advertising spend for this market-defining brand, making it the choice of a nation. In the overseas markets, competitors' unwillingness to match Cadbury's boldness in vaulting tariff barriers gave Dairy Milk the time to build powerful positions and define the chocolate preference.

Cadbury also benefited from two immensely powerful advertising ideas. *A Glass and a Half of Full Cream Milk in Every Half Pound'* had its inception in an initial advertisement showing a cup of milk pouring into a 2d bar. If it had remained this way, it is questionable that Dairy Milk would have reached the heights that it has. The creativity of the Glass and a Half symbol pouring into the half pound bar turbo-charged the idea. It immediately became even more potent for the company than had

THERE'S HALF · A CUP OF ENGLISH FULL CREAM MILK IN EVERY CADBURY 2ᴰ MILK BAR

been *Absolutely Pure, Therefore Best* a generation earlier. Each of these campaigns ran for decades – 'Glass and a Half' still features nearly eighty years after its inception – and was able to do so because they defined in a memorable way how consumers should view each category.

Cadbury did not just launch two strong brands; in each case the company moulded consumers' frame of reference. In both cases, the brands would only face problems due to shifts in those frames of reference decades later. As product adulteration became a long-distant memory, Van Houten redefined the cocoa category to be about taste, texture and aroma. Equally, for a long time it looked like Countlines would redefine chocolate bars to be all about variety in taste and texture. The threat to Dairy Milk worsened when cocoa became an inflation-prone commodity market, in contrast to the much cheaper and more stable prices of key Countline ingredients such as wafer, biscuit and caramel.

Either shift could have ultimately sidelined Cadbury as the key name in the category, but the Cadbury brand was able to evolve into the new world. This evolution was possible because, ultimately, Cadbury stood for more than the position of either Cocoa Essence or Dairy Milk

Capacity for Evolution

Cadbury's Cocoa Essence and Cadbury's Dairy Milk were the two defining brands in the development of Cadbury, but each was appropriate for the circumstances of the time. Cocoa Essence owned the high ground of what *wasn't* in the product. It made no direct claim about the provenance of their cocoa, or a special manufacturing process, but was entirely based on what Cadbury didn't add to the product. For the consumer of the latter part of the 19th-century, product adulteration was a big issue – even bigger as a result of Cadbury's evangelising. Cadbury not only addressed these worries by providing an additive-free cocoa, but refused on principle to manufacture an adulterated cocoa under another brand name.

Eventually, once labelling regulations and branded competition had seen the back of the charlatans, the consumer demonstrated that product adulteration was no longer an issue by happily buying Van Houten's alkalised cocoa. If Cadbury had not bitten the bullet and launched Bournville Cocoa when they realised that purity had run its course as a driver of the cocoa market, they would have become increasingly irrelevant as a cocoa house. It was the boldest of moves; Bournville Cocoa flew in the face of everything Cocoa Essence had stood for. Cadbury, by willingly pulling the plug on their number one brand, demonstrated a capacity to evolve their business in tune with the changing consumer. The Cocoa Essence brand still stood for purity, while Cadbury, in meeting consumers' evolving needs with Bournville, was on the side of the consumer, looking after their interests.

This is the benefit of a distinctive and powerful corporate-level brand, in that, by operating above the level of a simple product feature-benefit that can be overtaken by events, it can adapt to new circumstances in a way that individual product brands find almost impossible. And by being able to stand for different things, Cadbury has been advantaged over its competitors in achieving the next key element, that of ubiquity.

Part of Consumers' lives

Cadbury led the way in making chocolate a treat affordable to all by their forceful exploitation of the miracles of the second industrial revolution in the early 20th-century. The volume production of good value, high quality chocolate took the Cadbury brand to the masses and then overseas. By making the preferred chocolate both affordable and available, Cadbury moved from being an occasional indulgence for the few to the regular enjoyment for the many. The Swiss firms Lindt and Suchard, who were once direct competitors to Cadbury, did not go down this road and stayed appealing to the more affluent minority.

Cadbury also took many forms of chocolate to the masses. By marketing a

wide range of brands, from Freddo the Frog to large Christmas boxes of Milk Tray, the Cadbury name has a relevance not just in more lives, but in more stages of life, as explained by Dominic Cadbury,

People grow up with Cadbury...they continue that relationship through their whole life. Cadbury is a genuine brand as opposed to a 'me-too' product. Cadbury is unique. You can't buy it anywhere else, you can't buy it under an own-label, you can't buy Tesco chocolate and think its Cadbury chocolate. This is a unique brand that people enjoy throughout their lives.[1]

But as well as accompanying consumers through their entire lives, the ubiquity of the Cadbury brand was massively enhanced by an approach to marketing, which, apart from an enforced shift in the heyday of the television commercial, has achieved a depth of consumer engagement to complement its breadth. Experiential marketing is fashionable today precisely because of the longevity of impact that it can have. While usually being much more expensive per consumer versus a simple mass media strategy, the greater value comes with the loyalty that can last for decades.

That being the case, it is as well to remain recognisable to consumers over such a time-span. In a world where the average grocery store has 25,000 products and where we are assaulted by hundreds, if not thousands of advertising messages a day, standing out is a challenge that defeats most ordinary brands. But the purple wrappers, Cadbury signature and Glass and a Half logo are instantly-recognisable icons, and have been for decades. Each alone has become strongly associated with the Cadbury name even though, for the most part, the colour purple has been restricted to the Moulded products and the Glass and a Half to those made from Dairy Milk chocolate.

The three did not come together in the U.K. until 1952, when the Cadbury script logo became the only one used on the packaging across the entire product range. The company's devolved operating style also led to some divergences over time in the various markets, and the company has launched initiatives several times to bring the iconography around the world more into line. Research conducted in the 1970s demonstrated that virtually any seven letter word beginning with 'C', when written in the Cadbury script, is read as 'Cadbury' when viewed in a split-second. Such a strength, in what is primarily an impulse purchase category, could not be wasted, so the use of the Cadbury signature as the company logo on packaging in all markets was then mandated,

Complete consistency on all elements of packaging design was not achieved until 2003, after more research across key Cadbury markets showed a remarkable correlation between the colour purple and the Cadbury brand – four times the correlation between Kit Kat and the colour red. By being so instantly

---

[1] *Business Solutions* – West Midland edition, Feb/Mar 2004

recognisable, Cadbury has been advantaged over its competitors in being perceived as a consistent part of people's lives

The longevity and depth of loyalty generated by the Cadbury brand provides a bulwark against the tribulations that will eventually happen to any long-lived brand. As we have seen, no brand is immune from changing circumstances, and it is vital that a brand can survive the inevitable mishaps. Such survival is more likely if the brand in question is known and trusted for its integrity.

Company Values and Business Strategy

A key part of the success of Cadbury has been that consumer loyalty could be more prolonged through a deeper level of trust beyond simple product features and benefits. Cadbury has shown that the values of a company over time can greatly influence consumer purchasing, especially when they are clearly and consistently practised and communicated within the context of complementary business strategies.

It would be cynical and unfair to suggest that long-term consumer loyalty was the driving motive behind Cadbury's values. For the greater part of the company's history, they were derived from the passionate beliefs of the founding family, rooted in their Quaker upbringing. But there were many Quaker-run businesses who held similar beliefs but did not build a brand relationship to match that of Cadbury. Banks such as Lloyds and Barclays were originally Quaker-run. In addition to Cadbury's confectionery rivals of Fry and Rowntree, consumer goods companies such as Clark's Shoes, Bryant & May matches, Huntley & Palmers, Carr's Biscuits, Reckitt's and Horniman's Tea were also Quaker in origin, yet none matched the bond between Cadbury and their consumers.[2]

Cadbury, more than any other Quaker firm, integrated their beliefs into complementary and leading-edge business strategies, and then aggressively promoted the outcomes. Quakers' respect of the worth of every individual made them, as managers, open to suggestions from the workforce, but none implemented a scheme to facilitate the process on such a scale as did Cadbury. Many Quaker businesses provided recreational facilities for their workers, but none were as directed to improving work efficiency as were those of Cadbury. Quaker firms could always be counted on to provide humane working conditions, but none advertised and promoted theirs as diligently as did Cadbury.

The company Publications Department issued dozens of authoritative books on Bournville's social, educational and cultural activities and on its business philosophy. The advertising ceaselessly trumpeted not just what the firm manufactured, but where and in what conditions it did so. The Bournville factory, Bournville Village and the 'Bournville Experiment' – Cadbury's unique approach to engaging and empowering employees – became almost as famous as the chocolate itself, and added such attributes as integrity and ethical to the Cadbury name.

But the trust in the Cadbury name is not solely derived from a set of actions a century ago guided by admirable principles. Cadbury did not become the most trusted brand in Australia and New Zealand because of a factory in a garden half a world away. Skilled local managers in those markets built and developed relationships of trust independent from those pertaining in the U.K. They worked to the same guiding principles, reinforced by visits from Cadbury family members over the years, but then adopted them as their own, offering relevant and excellent products that fit consumers' differing lifestyles and in the process, built a very similar brand equity.

---

[2] Sir Adrian Cadbury; *Beliefs and Business: The Experience of Quaker Companies*; 2003, http://rps. gn.apc.org/leveson/resources/cadbury0503.htm, Accessed July 14th, 2007

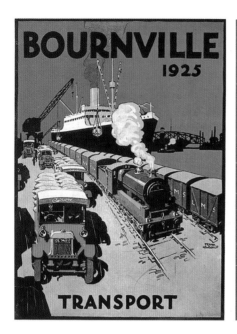

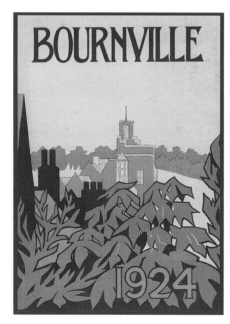

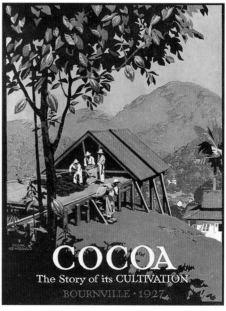

The Future

The future for the Cadbury brand is not for it to live on past glories. Henry Ford summed up the issue in a 1916 interview,

History is more or less bunk. It's tradition. We don't want tradition. We want to live in the present and the only history that is worth a tinker's dam(n) is the history we made today.[3]

But that quote, usually condensed into the somewhat misleading '*History is bunk*', misses the key part of the challenge: the creation of synergy between the history of the past and the history being made today. Brand equity is nothing but history; it is all consumers know of the brand. Any fool can throw out the old; the hard bit is seeing how the old can be updated in a way that is relevant to today and that adds to the brand.

Bold decisions are occasionally required to get to where the consumer is heading; decisions that leave competitors reeling. Making such leaps can be painful and risky – replacing existing strategies or even existing major brands – but they must be taken. The Cadbury brand was built through such moves as Cocoa Essence; cancelling non-pure cocoas; Bournville Cocoa sidelining Cocoa Essence; Dairy Milk; building the West African cocoa industry; the Bournville Experiment; slashing prices by 70%; re-conquering lost export markets; persevering in Australia and India.

As a result of such boldness, Cadbury now ranks as the world's fourth-largest global chocolate business. The only three ahead of them are Mars and Hershey – because of their dominant positions in the gargantuan U.S. chocolate market – and Nestlé, the only one of the three Swiss powerhouses to aggressively pursue a strategy of acquisition, which swallowed up the merged Rowntree Mackintosh in 1987. The brand names of Cadbury's great rivals of the past – Rowntree, Fry and MacRobertson – have almost been consigned to oblivion. That Cadbury should have outlasted them was not inevitable, it was as a result of Cadbury's philosophies, strategies and actions that built a stronger and more relevant brand.

It is tempting with a brand as venerable as Cadbury to play safe; after all, there is a lot at stake that can be lost. But the Cadbury brand will only continue to grow if, in addition to living up to the standards and values of its past, it continues to live up to the boldness of its past. Purple will then continue its reign as the leading colour on the chocolate fixture.

---

[3] Henry Ford; *Interview in Chicago Tribune, May 25th*, 1916; http://www.quotationspage.com/quote/24950.html; Accessed July 14th, 2007

Bibliography

The primary source for this book has been the Cadbury archives, located at the Bournville production site, which contain a wealth of material, both written and photographic, on all aspects of the Cadbury business. Since this provided at least 90% of the information contained herein, I considered it would have been tedious for both the reader and the author to list out sources along the lines of, "Box X, Shelf Y: Cadbury Archives." Only where I have sourced facts elsewhere do I reference them in the text.

Cadbury Publications Department – internally published

The Publications Department of Cadbury Bros. issued many interesting booklets. The following is a small selection of the total output.

Bournville: A Descriptive Account of Cocoa and of its Manufacture. 1880.

Thirty Years of Progress: A Review of the Growth of the Bournville Works. 1910.

Cadbury's of Bournville: The Building of a Modern Business. 1948.

Cadbury on the Gold Coast: A Brief Survey of the Commercial and Social Activities of Cadbury Brothers Limited. 1955.

Our 50 Years in the Gold Coast and Ghana. 1957.

The Organisation of a Large Business: The Development of Cadbury Brothers Limited. 1958.

Cadbury's Dairy Milk: The First Hundred Years. 2005.

Cadbury Publications Department – externally published

Cadbury Brothers was remarkably generous in sharing their various experiences in building the business with the outside world. The following are four books I found invaluable.

Rogers T.B., *A Century of Progress: 1831–1931,* Birmingham: Cadbury Bros. 1931.

Industrial Record 1919–1939: A Review of the Inter-War Years, Cadbury Bros/Pitman, 1945.

Sweet-Shop Success: A Handbook for the Sweet Retailer, London: Cadbury Bros/Pitman, 1949.

Industrial Challenge: The Experience of Cadburys of Bournville in the Post-War Years. London: Cadbury Bros/Pitman, 1964.

Books on Cadbury

Barringer E.E., *Sweet Success: The Story of Cadbury & Hudson in New Zealand,* Dunedin: Cadbury Confectionery Ltd, 2000.

Cadbury E., *Experiments in Industrial Organisation,* London: Longmans, Green & Co., 1912.

Chinn C., *The Cadbury Story: A Short History,* Studley: Brewin Books Ltd., 1988.

Crosfield J.F., *A History of the Cadbury Family,* Cambridge: University Press, 1985.

Gardiner A.G., *Life of George Cadbury,* London: Cassell and Company Ltd., 1923.

Hitches M., *Bournville: Steam & Chocolate,* Clophill: Irwell Press Ltd., 1992.

Marks W. & Cadbury C., *George Cadbury Junior, 1878–1954: A Short Biography,* Birmingham: Studio Press, Year unknown.

Williams I.A., *The Firm of Cadbury, 1831–1931,* London: Constable and Co. Ltd., 1931.

Books with Significant Reference to Cadbury and/or chocolate

Beauchampé S. & Inglis S., *Played in Birmingham: Charting the Heritage of a City at Play*, Birmingham: English Heritage, 2006.

Brenner J.G., *The Emperors of chocolate: Inside the Secret World of Hershey and Mars*, New York: Random House, 1999.

Cadbury A., *Corporate Governance and Chairmanship: A Personal View*, Oxford: University Press, 2002.

Casson H.N., *Creative Thinkers*, New York: Cosimo Classics, 2005.

Coe S.D. & M.D., *The True History of Chocolate*, London: Thames & Hudson Ltd., 1996.

Fitzgerald R., *Rowntree and the Marketing Revolution, 1862–1969*, Cambridge: University Press, 1995.

Harvey C.E. & Press J., *Studies in the Business History of Bristol*, Bristol: Bristol Academic Press, 1988 (Contains a chapter on the early history of Fry).

Head B. *The Food of the Gods: A Popular Account of Cocoa*, London: R. Brimley Jonson, 1903.

Robertson J., *MacRobertson, The Chocolate King*, Melbourne: Thomas C. Lothian Pty Ltd., 2004.

Witzel M., *Fifty Key Figures in Management*, London: Routledge, 2003.

General

Chandler A.D. Jnr., *Scale and Scope: The Dynamics of Industrial Capitalism*, Cambridge Mass: Harvard University Press, 1990.

Lacey R., *Ford – The men and the machines*, Boston: Little, Brown and Co., 1986.

Articles

'Face to Face – Sir Dominic Cadbury', *Business Solutions*, Issue 13, Feb/Mar 2004, pp26–30. Quotations from these interviews are reproduced by permission of *Business Solutions* Magazine.

Fitzgerald R., 'Products, Firms and Consumption: Cadbury and the Development of Marketing', *Business History*, Volume 47, Number 4, 2005.

Jones J., 'Multinational Chocolate: Cadbury Overseas, 1918–39', *Business History*, Volume 26, 1984.

'Hershey bars the American Way', *Financial Times*, Lex Column, March 23rd, 1988. Quotations from this article are reproduced by permission of the *Financial Times*.

'The Cadbury Schweppes Mix', *Management Today*, April 1970.

'Chocs Away', *The Sunday Telegraph*, September 8th, 1996, pp B5–6.

Websites

www.quotationspage.com/quote/24950.html; Henry Ford, Interview in Chicago Tribune, May 25th, 1916.

www.forbes.com/asap/1997/1201/070.html; Paterson T., 'The Dross of DOS'.

http://rps.gn.apc.org/leveson/resources/cadbury0503.htm; Sir Adrian Cadbury; 'Beliefs and Business: The Experience of Quaker Companies'.

www.Swissworld.org

www.ipa.co.uk/news/news_archive/displayitem.cfm?itemid=1752

www.nestle.co.uk/OurBrands/AboutOurBrands/ConfectioneryAndCakes/Yorkie.htm

Index